FIRST EDITION

THEORY AND APPLICATION IN SOCIOLOGY

READINGS ON CONTEMPORARY ISSUES

By **Stephanie Southworth**

Coastal Carolina University

cognella®
academic publishing

Bassim Hamadeh, CEO and Publisher
Kassie Graves, Director of Acquisitions
Jamie Giganti, Senior Managing Editor
Miguel Macias, Senior Graphic Designer
Jennifer McCarthy, Acquisitions Editor
Gem Rabanera, Project Editor
Elizabeth Rowe, Licensing Coordinator
Chelsey Schmid and Christian Berk, Associate Editor
Emily Guardado, Production Assistant

Cover image copyright © 2015 iStockphoto LP/woraput.
© 2016 iStockphoto LP/themacx.

Printed in the United States of America.

ISBN: 978-1-5165-0663-7 (pbk) / 978-1-5165-0664-4 (br)

www.cognella.com   800-200-3908

CONTENTS

SECTION II: STRATIFICATION

SECTION III: RACIAL INEQUALITY

SECTION IV: GENDER

SECTION V: DEVIANCE

SECTION VI: EDUCATION

SECTION VII: URBAN ISSUES

KEYWORDS BY CHAPTER

Understanding Youth Social Problems	Social Constructions, Variables, Symbolic Interaction, Conflict Theory, Functionalist Theory, Research Methods
Inequality	Race, Class, Gender, Social Class, Mobility, Inequality, Marx, Blau & Duncan, C. Wright Mills
The American Dream and Inequality	Wealth, Income, The American Dream, Inequality, Meritocracy
What's in a Name? Coverage of Senator Hillary Clinton During the 2008 Democratic Primary	Gender, Status Expectations, Sexism, Stereotyping
The Social Nature of Male Suicide: A New Analytical Model	Gender, Gender Roles, Escape Theory, Role Strain, Socialization, Masculinity, Masculinity Theory
Black Wealth/White Wealth	Income, Wealth, Race, Class, Redlining, Sociology of Race and Wealth
Language Oppression and Resistance:	Bourdieu, Race, Class, Latinos
The Case of Middle Class Latinos in the United States Contribution of Mainstream Theories	Routine Activities Theory, Deterrence Theory, Female Juvenile Delinquency Rational Choice Theory, Strain Theory, Control Theory, Gender, Labeling Theory, Delinquency, Persistent Offending Theory, Social Learning Theory, General Theory of Crime and Deviance, Gendered Theory of Crime and Deviance
The State of Public School Violence	Schools, Education, Deviance, Strain Theory, Differential Association Theory, Medicalization of Deviance, Control Theory
Modern Mass Education	Structural-Functionalism, Nation-Building, Credentialism
Social Class, the Commodification, and Space Through a Rural Lens	Education, Rural, Urban, Social Class
Portland's Response to Homeless Issues And Broken Windows Theory	Broken Windows Theory, Homelessness, Politics, Magnet Theory
No There There: Social Movements and the Urban Political Community	Political Sociology, New Institutionalism Conflict Theory, Marxism, Cyclical Disorder Theory, Social Movements, Politics

INTRODUCTION

Sociologists use theory and research to study society. They seek to understand the development of societies, collective behavior, and the ways social institutions affect human interactions. Sociologists explore the ways in which our social environment affects our opportunities, the decisions we make, and our life outcomes. So to study sociology is to study our lives, and the individual decisions we make, within the larger social environment in which we live. Although most Americans grow up believing our beliefs and the decisions we make are based on our own preferences and tastes, many do not understand the effects of institutions, social structures, and culture in guiding those beliefs and decisions.

Many social structures, such as the inequalities found in the educational and criminal justice systems, are obvious to those who study them, but less obvious to the general public. For example, a high school student who attends a school offering AP and Honors classes, small class sizes, and highly trained teachers has an advantage over the student who attends a poor rural or urban school with unsanitary facilities, large class sizes, and under-qualified teachers. Each student may work hard to obtain a diploma and both may be at the top of their respective classes. Their outcomes later in life, however, may be vastly different. Let's say each of the valedictorians from these hypothetical high schools apply to the same university. Both students have the same GPA and been involved in similar after-school activities. One student receives a congratulatory letter from the university and the other a rejection letter. Why? One student attended a high-class, state-of-the-art school, and the other a poor school with subpar academics and a bad reputation. The admissions officers, having a limited number of slots for incoming students, chose the student they believed would be the best prepared. The quality of the high school each student attended was used as a reference, resulting in unequal outcomes for similar effort. In essence, being at the top of the class has a different meaning depending on the school each student attended, and affected their outcomes through no fault of their own.

Sociologists use theories to explain social behavior. Not all sociologists, however, agree as to why social phenomena occur. This is one of the most exciting aspects of sociology. There are multiple ways of understanding human experiences. A theory is a statement as to why and how two or more concepts are related. The theoretical lens sociologists use guides the questions they ask about the social issues they are exploring and the methods used to conduct their research.

Theoretical Frameworks

There are three broad, overarching theoretical paradigms in sociology: conflict, structural-functionalist, and symbolic interaction. Each framework views the social world in a different way. The following is a brief synopsis of some of the concepts and founders of these three theoretical paradigms. As each of the readings in this text were chosen because they use one or more sociological theories, this summary is meant to give the reader an overview rather than a comprehensive explication of all the concepts in each theory.

Conflict Theory

Conflict theorists focus on inequality, power, and control. They see society as a structure rife with conflict stemming from inequalities based on gender, race, and social class. Sociologists who view the world through the lens of conflict theory seek to understand the ways in which dominant groups create and maintain their power. They also explore the ways conflict between dominant and nondominant groups can result in social change, which would equalize power dynamics.

Karl Marx (1818–1883) is very likely the most well-known conflict theorist. Writing in the nineteenth century, Marx observed the workings of the capitalist system and concluded that capitalism exacerbates inequality because power becomes increasingly concentrated in the hands of the elite. Marx was very critical of capitalism, arguing capitalistic societies separate people into "haves" and "have nots." In a capitalistic economy, the "bourgeoisie," or those who own the means of production, seek to increase their profits—often at the expense of the "proletarians," or the working class. Marx was certain as the "proletarians" continued to work harder for fewer benefits, eventually they would fight back and capitalism would be replaced with a more humane system of production.[1,2,3]

Max Weber (1864–1920), another key founder of sociology, argued that while social class is important, inequalities also are derived from differences in power and status. Whereas Marx attributed inequality to social structures, Weber focused on the relative ability of individuals to affect their own life chances. Because of inequalities in access to land and wealth, certain groups maintain more power and status than other groups. The result is there are inequalities between males and females (feminism or gender conflict theory) and dominant and nondominant racial groups (race conflict theory). These differences in power and status often reside not only between social classes, but also within them. For example, middle-class blacks in the United States have less wealth than middle-class whites due to current and past institutional discrimination, including housing policies such as redlining that made it legal to deny home loans to individuals based on their neighborhood or race. These policies continue to affect the wealth of blacks today and, in turn, affect the power they collectively hold. Differences in power and status are important considerations when analyzing gender as well. Females were the last group in the United States to be given the right to vote and own land. The result is, even today, within each social class an average female will have less wealth, power, and prestige than her male counterpart.[4]

Questions Conflict Theorists Ask

Who is in power and what are they doing to keep that power?

How do social institutions reinforce and perpetuate inequality?

How has institutional discrimination affected where and how people live?

Is institutional discrimination something people should consider important today?

Structural-Functional Theory

In contrast with conflict theorists' focus on inequality, structural-functionalists examine the ways social institutions and culture interact to keep society orderly and stable. They view the social world as made up of many interconnected parts that work together to provide a cohesive, organized society.

Herbert Spencer's (1820–1903) "social Darwinism" approach took the view that inequality is a result of the "survival of the fittest." If someone works hard and does what is needed to survive, he or she will benefit. Those who do not work as hard will not reap the same rewards. This theory was useful for the capitalists of the nineteenth century who used this ideology to resist implementing social programs for the poor. Rather, social Darwinism allowed the wealthy to blame the poor for their own problems. Although Spencer's views are not supported by most sociologists today, it is a useful framework for understanding the evolution of functionalist theory.[5]

Emile Durkheim (1858–1917) focused on the experiences and values communities share that allow people to feel they are part of a group and have a shared collective experience. He observed there was a division of labor in all societies, which worked to create efficient means for individuals to interact with their environment. As individuals find new and more effective ways to adapt to their environment, it causes cultural change. For example, Durkheim noticed people who live in urban areas have different patterns of interactions, social bonds, and division of labor than those living in rural areas. Individuals in rural areas are more likely to be connected to one another based on traits they have in common, and have similar values and morals (mechanical solidarity), whereas people in urban areas tend to be connected to people based on mutual need (organic solidarity) and have fewer close ties to one another, owing to the increased division of labor that urban areas produce.

Durkheim worried about people in urban areas developing anomie—a feeling of meaninglessness—stemming from work lacking in fulfillment and providing workers with no sense of purpose. Durkheim, however, thought these issues were temporary and an evolutionary stage that would be remedied when organic solidarity matured.

In addition, Durkheim argued even deviance can have positive benefits to society. He identified four positive "functions" of deviance: to affirm a community's values, create social change, increase social unity, and make moral boundaries clear. For example, after the September 11, 2001, terrorist attacks, most people in the United States felt they had something in common with everyone else; there was a common enemy, and citizens felt united. It also produced social change such as the increased security we now see at airports.[6]

Robert K Merton (1910–2003) argued every social structure has both manifest and latent functions. For instance, a manifest, or intended, function of going to college would be to gain knowledge or a degree. There are also unintended, or latent, consequences of attending college. Once a student enters college he or she is exposed to more people, gains new friends, and sometimes even finds a marriage partner. Although individuals are not paying college tuition to find friends, it is something that often occurs unintentionally as a result of attending a university.[7]

Merton recognized social structures are not stable all of the time and sometimes there are negative effects. He described the negative effects of social structures as dysfunctions. Dysfunctions are disruptions in society's operation. For example, Walmart provides low-cost goods to many individuals, but is also dysfunctional because to get those low prices Walmart produces many goods overseas, which reduces the manufacturing jobs in the United States and results in higher numbers of low-paid workers.

Questions Structural-Functionalists Ask

How does culture work in different societies to reinforce the values of that society?

How do rules and laws work to keep societies running smoothly?

What are the benefits of deviance to a community?

Symbolic Interaction

Whereas structural-functionalists and conflict theorists examine issues at the macro—or big picture—level, symbolic interactionist theories focus on micro—or individual—level interactions and symbols. George Herbert Mead (1863–1931) maintained that individuals actively create the world they live in. Through our interactions with others we shape our reality. In this view each gesture a person makes, or words used, trigger responses from others and shape social interactions. For example, imagine Selena goes to a party and stands in a corner with her arms crossed. People may perceive her as angry or closed off and not approach her. Selena leaves the party thinking it was boring and people were unfriendly. This will affect the likelihood of her attending a party the next time she is asked. Betsy, on the other hand, walks into the party smiling, and many people introduce themselves to her. Betsy leaves the party having a few new friends and may be eager to attend the next gathering. Learning theory and labeling theory are both symbolic interactionist theories that take their lead from Mead.[8]

Social learning theory is most often used to explain deviant behavior. According to learning theory, people learn the norms of appropriate behavior from those around them, but individuals can also learn to become deviant by associating with others who are deviant. For example, children who from a young age see their parents smoking are more likely to become smokers because they learned such behavior from their parents. The parents most likely never told the child that smoking is something they should take part in as an adult, but they modeled "adult" behavior that the child internalized and "learned."[9]

Labeling theory is another micro-level mechanism for explaining deviant behavior. The premise of labeling theory is that an act is only problematic if others define it as such. Labeling theorists also attest if a person is labeled, over time that person will respond to the label and it will become a part of who he or she is as an individual. From this perspective, deviance is defined by the group doing the labeling—the rich labeling the activities of the poor, the dominant racial group labeling minorities, or men labeling women. Even when two individuals complete the same act they may be labeled differently depending on their individual attributes. For instance, let's say there was a cat on a playground at school and ten-year-old Juan kicked the cat. Juan was a straight-A student and the teacher enjoyed his presence in the classroom. The teacher saw Juan kick the cat and took him aside, asking him what was wrong. She then encouraged him to talk to her if he was having a bad day. Later in the day, one of Juan's classmates, Shelly, kicked the same cat. Shelly came in late to school, usually had not bathed, and her teacher thought she was disrespectful. This teacher also saw Shelly kick the cat. Rather than asking Shelly what was wrong, the teacher told Shelly she was a bad girl for kicking the cat and sent her to the principal's office. Both students exhibited the same behavior, but the reaction of the teacher was quite different. The result is that one student was labeled a trouble-maker while the other was not. The "troublemaker" is now stigmatized and is more likely to be labeled by others as a "bad" girl. Eventually, she may begin to see herself as "bad" and begin living up to the poor expectations of others.[10]

Questions Symbolic Interactionists Ask

How do people experience their social world?

How do labels applied to people or objects affect social interactions?

How do people respond to negative and/or positive labels?

This introductory text uses readings published between 2000 and 2015 to explore social issues in the United States. This text is not meant to encompass every topic usually included in an introductory course, but the readings are intended to highlight how sociologists use theory to guide their research, and the usefulness of theories in explaining human actions. Students should read each selection critically, thinking about the theories and how they can be used to describe other social phenomenon.

Questions to Think About

1. How would a symbolic interactionist, a conflict theorist, and a structural-functionalist describe professional sports?
2. What are questions that someone using each theoretical perspective would ask if he or she were examining the social issue of poverty or homelessness?
3. What types of research would a sociologist be more likely to use a micro- rather than a macro-level approach?

Resources

Durkheim, Emile. 1997. *[1893] The Division of Labor in Society*, New York: Free Press.

The History Guide: Lectures on Modern European Intellectual History.
   http://www.historyguide.org/intellect/marx.HTML

Mead, George Herbert. 1913. "The Social Self." *Journal of Philosophy, Psychology and Scientific Methods* *10:* 374–380
   https://www.marxists.org/reference/subject/philosophy/works/us/mead3.htm

Calhoun, Craig. 2003. "Robert K Merton Remembered." *Footnotes*
   http://www.asanet.org/footnotes/mar03/indextwo.html

Perrin, Robert G. 1976. "Herbert Spencer's Four Theories of Social Evolution." *American Journal of Sociology,* 81:6 pp. 1339–1359. University of Chicago Press.

SECTION I
STUDYING SOCIAL ISSUES

Introduction

Reading 1, an excerpt from *Sex, Drugs and Death—Understanding Youth Social Problems,* by Tammy L. Anderson, was selected as an introductory chapter because it includes many of the tenants of sociology and sociological research and theory. It also includes focuses on a social issue many college students are very familiar with—teen drinking. Anderson introduces her book by exploring the ways in which social problems are also social constructions. Social constructionists focus on the ways the social world is created by individuals. Patterns of interaction, gender norms, and deviant acts are social constructs that change over time. For instance, what was "normal" in 1900 may be considered very deviant today. In 1900, females wore long dresses and could not vote, most people did not have cars, cocaine was an ingredient in Coca-Cola, and cell phones and televisions had not been invented. These aspects of material and nonmaterial culture created a social environment in which genders interacted with each other and people structured their free time much differently than they do today.

This reading describes the ways sociologists coming from the conflict, structural-functionalist, and symbolic interactionist schools of thought would study the underage drinking issue. Each discussion of the broader theoretical paradigms includes examples of several of the sub theories that fall under each theoretical umbrella. For instance, Emile Durkheim, Robert Merton, and Talcott Parsons all wrote in the structural-functionalist tradition, but each had a different focus of interest.

This chapter also includes the relatively new theoretical perspective of intersectionality, which explores the ways a person's multiple advantages or disadvantages intersect to either help or hinder his or her life chances. There are inequalities associated with gender, race, and social class, but if a part of more than one of these disadvantaged groups, it creates a dual disadvantage for them. For example, a person who is low income and female would have the disadvantage of being a female compounded by the disadvantage of having a low income.

The concluding section includes a discussion on the ways sociologists use theories to guide their research and the types of research they conduct. Sociologists use both qualitative and quantitative methods to explore patterns of human behavior. The type of research used depends largely on the research question and the theoretical perspective the researcher chooses to apply.

Reading 1: Understanding Youth Social Problems

By Tammy L. Anderson

Introduction

U.S. society in the 21st century is decidedly youth-oriented. The well-being of youth is one of the most central values of our society and culture. While birthing and raising children fundamentally shapes our existence, youth also signifies a lifestyle and aesthetic to which adults aspire. Increasingly, we wish to look, think, and act like young people as much as possible. Industries of all kinds sell older Americans products and services promising a return to youth or younger state. Symbolically then, youth is relevant to all of us since we live in a culture that prioritizes young people and strive to be like them, i.e., youthful.

While youth is both a group of people that demands top priority in society and a sort of 'state' or period with a highly valued aesthetic, lifestyle, and attitude, youth—in both of these forms—is also demonized and heavily monitored and controlled. The monitoring and controlling of youth makes some sense, given the societal importance placed on them/it. However, the viewpoint of youth, youth activities and styles as dangerous and problematic is more curious since they are simultaneously celebrated in our daily lives.

In this book, I look at three broad areas of youth behaviors that are deemed problematic, yet, at times, are celebrated as well: sex and sexuality, substance use, and suicide. Why focus on these three youth problems when there are many others (e.g., illiteracy, delinquency, and child poverty) needing attention? Three reasons justify my effort and serve as objectives of this book. First, sexuality, substance abuse, and suicide present an opportunity to teach readers about the unique ways sociologists study youth and the problems they face. This includes helping the reader understand how youth behavior gets defined as problematic in the first place, as well as learning the theories and methods sociologists use to study and address them. Unlike other disciplines, sociology allows us to comprehend how individuals and groups are connected to the communities, societies, nations, and cultures within which they live. Understanding this relationship is critically important for solving social problems.

Second, these three issues help elucidate how youth and other social problems are patterned (usually by social group) in our society and how sociologists can help identify what those patterns are so that effective remedies can be put forth. Third, and perhaps most importantly, sexuality, substance abuse, and suicide are linked in distinctive ways and highlighting this point will help readers see that such connections are common to social problems in general. My focus on the connections between these three youth problems, how-ever, means that there will inevitably be topics related to sex, drugs, and suicide that I can't discuss. Thus, the book should be read as a sociological treatment of three youth problems that are exceptionally patterned and interconnected.

How Sociologists View and Study Youth Social Problems

Many sociologists view youth problems as being **socially constructed** rather than absolute or objective facts. This means that matters such as teen pregnancy and under-age drinking are defined socially, not by nature, as problematic behaviors by certain people for a variety of reasons. People, usually influential or powerful ones, then use various techniques to convince the rest of us to see things their way and to accept their definitions of "youth problems." For example, it was not always against the law for 18-year-olds to consume alcoholic beverages. Between 1970 and 1975, 29 states lowered the minimum drinking age to 18, 19, or 20 (Wechsler and Sands, 1980). Scientists began studying the effects of the lowered drinking age in these places and found increased injury and death to teens from alcohol-related car accidents (Cucchiaro, Ferreira, and Sicherman 1974; Douglass, Filkins, and Clark 1974; Wagenaar, 1983, 1993; Whitehead, 1977; Whitehead et al. 1975; Williams et al. 1974). A **moral crusade** by parents' groups to change minimum drinking age laws followed under the guise of "protecting" the next generation. President Reagan used the 1984 Uniform Drinking Age Act to force the states to change their drinking age laws back to 21 in order to receive federal highway monies. All did by 1988.

Today, youth drinking is believed to cause many problems, not simply teen death and injury. Yet, youth drinking is condoned and even promoted by other institutions and alcohol stake-holders in our society. Consider advertising. The Center for Alcohol Marketing and Youth (2008) discovered that between 2001 and 2007, alcohol marketing on youth-oriented television programs had increased a whopping 38 percent. Their annual study found that "In 2007, approximately one out of every five alcohol advertisements was placed on programming that youth ages 12 to 20 were more likely per capita to see than adults of the legal drinking age." The shifts in minimum drinking laws and conflicting messages from private sector industry about youth drinking are, therefore, good examples to understand what sociologists call the social construction of social problems.

Sociologists use theories about how things in society or our culture (let us call them "environmental" factors) influence individuals and groups to explain youth social problems. Unlike natural scientists or even psychologists, sociologists do not explain or study sexuality, drug use, and suicide by looking exclusively at individuals and their characteristics. Instead, they most often focus on **environmental factors** that can influence our lives in ways we don't often recognize. Sociologists' explanations come in the form of **theories**. Whether grand or modest, theories feature **concepts** with relationships to each other. Concepts are abstract, mental images of phenomena that can usually be indicated by something more measurable in the real world. Peer pressure is one such concept and sociologists have theorized that it helps explain a variety of youth problems, including premarital sex, teen pregnancy, and substance use.

Let's go back to underage drinking to illustrate the sociological way of thinking. Student culture on most college campuses shapes motivations to drink and provides many opportunities for underage people to get drunk. So, if you want to know why young people violate drinking laws and engage in dangerous illegal behavior, sociologists might recommend looking not at the 18-year-olds' biological makeup or self-esteem, but rather to the cultural norms and values he or she is exposed to by certain social groups (e.g., fraternities and sororities) or in certain situations or settings (campus parties or local bars). In short, sociologists understand youth social problems as having cultural, social, and economic origins or ties. The causes that sociologists theorize to have an impact on things like underage drinking or suicide are often external to the individual, i.e., they are not biological, genetic or psychological traits possessed by them. Instead, these explanations direct our attention away from people to both the immediate and more distant social worlds in which they live.

While sociological theories often focus on environmental explanations, others look at individuals to clarify social problems. Such **micro-level** theories explain youth problems using the characteristics or experiences of people or those close to them, e.g., parents and peers. Such explanations are attractive, for many reasons, to both researchers and policy makers. For example, by focusing on individuals, micro-level theories lend themselves better to traditional scientific methods, e.g., quantitative studies using surveys and questionnaires administered to drug users. They enable young people under study to be targeted directly by programs and social policy.

Another important quality of **individual or micro-level explanations** is that they often, but not always, identify causes (i.e., **independent variables**) immediately preceding problem behaviors, instead of focusing on more distant precursors of them. For example, poor decision-making skills occur in close proximity to drug-taking, e.g., youth make "poor" decisions when they use drugs. Factors like this are perceived as more "direct" causes, making them attractive to policy makers when fashioning interventions.

Major Sociological Theories

Sociology has three main theories to explain youth and other social problems: **structural functionalism**, **social conflict**, and **symbolic interaction** (Allan 2007; Kimmel and Mahler 2007). Within each of these categories are numerous 'minitheories' that enrich the broader approach. Structural functionalism and **conflict theories** have focused mostly on the macro picture or things in the social, cultural, and physical environment to explain youth problems, while symbolic interactionism has focused more on social processes and individual interaction to explain the same. All three schools of thought illustrate how sociologists understand youth problems.

Structural Functionalism

To begin, the structural functional paradigm—credited largely to Emile Durkheim, Talcott Parsons, and Robert Merton—views society as a complex system whose parts work together to promote **solidarity** and stability among its population. Humans, especially young people, are believed to be able to thrive under these conditions. Chaos, instability, and **alienation** disrupt society's functioning and are considered undesirable (Durkheim 1933; Merton 1968; Parsons 1951, 1971). Agreement about morality and conformity to norms is required for society's smooth functioning (Durkheim 1947). Conflict about and deviation from norms and values challenge those things. Thus, while some conflict and deviation can be expected among people in a society, too much conflict and deviation will hinder solidarity and stability and thus throw society—and its people—into a state of chaos and alienation (Merton 1968; Parsons 1951, 1971).

Suicide was one of the first social problems to be analyzed from a structural functionalist viewpoint. Writing about societal change after the industrial revolution and the growth of capitalism, Durkheim (1933) warned about the rise of a condition called "**anomie**": the absence of social ties that bind people to society. For him, capitalism's ideology of individualism and preference for organic solidarity (specialized, fragmented social relations highlighting individual difference) weakened social ties among individuals, destabilized society and could lead to chaos.

While Durkheim discussed suicide and other social problems, he did not address youth directly. One of the unique traits of the sociological approach, and a central goal of this book, is the identification of behavioral patterns among groups, e.g., by race, age, gender, social class, and region of the country. Robert Merton (1968), another structural functionalist, targeted youth directly and extended Durkheim's ideas to other social problems with much youth involvement, e.g., crime and drug abuse. Merton was especially interested in explaining delinquency among poor and mixed race/ethnic youth. He discussed unequal opportunity, something that could produce alienation and, consequently, deviance for many. At issue was young people's access to opportunities for a full, productive life. Merton (1968) argued that such opportunities (economic and educational) were not equally available to all. Instead, access to them was largely a function of one's occupation, neighborhood, age, sex, race, education, and religion. Anomie, alienation or 'strain' emerged when there was a discrepancy between socially approved goals and access to their legitimate attainment. Groups and people with lower status sets suffered less access and, consequently, more strain. Social problems, including those affecting youth, were likely to escalate with increased anomie and unequal opportunity in society.

As indicated above, sociologists also focus on individual actions to explain social problems, including efforts that tie the types of structural explanations of Merton and Durkheim to more psychological issues germane to youth. Robert Agnew's (2006) general strain theory, for example, claims that important 'affect' or psychological variables influence the strain/deviance relationship. Agnew (2006) posited that strain was likely to result when youth place a high value on money, do not view adherence to legitimate norms as a source of status or prestige, and feel they won't be able to achieve financial success through legal channels. This predicament creates anger for some and can lead to problematic behavior. For example, the innovative response of selling drugs to attain goods or the retreatist response of using drugs to escape negative feelings (Anderson 1998a) depends on the individual's emotional response to strain.

Symbolic Interactionism

This brings us to a set of sociological theories focused more on how things happen or on the processes involved in sexual behaviors, drug use, and suicide. The **symbolic interactionist** perspective adopts a micro-level orientation to youth problems, focusing on human interaction in social situations. It sees society as a product of peoples' everyday interactions. In short, people act toward things based on the meaning those things have for them (Blumer 1969). Thus, society and reality are what people make of them.

The social construction of reality is important in understanding youth social problems. For example, interactionists maintain that deviance (i.e., teen sex, drug use, and suicide are types of deviance) is what is so labeled, or what people say it is (Becker 1963). Thus, nothing is inherently deviant or wrong. Such designations are defined by people, who reach those conclusions via shared and contested views of the world, society, and their own experience. This point was made above when reviewing the changing legal definitions of minimum drinking ages.

Symbolic interaction (e.g., **labeling theory**) and **social process theories** (e.g., **social control theory**) are concerned with how people interact and how deviance and drug use unfold over time. For example, these theories focus on how people or groups become involved in sexual behaviors or with drugs and alcohol, how their involvement changes over time, and what might initiate that change. Both social process theories discussed in this section, i.e., labeling theory and social control theory, adopt the structural functionalist tenets about consensus and solidarity.

According to labeling theory, youth drug and alcohol experimentation and use are, for example, not necessarily troublesome initially. Such behaviors become problematic when society officially brands youth as "delinquent" or "deviant" and punishes them harshly. This process of labeling threatens to enmesh young people in drug-abusing careers or lifestyles (Becker 1963; Denzin 1987; Lindesmith 1965, 1968). In other words, when youth are labeled and assumed to possess the negative traits, their involvement in deviance expands because they accept society's pejorative view of them. They called this the **self-fulfilling prophecy** (Cooley 1922, 1998; Lemert 2000). The internalization of negative labels leads to adopting deviant roles (i.e., tasks, behaviors) and identities (Lofland 1969). Interactionists maintain that negative social reactions (label or **stigma**) to individual drug use facilitated more, not less, drug use because individuals would likely internalize the negative labels applied to them and persist in deviant activities. Therefore, labeling theorists were more concerned about the social reaction (i.e., people, officials, agencies, etc.) to drug use, delinquency, and other forms of deviance than about what actually caused or influenced those behaviors in the first place.

When individuals adopt **deviant identities** or roles, they become greatly enmeshed in **deviant careers** (Becker 1963; Lofland 1969). Thus, the so-called middle period of the deviant career features heavy deviant behavior (Reinarman et al. 1997; Stephens 1991). This has deeply concerned both scholars and policy makers, who are interested in understanding and circumventing the experiences, activities, and consequences of active involvement in the illicit drug world, heavy alcohol consumption, promiscuous sex, or self-harm.

A second popular social process theory is social control theory (Gottfredson and Hirschi 1990). Its focus has been almost exclusively on deviant behaviors, such as delinquent acts (theft, vandalism, etc.) and drug use, rather than deviant roles and identities. Unlike labeling theory, social control theory explains original or primary deviance. It does so by asking a rather novel question: Why do people conform? This runs counter to the more common question—why do people deviate or break the law—asked by scholars and policy makers alike.

Intrigued by society's and sociology's innocuous expectation of conformity, Hirschi (1969) began theorizing about deviance by assuming people would violate norms and break the law unless they were actively prevented from doing so. The key to such prevention was effective socialization, which was a long process starting in childhood and lasting into adulthood. Thus, social control theory is considered one about process.

Who and what was responsible for this socialization? Hirschi (1969) and Gottfredson and Hirschi (1990) claimed families, peers, and schools had the most profound impact on each of our lives, especially as children and adolescents. They argued that close associations with parents and siblings, law-abiding peers, and teachers or other school officials, for example, were required to control individuals' behavior. The establishment of a strong moral bond between the juvenile and society, consisting of an attachment to others, commitment to conventional behavior, involvement in conventional activities, and a belief in the moral order and law, promoted conformity and prevented delinquency and other youth problems.

For Hirschi (1969), delinquent behaviors, like drug use, would be a likely outcome of ineffective ties to these things, i.e., improper socialization. Specifically, it is likely to occur if there is inadequate attachment (to parents and school), inadequate commitment (to educational and occupational success), inadequate involvement in conventional activities (e.g., scouting and sports leagues), and inadequate beliefs in such things as the legitimacy and morality of the law.

Social Conflict Theory

Unlike the two prior paradigms that embrace the idea of consensus, **social conflict theories** view society as an arena of inequality and conflict (Allan 2007; Kimmel and Mahler 2007). As indicated above, some interactionist work assumes the same. Conflict arises over disparities in things such as money, property, values, power, and ideology. In a diverse society like the U.S., there are many groups with different cultural values and customs. These cultural traits shape lifestyles, behaviors, identities, and life choices. All of this works to produce cultural conflict in society. Such cultural conflict is related to and exists in addition to more material forms of conflict such as money, wealth, and goods and services.

Conflict theorists are macro-oriented like structural functionalists, albeit they are nearly opposite on how that structure originates and functions. For conflict theorists, society's structure is controlled by those with the greatest economic, social, and cultural assets (Marx 1995; Marx and Engels 1992). Capitalism is an economic system characterized by private ownership of the means of production, from which personal profits can be derived through market competition. This capital enables individuals who own such means of production to rise to positions of power in the public and private sectors, where they continue to create structures that perpetuate their power and interests.

For conflict theorists, social problems, including those studied in this book, are theorized as a response to the alienating conditions of inequality and group (e.g., ethnic and racial minorities) marginalization (Ferrell and Websdale 1999; Quinney 1975). Two modern-day examples of conflict theory's utility in the drug use debate is official lobbying by harm reduction supporters to decriminalize marijuana in favor of individuals' rights to consume it and gang members who claim to sell drugs to empower themselves, their families and their communities (Bourgois 1996; Brotherton 2004).

Social reproduction theory, based on the ideas of the conflict approach, proposes that people acquire at birth and accumulate throughout their lives unequal shares of several types of capital (social, financial, human, and personal) that affect their life chances. Financial capital, i.e., tangible forms of wealth such as money, credit, investment, and assets—the kind Marx (1995; Marx and Engels 1992) discussed—are what most people think of when assessing inequality. Young people are dependent on their parents' financial capital for many things, ranging from basic sustenance needs to school tuition. Parents with greater financial assets can simply pay for better opportunities for their children. Poorer parents cannot provide these things. Thus their children are dependent on social supports (e.g., college tuition, loan programs) from the state. Absent such financial capital and the opportunities it provides, lower-class children may resort to alternative, illegal means to achieve the same things. This was a major premise of Merton's (1968) structural strain theory.

However, social reproduction theorists pointed to other types of capital that widened the inequality/goal attainment gap not previously discussed by Merton and others. One type was human capital, i.e., degrees, education, skills, training, and experience, which is required so that individuals can provide for themselves and others and alter their class position. This Bourdieu (1977) called attention to when criticizing the schools for reproducing class position via channeling youth to certain human capital training programs based on the class positions of their parents.

However, even when lower-class youth managed to attain advanced education and training, they lacked another critical form of capital possessed by the middle and upper classes: social capital, which are one's ties or connections to others who can do things for you or provide special treatment and access (Bourdieu 1977; Bourdieu and Passeron 1990). For example, many college students are unaware of the importance of this premise in understanding inequality and crime in society. Yet, they are aware that jobs or internships they secure often result from the connections their parents, relatives, teachers, and friends have to important others who make recommendations and hiring decisions on their behalf. Research shows that social capital (e.g., networking and access to powerful others) is critically important in securing valuable resources, including college admission and employment. It also shows such capital is not evenly distributed by class, race, ethnicity or gender.

Sociological Methods

Sociologists use a diverse set of research methods to investigate youth social problems empirically. In general, these methods can be classified into two broad categories: quantitative and qualitative. Surveys and experiments are called **quantitative methods** because they are designed to yield numerical measurements of important concepts. Participant observation and in-depth interviewing are called **qualitative methods** because they generally produce textual or non-numerical data. Both quantitative and qualitative methodologies stress that true knowledge is gained by gathering systematic evidence to elucidate a **theory**'s conceptual relationships. Each of the theories described above has concepts it attempts to explain and ideas about their causes. Scientists call outcomes that are to be explained **dependent variables**. Drug use and abuse, sexual behaviors (e.g., teen sex or pregnancy), and suicide are among the more common dependent variables that theories about youth attempt to elucidate. Independent variables are those believed, hypothesized, or discovered to play a role in producing such outcomes. At the theory stage, both independent and dependent variables come in the form of concepts (see page 3).

Understanding sociological theories begins with the discipline's unique focus on these matters. Sociologists have asked somewhat different questions about youth social problems. For example, they've investigated how drug and alcohol use and abuse vary culturally (e.g., by race and ethnicity or between societies), over time (historically), and by geographic location (e.g., the city versus the suburbs). Their objective has not been solely to explain individual behaviors. Sociological theories—like structural functionalism, symbolic interactionism, and conflict theory—utilize broader and often more abstract phenomena and concepts to explain social problems. Causality is more difficult to establish as researchers attempt to measure more abstract concepts and to specify their direct and indirect ties to youth behaviors. Inequality (usually economic) is one such concept. In some form, it is a component of several theories of drug abuse, suicide, and certain sexual behaviors, e.g., teen pregnancy. Yet, how inequality is measured and leads to youth problems is debated among sociologists. Sociological explanations are also challenging for policy makers to utilize and their proposed solutions are difficult to implement. This is because the solutions sociologists advocate require government and private sector resources and change, which is often unpopular with all parties involved.

Conclusions

In this chapter, I introduced the sociological approach to social problems. This approach recognizes that social problems are both subjectively defined and objectively observed. It is important to understand the differences between social constructions of social problems as well as the concrete consequences of them that impact our lives, society, and world. Ascertaining this distinction is made possible by using macro- and micro-level theories to understand how and why things become problematic in society, what patterns and connections exist, and how sociologists can use their tools and perspectives to derive solutions and interventions. These ideas will be considered in the next three chapters on youth sexuality, substance use, and suicide.

There is one last point to consider before we move on to the next chapter. It has to do with the patterning among people and groups. As indicated above, a central purpose of this book, and a unique characteristic of the sociological approach, is discovering that things like teen sex, underage drinking, and self-harm ideation are not randomly distributed among people in our society. Instead, they are patterned by important sociological phenomena, concepts, or variables. Sociologists have shown that demographic background traits (i.e., race, ethnicity, gender, social class, and age) not only help explain different levels of youth involvement in teen pregnancy, non-medical use of prescription drugs, and attempted suicide between whites and blacks, poor and rich, and males and females, but also why and how each group is implicated.

Sociologists' attention to **cultural diversity**—how people's values, lifestyles, and experiences differ by their race, ethnicity, social class, and gender—is a critically important way to understand the patterning of youth social problems. Comprehending such diversity comes by learning how our demographic traits constitute unique identities that connect us to other people and their cultural and social customs.

Intersectionality is a new way of understanding how multi-identities, based in one's race, class, gender, and sexual orientation, impact our lives (Collins 2007; Dill and Zambrana 2009). Intersectionality proposes that all experience is fundamentally structured and shaped by the multiple identities people embrace at any particular moment (Collins 2007; Dill and Zambrana 2009). This counts for youth social problems as well. For example, teen pregnancy may be a different experience for poor minorities than poor whites. **Non-medical abuse of prescription drugs** may impact middle-class whites in ways it does not any other group. The same could be true for coming out as homosexual or getting involved with illegal drugs. Early in my career, for example, I found that the personal identity change processes involved in getting into and out of illegal drugs was informed by the multiple identities of race and gender (Anderson 1998a–d). The point of intersectionality is that youth social problems are shaped by intersectional identities of things like gender, race, social class, age, and sexual orientation. Understanding this is a distinctive quality of sociology and a central objective of this book.

Discussion Questions

1. How could you use symbolic interaction theory and qualitative methods to study how teens get involved in drug dealing and gangs?
2. What are the benefits of seeing youth social problems as both socially constructed and observable facts?

Questions to Think About

1. What methods might people in power use to convince the public that a behavior is a "problem?"
2. Although teen drinking is illegal, there are places where it might be more acceptable than others. Where would you see more acceptance of teen drinking?
3. How do symbolic interactionist, conflict, and functionalist theories differ? What is the primary focus of each?
4. How are our ideas about race, gender, disability, etc. essentially social constructs?

Resources

Conrad, P. and Barker, K. 2010. "The Social Construction of illness: Key Insights and Policy Implications." *Journal of Health and Social Behavior* 51:1.

O'Connor, A. 2004. "Sociology of Youth Subcultures." *Peace Review* 16:4 409–414

Race as a Social Construct:

 http://www.theatlantic.com/national/archive/2013/05/what-we-mean-when-we-say-race-is-a-social-construct/275872/

SECTION II
STRATIFICATION

Introduction

Social stratification is a way to rank people in society. A person's position in a stratified system is a reflection of that person's power, wealth, and privilege relative to those around them. The primary stratification systems are caste systems (positions are inherited and do not change) and class systems (primarily inherited, but can change over the course of a lifetime). Class systems, such as those found in the United States, offer opportunities (at least theoretically) for individuals to move up in social class through a combination of schooling, occupation, and effort. While most people in the United States identify themselves as middle class, sociologists have identified many social classes derived from factors that include wealth, income, values, beliefs, and occupational prestige. The achievement ideology, which correlates hard work with achievement, is a very strong motivator and keeps even those who are low income believing they can gain wealth if only they work hard enough. In this view, the house one lives in, one's income, and one's wealth is a function of the effort that individual puts into succeeding. In part, this is true. For most people it is difficult to obtain their goals without putting in some effort; however, even in class systems, the strongest indicator of the social class of most adults is the social class of the family they were born into. People in different classes pass on their values, beliefs, and expectations to their children, which affects children's personal expectations. Think about it, if a person is raised in a community where all the adults work in the nearby factory, and there was an expectation most kids would grow up to work in the same factory, where is the incentive to go to college? On the flip side, if everyone in the community was going to college and it would create embarrassment and shame not to go to college, why would a person find it logical to work in a factory after high school?

The chapter "Inequality" gives an overview on the depth of stratification both in the United States and also globally, and outlines current theories on stratification.

Although originally published as a chapter on inequality in a sociology textbook, it is included here because, in a relatively short space, it offers a very comprehensive overview on many of the dimensions and structural aspects of inequality, which will help the reader to understand subsequent articles included in this text.

In the next reading, "The American Dream and Meritocracy," author Heather Beth Johnson argues the idea of the United States as a meritocracy conflicts with the reality of intergenerational wealth and the cumulative advantages enjoyed by higher classes. These advantages are not based on hard work, but on the traits ascribed to an individual from the time he or she is born. This chapter, an introduction to *The American Dream and the Power of Wealth*, summarizes interviews with individuals of all social classes. The author finds people of all social classes believe strongly in the American Dream. They believe the United States is a place where people receive just rewards for hard work. Rather than being a statement on how society functions, the author argues the idea of the American Dream serves to legitimate wealth inequality by giving lower income individuals a sense of hope and a belief opportunities are out there, and upper classes the belief their hard work is paying off. Although the author does not articulate the theoretical perspective she is writing from, this article is an example of conflict theory guiding the research questions posed in the section and framing the arguments the author makes.

Reading 2: Inequality

By Jeffrey C. Alexander and Kenneth Thompson

An Individual or a Social Story?

The Nike advertisement calling upon Americans to "just do it" illustrates the American belief that individuals can achieve anything they want to, if they have intelligence and motivation. Even those who have not achieved the "American dream"—such as Edna, a black woman in North Carolina, and Peggy, a white woman from a poor section of Philadelphia, both of whom were featured, among others, in a study by Wendy Luttrell (1997)—sometimes tell their life stories in ways that suggest they must have lacked the right kind of intelligence or had not tried hard enough (see box titled "Why Only Some Make It"). If they look beyond themselves, it is often to praise or blame other individuals—teachers or mothers—who had helped or blocked them. And even when they look beyond the people in their lives to the system in which they operate, they believe that a certain kind of intelligence and motivation is what divides people and sustains social inequality: "The important point is that the system is not working. People's mobility is very limited. People need education in order to get out of the ruts. The system keeps people in their place, in their class. You need intelligence to get out of your place" (Cheryl, a Philadelphia woman, quoted in Luttrell 1997: 28).

This phenomenon has been described as the **American individualistic success model**—a cultural model that combines individualism with optimism and a belief in self-discipline and hard work (the "work ethic"). All Western societies share elements of this model, but Americans are more inclined than others to explain success or failure in individualistic terms. For example, when asked the question "Why are there people in this country who live in need?" more Americans chose "personal laziness" (39 percent) over "societal injustice" (33 percent) as an answer. In France the figures were 15 percent and 42 percent, respectively (World Values Study Group 1994).

Does it matter what people believe about inequality? Americans' celebration of freedom, individualism, and the quest to "become somebody" may seem a worthy cause, but not when it leads to indifference toward inequalities among groups and the differences in power that perpetuate those inequalities. Knowledge and beliefs—the ingredients of culture—play a vital part in shaping and reproducing the patterns of inequality and power. Twentieth-century sociology developed useful methods for mapping the structures of inequality, and the "cultural turn" is now furthering our understanding of the part played by knowledge and beliefs.

In the first part of this chapter we examine some of the main concepts and theories concerning social inequality that are common to sociology as a whole, irrespective of different national traditions. Next, we describe some of the main findings about patterns of inequality in America and in other parts of the globe. Finally, we look at developments in the cultural approach to inequality and at forecasts about what kinds of inequality will develop in the future. For example, we consider the question of whether old social divisions based on position and occupation in the system of economic production (class) are becoming less important than cultural differences based on consumption (lifestyle), gender, or ethnicity. An even more radical suggestion is that we are now entering a postmodern era in which there are no fixed social positions and identities—"all that is solid melts into air."

Social Stratification

The focus on individual responsibility for inequality can be seen as a reflection of American culture, but it is also an example of nonsociological thinking more generally. As individuals, we are all unique. And, of course, each of us is different from others in various ways. At the same time, we are all alike in certain respects. At the most fundamental level, we are all human. Below that level of shared likeness, however, we begin to encounter a rich variety of differences—some based on physical attributes, such as skin color, body type, and male or female sex organs, and others based on social and cultural characteristics, ranging from wealth and occupation to lifestyle and consumer tastes. The sociologist becomes interested when these various differences appear in patterned combinations that persist and get reproduced from one generation to the next and, ultimately, have significant social effects.

Social differences become **social stratification** when people can be ranked hierarchically along some dimension of inequality, such as wealth,

American individualistic success model The cultural model shared by many Americans whereby success and failure are believed to be the result of individual qualities and efforts, and inequalities are assumed to be based on merit and personal shortcomings.

Social stratification The hierarchical ranking of people on the basis of social difference—specifically, with regard to their access to desirable resources, their life chances, and their social influence. Various theories of social stratification have proposed different understandings of how these strata are defined and arranged. Marx, for example, maintained that class was the basis of stratification in modern capitalist society. Weber, on the other hand, distinguished among three different types of strata—class, status, and power. Other theories of stratification might consider gender or race to be the basis of stratification.

income, prestige, power, gender, sex, religion, or ethnicity. People at each of the levels constitut-
ing the stratification hierarchy tend to have **life chances** in common; in other words, they have
similar chances of sharing in material or cultural goods. Members of the same social stratum
may have similar lifestyles, such as going to the opera or taking vacations overseas. They may
even have a sense of shared identity with "people like us." On the other hand, the chances
of getting a higher education and of living into old age are examples of life chances that are
unequally distributed in society.

An important factor in maintaining hierarchies and inequalities is power—the capacity to
get things done even against the wishes of others. The possession of power depends on the
unequal distribution of resources such as wealth, prestige, strength, and force. Sometimes
power is given institutional recognition and becomes "authority," which denotes a formal position or official status, as in the case of organizational officeholders—chief executive officer,
governor, police chief, and so on. At other times, power becomes much broader than a particular
organization and is accumulated in a social stratum, such as an elite. When power gains acceptance in the eyes of those subject to it, we may say that it has secured "legitimacy." The question
of how this legitimacy is achieved is a subject addressed by the sociology of culture and by the
cultural approach to politics.

It is important to recognize that an objective **social structure** of inequality may exist
independently of people's conscious awareness of it. To an extent, structure and consciousness
have to be kept analytically separate. However,
consciousness—what people think—is a significant factor in the creation and maintenance of
social stratification, even though the latter may
involve mere acceptance of the routine necessities
of everyday life rather than an active endorse-
ment of the social order. Alternatively, acceptance
of the unequal social order may be due to a lack
of knowledge of any possible alternative, and
acceptance of the way things are ordered, whether
positive or passive and fatalistic, may be the result
of the persuasive influence of an ideology—a set
of assumptions and beliefs justifying the existing
social order. This ideology does not have to be set

> **Life chances** The opportunities for sharing in material
> or cultural goods during one's lifetime. Life chances are
> affected not only by personal merit and accomplish-
> ment but also by race, gender, and socioeconomic status.
>
> **Social structure** The enduring, orderly, and patterned
> relationships among elements of society that shape
> and, at times, regulate social behavior. Social structure
> influences not only our actions and behavior but also
> our possibilities for action and behavior. The enduring
> theoretical debate, of course, is that between social
> structure and human agency.

out in formal documents as a set of doctrines; indeed, it can be implicitly conveyed through
popular culture, as in the individualist sentiments of a popular song such as Frank Sinatra's "I
Did It My Way" or in the "rags-to-riches" theme of many TV game shows and soap operas.

Dimensions of Stratification

One way of thinking of social stratification is to see it in terms of how individuals fit into set positions or locations in a pre-given structure of hierarchies. The hierarchies may take various forms, with different degrees of opportunity for movement up or down the hierarchy.

The most rigid form of stratification is that of **caste,** and, historically, India has provided the best illustration of how caste should be understood (Milner 1994). Indian society still has traces of the caste system, according to which one's lifestyle and possible occupation are set from birth on the basis of the family's societal status. The caste system was supported by Hindu scripture, which identified a hierarchy of castes separated by rules of ritual purity. Each caste was ritually purer than the one below it, and members of one caste could not marry someone from a lower caste. At the bottom of the hierarchy were the "untouchables"—so called because they were excluded from rituals that conferred religious purity. They were denied the right to enter Hindu temples or to draw water from the same wells as members of higher castes, who feared they would suffer ritual pollution if they came into contact with an untouchable. The Enlightenment values that inspired India's anticolonial struggle against Britain informed the new nation's decision to officially abolish caste—indeed, the Indian Constitution officially abolished "untouchability"—and an untouchable was elected president in 1997. As noted earlier, the caste system still exercises an influence on Indian social stratification; however, that influence is diminishing in the face of India's rapid economic expansion in recent years, accompanied by increasing levels of higher education and social mobility—not least in the regions where the expanding computer industry is located.

An interesting feature of the caste system is that it represents a hierarchy of social statuses based on **prestige**—in this case, religious prestige. Members of the higher castes do not necessarily have greater economic standing or power than those below them, although it is often the case that they do. It was perhaps because Max Weber had so thoroughly studied India that, upon turning his attention to modern societies, he emphasized the need to distinguish among three hierarchies or dimensions of stratification: class, status, and political power. These categories were often related, but sometimes they were clearly separate. For example, a minister of religion might have high status based on prestige, but low income from his or her class position and little political power.

Caste The most rigid form of stratification. In a caste system, individuals are born into their social position and have few, if any, opportunities for upward or downward mobility. Traditional Indian society, in which the Hindu religion was dominant, is often cited as an example of a caste system.

Prestige The esteem, honor, or deference assigned to one's social position.

Class, Race, and Gender

The three hierarchies of stratification that have drawn the most attention and controversy are class, race, and gender. (1) The class structure is composed of positions in the system of economic production. (2) In the racial structure, people are distinguished according to their skin color. Race is distinct from ethnicity, which refers to a shared cultural identity, often involving shared language, religion, and other cultural factors that lead people to believe they have a common origin, as in the case of immigrant groups such as Italian-Americans and Polish-Americans. Race and ethnicity may overlap, and various ethnicities exist within racial categories. For example, both Italian-Americans and Polish-Americans would be classified within the category of the white race. Some ethnic groups have been found to be more difficult to categorize, such as Hispanics in the United States, who may choose to classify themselves as "white." The increasing numbers of Asian ethnic groups present a similar problem. Apart from skin color, which itself is variable (no group is really "white" or "black"), it is difficult to find a physical factor that would differentiate so-called races. (3) Finally, a gender structure exists to the extent that people are distinguished according to whether they have a set of characteristics that lead them to be classified as either male or female and are expected to behave in ways deemed appropriate to their gender.

A key question is whether class is the fundamental source of modern stratification (see Table 8.1). In the nineteenth century, when the modern industrial system was being established, large numbers of former rural agricultural workers moved to the growing cities to become factory workers. Their living and working conditions were often harsh and they were subjected to tough work disciplines, with wage stoppages as punishment for lateness or slowness. Women and children worked in conditions that would now be unacceptable in Western societies, although they are still widespread in some developing countries. Violent conflict often erupted between owner-managers (capitalists) and their workers—one group attempting to increase production and reduce costs, the other group trying to resist **exploitation.** It was in these circumstances that Karl Marx developed an analysis of modern society that viewed social classes and the conflicts between them as the most important determinants of stratification (Marx and Engels 1848/1964).

Much of the discussion of social class in twentieth-century sociology could be described as a debate with the ghost of Marx. This is especially true of the Weberian approach, which has been so

> **Exploitation** The manipulation of one person or group by another for the latter's own benefit and profit. Marx argued that exploitation is inherent to modern capitalism. The wages of workers, he said, are always lower than the value of their contribution to the finished product, thereby benefiting the capitalist at the expense of the workers.

formative for analyzing stratification in modern sociology (Parkin 1979; Weber 1968). The debate hinges on whether Marx was right to single out class divisions, based on relations in the production system, as the most fundamental source of stratification in modern society. Weber and his successors have argued that other sources of stratification, such as prestige (status) and political power (party), can be equally important. In recent years some commentators have argued that class is declining in importance compared with gender, race, and consumer lifestyles; others disagree (Grusky 1998; Lamont 2000).

Those who follow Marx's approach to class insist that the central feature of the capitalist economic system is the exploitation of workers by capitalists. By *exploitation* Marx meant a situation in which wages were consistently lower than the value that workers contributed to the finished product, and the capitalist pocketed part of the workers' "share" (the surplus value) as profit. Consequently, there was always some conflict between the capitalist class (the bourgeoisie) and the working class (the proletariat). Exploitation, according to Marx, had existed in various forms in all types of economic systems (modes of production)—including ancient slavery (in the relations between slaves and their owners) and feudalism (in the relations between landowners and serfs). Although there were more than two classes in capitalist society, including intermediate classes such as the petit-bourgeois class composed of the self-employed and others who mainly exploited their own or their family's labor, the main division was between the exploiting class of capitalists and the exploited class of workers. (Some contemporary sociologists have also attempted to distinguish subclasses according to such criteria as how much autonomy and power workers have in their employment situation [e.g., Wright 1985].)

For Weber, too, property ownership and lack of property were basic categories of all class situations (Weber 1948: 182). However, he also maintained that class situation could vary within those broad groupings, depending on what the individuals in question had to offer in the market (e.g., skills, labor, and property). In practice, this approach has been used to develop a list of classes that, in turn, consist of lists of occupations at similar income levels. This multiple-classes categorization is useful to policymakers who need to know how various income groups are faring and whether opportunities for **social mobility** exist. The amount of social mobility may be affected by state policies aimed at increasing opportunities for individuals—for example, by providing more educational facilities. It is also affected by the ability of occupational groups to practice *closure*, which involves closing off access to new entrants by raising barriers, as when higher educational qualifications are demanded

Social mobility The ability of individuals or groups to change their social position or status, either for better or for worse, within a social hierarchy. Societal myths such as the "American dream" imply that society is open and meritocratic, and that social mobility for the better is simply the result of hard work; however, long-standing inequalities suggest that this is not the case.

Social Inequality in the United States

Wealth and Poverty

U.S. median household income[1]	$40,816
Average household net worth of the top 1% of wage earners	$10,204,000
Average net worth of the bottom 40% of wage earners[2]	$1,900
Definition of middle-class in terms of income[3]	$32,653 to $48,979
Percentage of U.S. children who live in poverty[4]	20%
Percentage of U.S. adults who live in poverty[5]	12%
Percentage of single mothers who live in poverty[6]	37.4%
Rank of the United States among the seventeen leading industrial nations with the largest percentage of their populations in poverty[7]	1
Portion of U.S. stock owned by the wealthiest 10% of Americans[8]	9/10
Median hourly wage of a former welfare recipient [9]	$6.61
Percentage of former welfare recipients who have no access to a car[10]	90%
Bill Gates's hourly wage[11]	$650,000

Attitudes About Wealth and Poverty

Percentage of those earning $15,000 a year who call themselves middle-class	36%
Percentage of those with incomes between $35,000 and $49,999 who call themselves middle-class	49%
Percentage of those with incomes above $75,000 who call themselves middle-class[12]	71%
Percentage of 5,000 American adults polled who cited "lack of effort" as a reason people are poor	43%
Percentage who cited "strong effort" as a reason some people are rich[13]	53%

Effects of Class, Race, and Gender on Income

Median net worth of a white American	$81,700
Median net worth of an African-American [14]	$10,000
Number of white people living in poverty	21,922,000
Number of black people living in poverty[15]	8,360,000
Percentage of men earning poverty-level hourly wage	19.5%
Percentage of women earning poverty-level hourly wage[16]	31.1%

Males	
White-collar	47% (of workforce), avg hourly wage = $22.20
Service	10.4%, avg hourly wage = $10.92
Blue-collar	40.1%, avg hourly wage = $13.71

Females	
White-collar	73.4%, avg hourly wage = $14.90
Service	15.2%, avg hourly wage = $8.17
Blue-collar[17]	9.6%, avg hourly wage = $9.94

Median income by type of household	
Family households (all)	$49,940

Married couple families	$56,827
Female householder, no husband present	$26,164
Male householder, no wife present[18]	$41,838

Education

In October 1996, 48.6% of 16- to 24-year-old high school completers in lower-income families were enrolled in college, compared with 62.7% from middle-income families and 78% from higher-income families.[19]

Mean verbal SAT score for children in households with income below $10,000	427
Mean verbal SAT score for children in households with income above $100,000	559
Mean math SAT score for children in households with income below $10,000	446
Mean math SAT score for children in households with income above $100,000[20]	572
Median household income for those with less than a ninth grade education	$17,261
Median household income for those with a ninth to twelfth grade education (no diploma)	$21,737
Median household income for high school graduates	$35,744
Median household income for college graduates, B.A.	$64,406
Median household income for college graduates, M.A.	$74,476
Median household income for professional degree holders[21]	$100,000

Housing

Number of American households that spend more than 50% of income on housing[22]	14 million
Number of families or primary individuals who live in mobile homes or trailers[23]	6.8 million
Percentage change in the number of rural Americans living in mobile homes between 1980 and 1990[24]	+ 52
Number of U.S. households earning less than $10,000/year	7.6 million
Number of affordable housing units available[25]	4.4 million
Number of gated communities in America[26]	approx 20,000 (housing approximately 8.4 million people)
Number of gated communities in 1950[27]	2,500

Interesting fact: In 1995, homeowners earning more than $100,000 a year received a total of $28.9 billion in federal income tax deductions on mortgage interest payments. The entire 1996 budget of the U.S. Department of Housing and Urban Development was only $19 billion.[28]

Sources:
1 U.S. Census Bureau, 1999.
2 Edward N. Wolff, "Recent Trends in Wealth Ownership, 1983–1998," April 2000.
3 Economy.com, "The Dismal Scientist," 1999.
4 U.S. Census Bureau, 2000.
5 U.S. Census Bureau, 2000.
6 U.S. Census Bureau, 1999.
7 UN Human Development Report 1998.
8 Economic Policy Institute, Washington, D.C., 1999.
9 Urban Institute, 2000.
10 Surface Transportation Policy Project, 2001
11 Bill Gates's net worth page, average since 1986.
12 National Center for Opinion Research, 2000.
13 Gallup Poll Social Audit, 1998.
14 Edward N. Wolff, "Recent Trends in Wealth Ownership, 1983–1998," April 2000.
15 U.S. Census Bureau, 1999.
16 Economic Policy Institute, 2000.
17 "The State of Working America 2000–2001," Economic Policy Institute; statistics are for 2000.
18 U.S. Census Bureau, 1999.
19 U.S. Department of Commerce, Bureau of the Census, Current Population Survey.
20 SAT Program information, 1998.
21 U.S. Census Bureau, 1999.
22 Habitat for Humanity, 1999.
23 U.S. Census Bureau, American Housing Survey, 1999.
24 Housing Assistance Council, Washington, D.C.
25 Low Income Housing Information Service, 1995.
26 *Fortress America: Gated Communities in America*, Edward J. Blakely and Mary Gail Snyder, Brookings Institution Press, 1997.
27 *Fortress America*, 1997.
28 "The New Politics of Housing," Peter Dreier, *Journal of the American Planning Association* 63, no 1 (winter 1997).

Average Executive to Average Production Worker Pay Ratio, 1990–2003

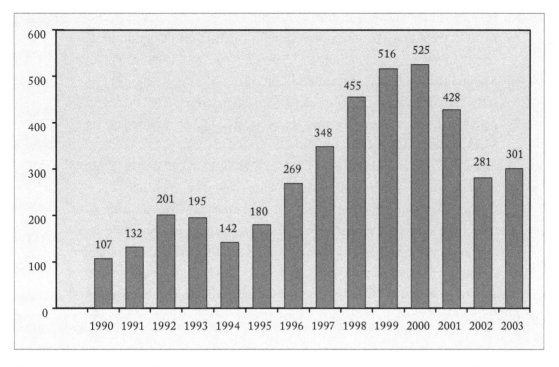

Note: Total executive compensation: Includes salary, bonus, restricted stock, payouts on other long-term incentives, and the value of options exercised (*Business Week* annual compensation survey, 1991–2005). Average worker pay: Bureau of Labor Statistics, Employment, Hours, and Earnings from the Current Employment Statistics Survey, Table B-2.

Source: Anderson, et al. (2005).

(Parkin 1979). Randall Collins (1979) refers to this practice as "credentialism." Alternatively, a group may seek to usurp the position of a more highly ranked occupation and secure recognition within it, as in the case of nurses in the medical profession.

The result of these different starting points is that sociologists who follow Marx's lead are concerned with revealing how the changing capitalist economic system is affecting class relations and whether his prediction of increasing polarization of the two main classes—capitalists and proletarians—is occurring. Three developments that might bring this about are (1) an increasing concentration of wealth in the hands of the rich and in large corporations (see Figure 8.1); (2) the de-skilling of labor as a result of new technology in which the skills are built into the machinery (Braverman 1974); and (3) a weakening of labor's position through changes in the market, such as increased employment of nonunionized workers or foreign labor. It can safely be stated that (1) and (3) have been occurring in U.S. society in the last ten years or so, whereas with regard to (2) the evidence is more mixed, varying among occupations and sectors of the economy.

The twelfth annual CEO compensation survey by the Institute for Policy Studies and United for a Fair Economy yielded these findings:

- In 2004, the average total compensation for CEOs of the 367 leading U.S. corporations was $11.8 million, up 45 percent from $8.1 million in 2003 and $2.0 million in 1990 (Anderson et al. 2005: 2).
- If the minimum wage had risen as fast as CEO pay since 1990, the lowest-paid workers in our country would be earning $23.03 an hour today, not $5.15 an hour (Anderson et al. 2005: 2).
- Since 1990, the cumulative pay of the ten highest-paid CEOs in each year together has totaled more than $11.7 billion (Anderson et al. 2005: 3).
- Of the 150 possible slots for the highest-paid executives over the same period, not a single one was filled by a woman, and only one non-white male appeared on the list: Charles Wang, founder and former CEO of Computer Associates (Anderson et al. 2005: 3).

Based on their analysis of CEO compensation-package information, Sarah Anderson and her colleagues (2005) concluded that the current ratio of CEO compensation to worker pay is 301:1.

In contrast to sociologists influenced by the Marxian approach to class, those in the tradition of Weber are concerned with mapping the changing market positions (e.g., level of qualifications and skills) of different groups of occupations that constitute classes and investigating how these changes affect "life chances," such as educational attainment, health, and income. Professionals and managers tend to have higher qualifications and can command higher incomes than workers in blue-collar occupations. Similarly, skilled workers are more marketable and earn higher incomes than workers in unskilled occupations. Given the importance of the possession of qualifications and skills (credentials), a key topic is that of educational opportunities. Are educational opportunities increasing for the lower classes, and is there more social mobility as a result? "Weberian" questions like these, concerning social mobility, have occupied American sociologists to a greater degree than "Marxian" questions.

Social Mobility

Most Americans accept a certain amount of inequality as functional for society. Inequalities are thought to supply motivation to work hard and get ahead—high earnings should go to those with skills and talent, low earnings to those who have less to offer. This is consistent with the structural-functional view of social stratification, whereby various occupational roles are rewarded according to their perceived worth in line with society's values (Parsons 1949).

The structural-functional view is sometimes referred to as the Davis-Moore Thesis, because it was first presented by Kingsley Davis and Wilbert Moore (1945). Critics, such as Melvin Tumin (1953), have asked how such estimates of worth could be related to social values. For example, are society's values upheld if a basketball player is paid more than the president of the United States? Or is there a gap between the economic market mechanism and other sets of values?

Criticisms of inequalities occur when it is thought that people are being denied opportunities for social mobility, because of either discrimination against certain groups (e.g., race or sex discrimination) or lack of facilities (e.g., inadequate schools and scarcity of good teachers). Policymakers have been sensitive to this issue of equality of opportunities for social mobility, so a great deal of effort has gone into developing measures of social mobility, especially in relation to education.

The first major study in America was carried out in 1967 by Peter Blau and Otis Dudley Duncan in association with the U.S. Bureau of Census (Blau and Duncan 1967). Using a sample of more than 20,000 men between the ages of 20 and 64, the authors compared respondents' occupations with those of their fathers. Initially, they drew up a list of occupational categories, which they ranked in a hierarchy of prestige, using as the mean indicator of prestige the level of income in each occupation. What they found were a high level of upward mobility from blue-collar to white-collar occupations and a low level of downward mobility. The high level of upward mobility was seen as a consequence of the massive growth in the number of white-collar and service jobs. Most of the mobility was short-range, between manual and white-collar jobs, and there was only a small amount of long-range upward mobility from the bottom of the occupational hierarchy to the top—from "log cabin to riches." The most important factor correlating with upward mobility was education—both the father's level of education and that of the son. Another finding was that African-Americans were disadvantaged in terms of securing upward mobility, with respect to both educational opportunities and competition for jobs with similarly qualified white Americans.

Blau and Duncan's findings regarding social mobility in the 1960s have been found to hold true in subsequent periods, with little change. Moreover, comparative studies of social mobility in other Western societies show rates of social mobility that are broadly similar to those in the United States (e.g., Erikson and Goldthorpe 1994).

In the past, findings about social mobility between classes tended to be based on changes in men's occupations over their lifetime or compared with their father's occupation. Women's social mobility was often ignored that many women were not in paid employment or because married women were assumed to share the class position of their husbands. However, now that many more women are in the workforce, it is important to investigate patterns of inequality and opportunity as they relate to women. One of the main avenues of upward mobility is education. The more education people receive, the bigger their paychecks are likely to be (U.S. Census Bureau 2002). However, at each level of education, women earn less than men do and the inequality shows little variation (U.S. Census Bureau 2002). Among professional-degree holders, for example, women earned on average half the salary of men in 1993, although the gap appears to be narrowing a little (U.S. Census Bureau 1993, 2002). Moreover, some degree fields are dominated by men (e.g., engineering) and others by women (e.g., nursing). The earnings of people with bachelor degrees in engineering were at the top of the earnings league, while those with the equivalent degree in education were next to the bottom. So, although educational opportunities have increased for women, their incomes still lag behind those of men with comparable levels of education.

Race and ethnic background also affect one's chances of getting a good education and experiencing upward social mobility. Poor, black, and Hispanic students are more likely than white, middle-class children to be physically punished, suspended, expelled, or forced to repeat a grade (Eitzen and Baca-Zinn 1991). Even the standardized intelligence tests used to measure supposedly innate intelligence have been found to be culture-bound, tapping into an individual's familiarity—or unfamiliarity—with a range of white, middle-class experiences (Curran and Renzetti 1996). The schools and educational facilities available to racial and ethnic minorities in poor school districts tend to receive much lower funding than those in predominantly white, middle-class districts with higher property values. Consequently, black Americans do less well in terms of securing upward social mobility through education than whites and certain other ethnic groups, such as Asians.

The Class Gap

Arguably, the really major inequalities of opportunity are not in the middle of the social stratification hierarchy but at the top and the bottom. It is certainly more difficult to gain entry to the top positions and to escape from the bottom than to move up or down a few positions in the middle. Accordingly, many sociologists have felt it necessary to focus on what distinguishes those at the top from those at the bottom. As we will see, it is not class position alone that accounts for this distinction but also the factors that Weber referred to as power and status. Ownership of property is always an important source of power, but it is not the only source. It has been argued that, on the one hand, there is an **elite** whose power grows out of corporate hierarchies—chief executives of corporations, top government officials, senior politicians, military leaders—and that these constitute a power

Elite A social group that occupies a position of prestige and power in society and is dominant as a result.

elite and, on the other hand, that at the bottom of the stratification system are groups below the working class whose constituents have the status of welfare recipients—the so-called **underclass.**

The Elite

The idea that society is divided between a small and organized power elite and an unorganized and powerless mass was offered as a response to the rise of fascist and communist dictatorships in Europe during the first half of the twentieth century. The fascist regimes of Germany and Italy in the 1930s and 1940s, and the communist states of the Soviet Union in the 1920s and then of China and Soviet-dominated Eastern Europe after 1945, subjected property and markets to the control of the political power elite.

The elite-mass model of stratification was also used by some sociologists to describe the post–World War II American power structure. According to Columbia University sociologist C. Wright Mills (1956), the fusion of executive-governmental, corporate, and military power during the Cold War gave rise to a power elite that reached the top of the corporate hierarchies of the state-militaryindustrial complex—and, from there,

> **Underclass** A segment of society that, unlike other classes that are defined by property ownership or occupation, is composed of people who are underemployed or unemployed and may be dependent upon welfare benefits from the state. It is because of their dependency that members of the underclass are often negatively stigmatized.

ruled America. Although Mills accepted Marx's ideas about the power of property and the importance of class relations, he was also influenced by Weber's insistence that organizational-political power could, to some extent, operate independently of class.

Has the existence of such a power elite been verified? In fact, during the Cold War period, which lasted from the end of World War II in 1946 until the fall of the East European communist regimes in 1989, there was plenty of evidence of close decisionmaking ties between corporate elites in the state-military-industrial complex. This is probably not surprising in view of the perceived threat posed by the nuclear arms race and the need for secrecy in matters of strategic importance. Since the end of the Soviet regime and its military power, the issue of the military's role in the American power structure has become less prominent. Concerns about a power elite have become more focused on the question of whether the super-rich and those in charge of large corporations have too much influence, especially over major institutions (including universities), politicians, and the mass media (Domhoff 1998). It is easy to find examples to support this view. The most obvious ones are multimillionaires, such as H. Ross Perot and Steve Forbes, who used their vast wealth to fund their presidential campaigns (in 1992 and 1996, respectively). Wealthy donors to political campaigns have also gained privileged access to the White House and to high-level members of Congress (Van Natta and Fritsch 1997). However, we can also cite examples of divisions within the ranks of the rich, suggesting that there may not be a single power elite. For example, even the great wealth and influence of Bill Gates of Microsoft were not enough to spare him the federal court proceedings that led to a judgment requiring the partial breakup of his company. Nor did the corporate riches of Enron and its close connections to local and national political power prevent its corrupt executives from being prosecuted and spending a good part of their adult lives in jail.

The claim that the power elite manipulates the masses through the mass media has also been disputed. Although those who control large media corporations exercise great influence, their power is often limited by the competition and diversity that exist in the media themselves. There is strong evidence, moreover, that the professional ethics of news journalists provide a powerful counterweight against the temptation for newspaper owners to manipulate their stories. And, finally, there is reason to believe that the consumers of the mass media are not passive receivers of the media's messages but, rather, play an active role in selecting and interpreting them. In sum, the problems with the power elite thesis are (1) that it overemphasizes the consolidation of stratification to the neglect of its multidimensionality and fragmentation, and (2) that it moves directly from this distorted characterization of inequality to make claims about political governance. We explore the first of these problems in the present chapter.

The Underclass

A key development in twentieth-century industrial societies was the expansion of state activity, including the growth of the welfare state. As a response to political pressure from organized labor and other groups, the state began to provide a "safety net" of welfare benefits to the unemployed, who suffered disproportionately from illness, homelessness, and old age. Eventually, such benefits were directed not only to the unemployed but also to the underemployed (in part-time or irregular employment), the physically and mentally disabled, many female heads of households, and all elderly people. Once people become part of this underclass, they tend to remain in it, as do their families. This is especially true in cases where membership intersects with age, female gender, race, or ethnicity.

Strictly speaking, the underclass is not a class, because it is defined neither by property or non-property ownership (Marx) nor by occupation (Weber). Rather, it is defined by status: the status of being a citizen dependent on welfare benefits. Because of the prestige attached to wealth and consumption in society, those who have little to spend except for welfare "handouts" are negatively stigmatized. This, in turn, may combine with the stigma attached to their race, gender, or family circumstances (e.g., single mothers), causing them to experience further discrimination and exclusion. Indeed, they can become stuck in a "culture of poverty," which makes it hard for them to break out (Lewis 1961). Educational opportunities are less available to them than to those in families that are not dependent on welfare. And the situation is made even worse when an area, such as the inner city, is deserted by members of the community who have managed to prosper and move out. The effects of this isolation of the inner-city black underclass from the more affluent parts of the black community is the focus of William Julius Wilson in his book *The Truly Disadvantaged: The Inner City, the Underclass, and Public Policy* (1987), on race and ethnicity. The removal of the more successful members of a community from an area also re-moves their spending power, leadership abilities, and the chance for them to be seen as role models.

The concept of the underclass is controversial because it can be used as a blanket label covering people with a variety of circumstances and needs (e.g., single parents, low-paid part-time workers, the elderly, the physically or mentally sick, the unemployed). It also has the potential to stereotype people, implying that their poverty is their own fault rather than possibly the result of absent economic and educational opportunities.

Beliefs and Attitudes

Sociologists who have conducted surveys of beliefs about inequality in America have found that there is a "dominant ideology" involving three key beliefs: first, that opportunity for economic advancement is widespread in America today; second, that individuals are personally responsible for their circumstances; and third, that the overall system of inequality is therefore equitable and fair (Bullock 1999; Cozzarelli, Wilkinson, and Tagler 2001; Kluegel and Smith 1986: 23).

This dominant ideology is said to dispose people to a conservative evaluation of welfare policies, inasmuch as these policies are deemed unnecessary on the grounds that the stratification system presents ample opportunities to better oneself through individual effort. However, social liberalism has increased somewhat in response to social and political struggles and events of the past forty years, such as the civil rights movement and the women's movement. Social liberalism entails an attitude of acceptance of social and political equality with groups such as blacks and women, although without necessarily calling into question the fundamental bases of economic inequality. As a result, beliefs and attitudes regarding some aspects of poverty, race relations, and women's role in society have become markedly more liberal. The growth of social liberalism has not been uniform, however; some groups—such as the "babyboom" generation—are more liberal than others. In addition, there are regional differences with regard to social liberalism and conservatism, as indicated by the use of terms such as *red states* and *blue states* to distinguish among the prevailing attitudes and values of voters in the 2004 presidential election.

People in different social positions in the hierarchy of inequality react differently to the social inequalities affecting them; hence the mix of beliefs about inequality is likely to vary from group to group (Bullock 1999). In other words, although certain key beliefs are widespread, the overall set of ideas or beliefs is not internally consistent and may include contradictory elements. A person's set of beliefs serves more than one function. For example, some beliefs are based on individual experience or the accepted wisdom of the group, whereas others may act as defense mechanisms to bolster the individual's or group's interests. A belief in one thing (say, that the poor are generally the helpless victims of unfortunate circumstances) may coexist with a contradictory or inconsistent belief (that the poor could lift themselves from poverty if they tried hard enough). Facing up to such inconsistencies of this sort and attempting to resolve them may be too psychologically costly for the individual, whereas just living with the potential contradictions carries few if any costs in everyday life. It is perfectly possible to live with such inconsistencies because the different beliefs come to mind only in response to cues that trigger them. For example, thoughts about the "helpless poor" might be triggered by television images of racial minorities facing job discrimination, just as images of welfare recipients driving Cadillacs may bring to mind the belief that poor people are undeserving.

Americans of all classes and ethnic groups generally accept the ideology of individualism and the American dream, both of which advance the belief that hard work, perseverance, individual achievement, and upward mobility are inherently linked (Hochschild 1995). When the members of a group succeed, the ideology behind the American dream attributes their upward mobility to individual effort, hard work, and grit. However, when people feel that a certain group has violated the traditional American value of individualism, prejudice against this group is a likely result. For example, the persistence of anti-black prejudice among whites has been found to be based in part on whites' perception that blacks violate the principle of individualism in cases where they are believed to have received preferential treatment in the form of government set-asides or affirmative action (Kinder and Sears 1981; Lamont 2000; Lipset and Schneider 1978). But the question of who is deserving and who should legitimately receive preferential treatment varies enormously with respect to the various groups. Most white Americans do not object to preferential treatment for veterans or those who have disabilities, but they firmly draw the line when it comes to blacks. And whereas whites in mainstream middle-class America feel that blacks violate the tenets of individualism, in black, urban America it is not African-Americans but rather foreign-born individuals who may receive the blame. Indeed, resentment is often directed against foreign-born store owners, such as

Koreans and Asian Indians, who set up shop in black communities. The (mistaken) belief is that they must be receiving preferential treatment from the government or from U.S. banks, and this violates the belief in the link between American individualism and upward mobility (Lee 1999).

To summarize: The interpretation and application of the ideology behind individualism, meritocracy, and the question of who is "deserving" vary according to the circumstances—they are context- and group-specific (Skrentny 1996).

...

Reading 3: The American Dream of Meritocracy

By Heather Beth Johnson

The American Dream has been continually re-invented over time, so that for each generation of Americans it has held different meanings. And since the phrase "the American Dream" could mean different things to every one of us, it might be more accurate to call it "the American Dreams." At its core, however, some aspects of the Dream (or Dreams) are consistently fundamental. Simply, the American Dream explains the logic of our country's social system. *It is a way (or perhaps the way) we are to understand how American society operates.* It is how we make sense of our particular social structure. The American Dream rests on the idea that, with hard work and personal determination anyone, regardless of background, has an equal opportunity to achieve his or her aspirations. The American Dream promises that our system functions as a meritocracy. *Within a meritocracy people get ahead or behind based on what they earn and deserve, rather than what circumstances they were born into.* This notion of is central to the American Dream, and is the central logic of how our system is supposed to operate. The American Dream, in many ways, defines us and sets our system apart from others.

Given the importance of the American Dream to our national identity, and the enormity of it in shaping our core ideologies, it is curious how little attention the idea has received in academe, especially in the social sciences. Until relatively recently, no one had traced the history of its origins, meanings, or cultural impacts. In the past decade, however, groundbreaking scholarship on the American Dream has yielded important understandings. We know, for example, that the principles of the American Dream were promoted by even the very first settlers to arrive from Britain. Later, the American Dream was central to the charter of the United States when the Declaration of Independence was created. And although the phrase "the American Dream" does not appear to have been coined until around 1931, it has quickly become recognizable the world over. The American Dream is, for better or for worse, the central creed of our nation.

As a creed, the American Dream represents a basic belief in the power and capacity of the individual. Deeply embedded in this belief is a particular notion of individual agency—the idea that over the course of our own lives we are each accountable for whatever position we find ourselves in. Full collective potential for this agency, though, depends on exactly that which the dream promises: A system of opportunity, so that regardless of background each individual has an equal chance to prosper. The American Dream promises that an egalitarian system will allow individuals to advance based on their own merit. This promise resonates throughout contemporary American society telling us—through multiple variations on a theme, through school assignments and television advertisements, through song lyrics and newspaper stories—that in a meritocratic process we rise or fall self-reliantly. So, despite differences across generations and regardless we each have unique hopes and dreams, we share the American Dream of meritocracy in common: That is, we are each subject—in one way or another—to our nationalist ideology of meritocracy.

Meritocracy explains not only how our society works but how inequality exists. The idea is that what we reap—good or bad—is merited; whatever we have, whatever our status, whatever our place in the social world, we earn. A system of meritocracy does not assert equality *per se*—within any social hierarchy some individuals will inevitably be positioned higher and some lower—rather, it justifies inequality of social positioning by the meritocratic process itself. Inequality of outcomes is justified and legitimized by equality of opportunity. This meritocratic idea has roots dating back to the British colonialists' aspirations for a society founded in a "natural aristocracy." In their vision upward mobility and prominence would be merited and achieved, rather than ascribed. For those first families settling from Europe, this vision was a defiant rebellion from other forms of social structure where social rank was inherited based on such distinctions as family lineage, royalty, and caste. Although they never precisely defined how merit should be measured, it was always clear how it should not be: achievement based on individual merit is not unearned advantage; it is not inherited privilege. A meritocratic system is contingent upon a societal commitment to fair competition so that no individual or group is advantaged or disadvantaged by the positions or predicaments of their ancestors.

The American Dream of meritocracy is at once a simple idea and a complex national ethos. For some people the American Dream may simply represent owning a home, while for others it might represent striking it rich. Although those may be part of what the American Dream means for many people, as a foundational ideology it is about more than material abundance or a place with streets-paved-with-gold. It is about opportunity—not just an opportunity, but equal opportunity. It is about not just a chance, but equal chances. In her landmark book, *Facing Up to the American Dream: Race, Class, and the Soul of a Nation*, political scientist Jennifer Hochschild explicates the American Dream and identifies its main tenets. She distinguishes key premises which interlock to form its philosophical foundation. These premises include meritocracy, the notion that in our social system upward and downward mobility is based on personal achievement so that people get ahead or behind based on merit; equal opportunity, the notion that all members of society are given equal opportunity for social mobility; individualism, the notion that each individual makes it on his or her own; and the open society, the notion that the United States is a free country, the melting pot of the world, the land of opportunity for all people. As Hochschild outlines, the American Dream is a set of deeply held beliefs, a particular mindset. It is a particular way of viewing the world, and it is a particular way in which we want the world to view us. For many Americans, the American Dream is a great source of pride. But even many who question it as an accurate portrayal of social life believe strongly in the egalitarian and inclusive principles for which it stands.

As a dominant ideology the American Dream echoes throughout our nation, it carries on through generations, and can cement in crystal form in our minds. But it can also be easily taken for granted. For as central the American Dream is to our national identity, we don't consciously reflect on it often. As historian Jim Cullen has noted, the American Dream is "an idea that seems to envelop us as unmistakably as the air we breathe." We can be reminded of it, without even being aware, every time we are told that we will achieve if we work hard enough, or that we could have achieved if we had only worked harder. The American Dream can inspire great aspirations and explain great achievements, and it can depress us as we ponder our regrets. It is malleable enough to fit in almost any social situation. We can use it to justify our accomplishments: I earned it on my own. This is the result of my hard work. I deserve this. And we can feel the sting of it as we question ourselves: Should I have worked harder? Could I have gone farther? Why am I not where he is? And, we can use it to question others' social standing: Why doesn't she try harder? Doesn't he want more? Why don't they make better choices? The American Dream is all around us, and, in many ways it is in us.

Ultimately, the American Dream is an explanation for the hierarchical ordering of our class positions in our social world. It explains our relative rank as the result of solely our own doing, not as the result of social forces or the circumstances we find ourselves in. It is not surprising, then, that Americans might genuinely believe that they independently earn and deserve their class positions—the dominant ideology of our culture tells them so. This internalized sense of class positioning has been the subject of scholarly research, especially in regards to working-class and poor families. In Richard Sennett and Jonathan Cobb's pivotal book *The Hidden Injuries of Class*, for example, they discuss the "hidden injury" of the internal class conflict experienced among working-class men. They wrote that "Every question of identity as an image of social place in a hierarchy is also a question of social value. … This is the context in which all questions of personal and social legitimacy occur." The American Dream helps to sustain these "hidden injuries" by bombarding people with the message that their social place—and their social value, their self-worth—is directly and exclusively the result of their own actions.

In their interviews for this book, people spoke in depth and at length about the American Dream, despite the fact that in the first 182 interviews the families were not even asked about it. Those parents were told that the project was to study assets and inequality, and during the interviews they were asked to speak about the communities they lived in, their children's schools, and their families' financial histories. Over and over, however, the focus of the interviews turned to beliefs in meritocracy as families repeatedly brought up the subject and wove it into the conversations. I must admit that I myself was surprised with the extent to which the interview findings were so ideological in nature. And I was even more surprised when interviews—including those interviews from the second phase which did directly ask people about their thoughts on the American Dream—revealed the depths of people's commitment to, and belief in, meritocracy as a real and valid explanation for how contemporary American society operates. People from all walks of life spoke forthrightly of their belief in meritocracy, not just as rhetoric, but as an accurate explanation of our social system.

Trying to confirm these findings has been frustrating due to the lack of qualitative studies that have asked people in-depth about their perspectives on the American Dream. Curiously, even in terms of quantitative studies, surprisingly few public opinion polls have been conducted on the subject of the American Dream. However, related social survey data that do exist reflect that Americans overwhelmingly believe that their country operates as a meritocracy. Indeed, after his review of the data political scientist Everett Carl Ladd concluded that survey research "shows Americans holding tenaciously and distinctively to the central elements of their founding ideology." He found Americans' belief in the American Dream to be more intense, pervasive, and firmly entrenched than generally recognized. Very recent qualitative research on post-civil rights views also finds that in in-depth interviews people are remarkably insistent in their beliefs that the playing field is level, that meritocracy is real. While these findings are definitely in line with my own, perhaps the most compelling affirmation for me has been to discover that other sociologists doing in-depth interviewing on subjects not explicitly focused on the American Dream are finding, as I have, that respondents consistently evoke the American Dream—specifically the notion of meritocracy—as their own theme in interviews. In the 200 interviews conducted for this study, what families said, their views, their decisions, and their experiences, were explicitly framed by their belief in meritocracy. These families' perspectives give a vivid account of the place and significance of the American Dream in contemporary life.

The reality of wealth in America though—the way it is acquired, distributed, and the way it is used—is a direct contradiction to these fundamental ideas. In interviews with American families we have seen a way how that plays out. Examining school decision-making (just one arena wherein families potentially experience the ramifications of wealth inequality), those parents from backgrounds of even moderate wealth had a significant advantage over parents with family histories of wealth poverty. Disproportionately white, wealth-holding parents used the financial assistance, intergenerational transfers, and security of their family wealth to help access schools for their own children that were viewed as advantageous by all of the parents. Meanwhile, parents without family wealth to rely upon, who were disproportionately black, were navigating the same arena unaided, with relatively limited resources and constrained capacities. *A central incongruity surfaces when families' school decisions are considered in the context of the American Dream: the assets that the wealth-holding families had owned, relied upon, and utilized in choosing schools had most often originated from non-merit sources.* Inherited wealth and the security of family wealth were critical advantages being passed along to the next generation—advantages often unearned by the parents themselves, and always unearned by their children.

A foundational conflict exists between the meritocratic values of the American Dream and the structure of intergenerational wealth inequality. Simply, advantageous resources inherited and passed along in families are not attained through individual achievement. Although wealth can, of course, be earned by an individual entirely independently, in the case of the families we spoke with it had not. This is the aspect of family wealth that concerns us here. Family wealth generates unearned advantages for those who have it. It is a form of privilege. In light of their beliefs in the American Dream, how do those families who present the most transparent contradiction to the idea of meritocracy—families with wealth privilege—understand their positioning and the unearned advantages they pass along to their children?

We could presume that as with other forms of privilege (such as race privilege or gender privilege) wealth privilege would generally appear invisible and be taken for granted by those who have it. However, one of the most striking aspects of the interviews was the acknowledgement of wealth privilege on the part of wealth-holding families. The parents who had benefited from family wealth acknowledged a structure of wealth inequality that grants privilege to some families and disadvantage to others, and they acknowledged the advantages they were passing along to the next generation through the schools that they chose.

Acknowledging Advantage: A Structure of Wealth Inequality

Given the fact that these families had so vehemently expressed their beliefs in the legitimacy of the American Dream, it was startling to hear them so openly discuss the reality of structured wealth inequality in American society. Not only did parents talk openly about this, they expressed specific views concerning the advantages conferred by wealth. Wealth-holding families thought of wealth as a distinctive resource to be used in particular ways, and even asset-poor families had concrete opinions about how they would use wealth—as opposed to income—if they had it. *Regardless of whether a family had a lot, a little, or none, wealth was thought of as a special form of money, different from income.* Wealth was perceived as a vehicle to provide opportunities, experiences, and material things, as well as a source to provide other less tangible advantages that were harder to articulate but no less important (a sense of security, or confidence about the future, for example). *As a whole, families' perspectives on the advantages of family wealth centered around two notions: wealth as a push and wealth as a safety net.* While families across the board alluded to these ideas, they were especially prevalent among the wealthier families, who emphasized them repeatedly. The first notion— a "push"—or an "edge" as some referred to it, was used by parents to explain how family wealth put some people "ahead" of others right from the start and "paved the way" for them over time.

Int: Do you believe that you would have achieved the same social and economic situation that you have today if you weren't given the same financial support from your parents?

James: I would say no, because I feel what it has given me is the edge today. But for us today—for what I am, where I work, my abilities as well as my level of education— I feel without that I don't think I would be where I am today. Because the son would not have been successful without his father doing this—

Pamela: Paving the way for him—

James: [Nods] So, his father paved the way for him to start off and climb up the ladder to be what he is right now. Each kid has the potential, aspiration, a dream. And with wealth you can guide them, you can steer them that way. And you can help them, smooth the way for them, open up doors which they had never seen before.

Pamela and James Gordon, just as the other parents from backgrounds of family wealth, had experienced how that wealth had given them a push and believed it had made a positive difference in the trajectory of their life course. And they believed that this same push they were now giving their own children would make a difference for them too down the road.

Some of the wealth-holding families interviewed were more resistant than others to explicitly conceptualize that "push" they referred to, or those "difference down the road," as concrete "advantage." Joel, for example, asserted right away that wealth passed on to children is "not advantage." He did, however, believe that "it helps." While he described the wealth passed along in families as "a pushing factor," he was careful to not suggest that this translated into actual advantage.

Int: Does the financial help in terms of wealth that some people receive from their families give them certain advantages?

Joel: Not advantage, but it helps. It will help.

Int: Do you think it's significant?

Joel: Depends on what kind of financial help you're talking about.

Int: I'm not talking about billionaires. I'm talking, like, giving a kid after he graduates a $45,000 car. Or giving him, like, $30,000 for his wedding gift.

Joel: That helps, yeah, that does help. Yeah, the normal help that the parents give to the children, that is a pushing factor. Just puts you ahead a little bit.

Int: Do you believe those without stable economic situations have a harder time achieving success?

Joel: Yes, I do. That's the rule of life. I mean if you have the money you have peace of mind. So you probably can make better decisions. If you're under pressure for lack of money you could go wrong, you could make wrong decisions, definitely.

Here we see a tension between the ideology of meritocracy and the reality of structured wealth inequality in the nuances of how Joel Conrad talked about, perceived, and made sense of family wealth. While a few other parents expressed similar resistance to acknowledging that the "push" of family wealth was a form of privilege, most families did not. Victoria and Abraham Keenan, for example, conceptualized what they were doing for their own children as "absolutely" giving them advantages. While they were careful to point out that they were not "multi-millionaires" like other people they knew, they did fully believe, and acknowledge, that their family wealth was giving their children "a better chance of becoming successful." Implicit in the way they discussed the passing along of their wealth was their acknowledgement that by doing so they were passing along advantage.

Family wealth was believed to give children a push that, as Abraham said, "gives them a better chance of becoming successful." Some families, of course, can give bigger pushes than others, but even small pushes are clearly advantageous. Children who get the pushes of family wealth benefit from advantages they did nothing to individually earn. The acknowledgement of this on the part of the families who were passing advantages along is an important part of their perspectives on wealth privilege and an important insight to how they think about inequality. The second major way that parents depicted the advantages of family wealth was that it acted as a "safety net" for them in important decisions and throughout their lives. Parents from wealth-holding families repeatedly articulated their sense that family wealth was a "safety net" that gave them tremendous "peace of mind." The Barrys, a white couple whose families on both sides had given them significant financial assets over the years, described their wealth-holdings, and the family wealth they believed they could rely upon in the future, as "a sense of economic security." When asked what that sense of security provides for them, Briggette answered:

> Briggette: Sleep at night. It's very non-tangible things. Being able to give my children a sense of peace. Being able to live worry free. It's really non-tangible things. Knowing that I will probably never have the income that my parents had, but still being comfortable with that and being able to provide for my children what they need.

Another parent who explicitly described her family's wealth as a "safety net," went on to explain, "Well, I think just having, um, the assets, just gives us a certain freedom. … You know? You're more freer and more comfortable." The sense of security parents felt from the safety net of family wealth, their desire to re-establish that safety net for their own children, and their ability to rely on it and expand on it in investing in their children's futures cannot be overemphasized. This was a major way that individuals we interviewed—for example Cynthia and Paul Perkins, a white middle-class couple with three children in Boston—acknowledged the power of wealth and wealth's associated privileges.

When a "safety net" of wealth—or, "a cushion for the future"—could not be relied upon, families without it felt the insecurity of having nothing on which to fall back. This is where the difference between wealth and income is perhaps the clearest. As Lenore Meehan, a young black mother from Boston explained it: "You know, if you look on paper, I make a lot of money, but it doesn't feel like it. … I mean, I don't feel like I'm economically secure at all." While she was up-front about the fact that she felt she made quite a lot of money working as a dispatcher for the police force, Lenore's income simply could not provide the sense of security that family wealth was granting to other parents who had it. The families interviewed from all race and class backgrounds made a clear distinction between wealth and income and had concrete understandings of the kinds of advantages that family wealth can provide. Their conceptualization of the "push" and the "safety net" that wealth affords for families and children (and that lack-of-wealth prohibits) reveals their intrinsic awareness and understanding of the power of wealth. *Their acknowledgement of the role of wealth in shaping opportunities, life trajectories, and future chances reveals their awareness and understanding of a structure of wealth inequality.*

As Abigail Connor said, "for someone like her" (someone from a wealthy white family with accumulated, historically rooted race and class advantages), intergenerational transfers of wealth along the way had created a real form of contemporary privilege: family wealth advantage that is not earned entirely independently but which make opportunities relatively easier to attain, aspirations relatively more achievable, and life chances relatively more optimistic. When asked to reflect on the way this had played out in their own lives Abigail and others "like her" (others from families of relative wealth privilege) were quite aware of the essential role that their family wealth had played in their lives. Here Emily Mitchel explains:

Int: Do you believe that you would have achieved the same social and economic situation that you have today if you weren't given the same financial support from your parents growing up?

Emily: No.

Int: [silent pause] How essential, if at all, do you believe family wealth is in attaining success?

Emily: I think it certainly helps. I think more people who have money tend to excel than people who have no money. It gives you the education, it gives you the contacts, it gives you the clothes, the way of talking. The things that make life easier. Can you do it without it? Yes. Is it as easy? I don't think so. … I think early in our history hard work was really important. But I think money—you can work really hard and be the best foreman on a construction job, but it's not gonna get you a villa in France or a villa in Tuscany. It's just gonna get you whatever kind of advance you want, and a place to live. So I really think that wealth or family money is one of the essential ingredients.

Parents who had benefited from the advantages of family wealth consistently expressed their beliefs that they would not have achieved their same level of success without the financial support that they had received. Of the families who had benefited from family wealth, in only two cases did a parent insist without any compromise that they would have ended up in exactly the same position without any of the financial support that they had received from their family. And in the two exceptions it is possible, of course, that they are correct. It is also the case that we have no way to really know.

In addition to talking about how it had impacted them, parents with family wealth also discussed how they were using that wealth to shape their own children's lives. They were consciously aware that their own relatively privileged positions were enabling them to pass advantage along to the next generation. From these parents' perspectives, family wealth provided specific advantages such as educational opportunities that without it their children would not have. Elizabeth Cummings, a white mother from a wealthy St. Louis family, explained her perspective:

Elizabeth: No question about it! I mean, if my parents hadn't had the money to send my kids to *The Hills School*, we couldn't have considered it. We would have had to really do belt tightening, and financial aid, and many more loans, more mortgages. It would have been very difficult and a real strain on us, especially with two. And we probably would have felt like we just couldn't swing it as a family. So, I don't know, I would have had to gone out and gotten a job that would pay enough to justify two kids in private school. With that, it would have meant not being able to mother them as much myself. Or my husband having to change work, and all the soul searching that would have meant for him. It's unimaginable. I can't envision a path that we would have been able to so comfortably just sail on over to *The Hills School*.

The idea that "you have to have wealth to get it" (or, at least, that having wealth makes it relatively easier to get more) and the idea that "wealthier people have better life chances" (or, at least, that wealth confers relatively better chances for success), stood at the heart of the matter in the interviews. And these concepts stand at the heart of the matter here: If family wealth makes the next generation's wealth relatively easier to acquire, and if wealth makes success (however defined) relatively easier to attain, then people born into families with wealth are born with a distinct, unearned advantage. They are born with privilege that others do not have.

Conviction in Meritocracy: Hard Work or Lack Thereof

Carter: The fact of the matter is because you get some assistance from your parents doesn't mean that you haven't primarily achieved anything on your own. The fact of the matter is getting a down payment on a house means you were able to get a house sooner, but you still have to make the payments on the house, you still have to do everything necessary to maintain that house. So yeah, it's a help, but it's not the over-riding factor.

Int: You think the overriding factor is your own—
Carter: Your own psyche. ... At the end of the day, hard work is the most important ingredient—in anybody's success.

Int: Think so?

Carter: Yes. The determination to be successful is like the tide, you know? You can't stop it.

Faith & Carter Martin, Homemaker &
Attorney, White, Washington, D.C.

Tracei Diamond, a black single mother from St. Louis, spent much of her interview answering "no" to every question regarding any financial assistance she might have received and explaining the lack of any family financial resources available to her. As a full time banquet waitress at a private country club, Tracei's annual income was $24,000, she had zero net financial assets, and held only a high school degree. Tracei talked about how she sees the members of the country club at functions and events and thinks about how they and their children had advantages that she and her three children simply did not have. She spoke at length, for example, about how the schools "out there" (where the country club was located) were "good schools," how the teachers "really work with them" (the students), and how overall "the education is better." In Tracei's view, for as much as she would like to be able to give her kids those same kinds of opportunities, she simply cannot afford the move to such an area. On top of supporting her three children on her own (she was receiving no child support), Tracei also was doing whatever she could to financially support her younger sister and their mother.

Tracei's interview was typical in that she articulated clear recognition of a structured inequality amongst families that blatantly and categorically translates into unequal educational opportunities for children of different family wealth backgrounds. Yet also typical was Tracei's outright rejection of this inequality and of unequal opportunity. Tracei recognized it and rejected it at the same time. After Tracei had talked about how "wealthy families" get the "better schools," she was asked about how a family's wealth plays a factor in their children's access to quality education. She replied: "It really doesn't have an impact on it. I guess pretty much it depends on you, as far as what kind of life you will have for your child." When she was asked if wealth has any impact, she said "I don't really look at it like that. So, like I say, money definitely doesn't have anything to do with it." When asked to explain further, Tracei did: "It's basically what the parents want or whatever, that's the only thing I really can see. It just depends on how they raise them really." Despite their perspectives that class inequality structures life chances, Tracei and the other families maintained their belief that merit—not money—is what matters; they maintained with conviction their belief in meritocracy.

It was striking to hear disadvantaged parents talk so vehemently about meritocracy, to hear them assert repeatedly that positions in society are earned entirely through hard work and personal achievement, and to hear them deny family wealth inequality as a legitimate explanation. But considering that many of these parents had no direct experience with wealth privilege, that they had no awareness of the extent to which wealthy families are using and extending intergenerational transfers of assets, that they did not know for sure how much others are advantaged by unearned resources, then it makes sense how they clung so resolutely to the dominant ideology. What was most remarkable, however, is that those parents with family wealth who had spoken openly of their unearned advantages, who had so plainly seen and felt and known wealth privilege in motion in their own lives, were, at the same time, insistent that meritocracy is an accurate and realistic explanation for social stratification in America. In an interview in St. Louis, Briggette and Joe Barry spoke in detail of the financial help they had received from their parents. *They openly declared that these resources had allowed for a lifestyle they would not otherwise have had. After listing extensive financial assistance, the security of family wealth, and the many advantages they have had, the Barrys insisted that the way they had earned their assets was through hard work.*

The Barrys were not atypical of the white middle-class families interviewed; on the contrary, they portrayed the sentiments of families like them in the sample. Their socioeconomic positions were due, in large part, to the inheritance and accumulative advantages of family wealth, yet at the same time they were adamant that they singlehandedly earned and deserved their places in society. These families' insistence that they had, "worked their butts off" for what they had was astonishing. They listed in detail the help they had received from their families: Financial assistance with major purchases, down payments on houses, school tuition for children, "loans" that were later forgiven, etc. They catalogued the gifts they had received from family members for birthdays, graduations, weddings, and births of children. They discussed the numerous ways their extended families had been financially generous over the years by providing used cars, old furniture, flight tickets home for holidays, family vacations, dining out, kids' back-to-school clothes, and groceries, to name a few. They described the "push" and the "safety net" that comes with family wealth: Feeling that they have had "a head start" or "an edge" over others, knowing they would have something to fall back on in a financial pinch, and the expectation of future inheritances. While they talked about, listed, and described these things when asked, they repeatedly emphasized how hard they had worked for all that they owned and how much they deserved their stations in life.

Regardless of background, families used the American Dream of meritocracy to explain their assertion that anyone can be anything and do anything and get anywhere with hard work. They stressed that hard work or lack thereof was the determinant of each individual's position in society. But for those with family wealth, what was most notable was how they implied, implicitly and explicitly, that their own advantages as well as the advantages they were passing along to their children were earned and deserved autonomously—through hard work, perseverance, and determination alone.

Another example comes from our interview with Chris and Peter Ackerman, a white couple in their early thirties who lived in a white suburb of St. Louis. They had three kids, ages six, three, and two. They had been married for ten years and both worked in management positions on the staff of a local university. Their combined annual income was $83,000, their net worth $210,000, and their net financial assets totaled $91,500. This couple owned savings accounts, savings bonds, small trust funds for each child, and a boat worth $12,500. They had received significant financial assistance from their families, including help with a down payment on their first home, which they bought when they married. The equity from that house was later used as a down payment for an upgraded home when they had their children. Chris and Peter's parents financed their college educations; they never had to take out student loans; their children regularly received cash gifts and savings bonds from their grandparents on holidays and birthdays; Chris's parents had often paid for the family to vacation with them; Peter's parents had bought many of their major household appliances for them, as well as their car; and so on. They talked about how appreciative they were of all this help, about how they would not be in the position that they are without it. Despite this acknowledgement, Chris and Peter continually insisted that their wealth had been achieved single-handedly:

Int: How did you acquire the assets you own?
Chris: By working.
Peter: Saving, working.
Chris: Working and saving, working and saving. That's basically how we do it.

The Ackermans and many of their peers simultaneously acknowledged the power of their wealth privilege and avowed that it does not really matter. They were resolute in their explanation that hard work and determination had gotten them to where they are. For as much as they were upfront about the structure of wealth, they also depicted social positioning as independently earned and deserved. As one young mother from just outside of New York City put it, "You know—and I'm not bragging, I'm not saying anything—but it just comes from setting your priorities straight, and taking care of business!" In discussing hard work and individual achievement people often spoke louder, quicker, and sometimes at a higher pitch. People leaned forward or moved in toward the tape recorder's microphone as if to want to be sure they were heard clearly on this. They spoke with fervor and conviction when crediting themselves with their own success. For example, in talking with Lily and Jonathan Boothe, a white wealthy family from the New York City area, Jonathan had been quite serene throughout the interview. However, when we began talking about the Boothes' perspectives on success and achievement, Jonathan became noticeably more vivacious.

Just as people with wealth credited themselves for their success, conversely, those who lacked family wealth blamed themselves. Conviction in meritocracy worked both ways, and meritocracy could justify both positions. The themes of "sticking to one's ideals," "being focused," "motivated," and "willing to work hard" were as consistent in interviews with working-class and impoverished families as they were in affluent families. People blamed themselves for their inability to attain what they wished for and wanted for themselves and their children, even when they were starting from the most disadvantaged backgrounds. One parent from Boston explained that, compared to others, she comes up short because "I did a lot of fooling around." A mother from St. Louis said, "I would say that I am a little bit limited. But it's nobody's fault but my own. So I can't complain." And still another parent lamented, "If I was to make more, better, wiser decisions along the way, I wouldn't have the debt that I have now."

Most people have regrets in life, and maybe if the families who were struggling to make ends meet had made "more, better, wiser decisions along the way," things would have turned out differently for them. Maybe not. But one of the things that stood out the most about this explanation was that many of these families had in fact done extraordinarily well for themselves. More often than not, however, the fruits of unaided self-achievement simply paled in comparison to the results of self-achievement combined with the advantages of family wealth. Still, throughout the interviews, parents from poor and working-class family backgrounds compared themselves to more "well-off" others, blamed themselves, and legitimized their situations by saying they should have worked harder. While to some extent they understood that a structure of wealth inequality existed, and while they recognized the real advantages for those with family wealth, they simultaneously blamed themselves for not having worked harder and done better than they had.

The interviews also show the power of hope. For these families the American Dream was hope. It held out hope that what is wanted will happen, and that what is wanted can be expected. It held out hope that children's life chances were all equally unconstrained. It held out hope that the world is just. To think otherwise (to think that the world is not just) would be heart-breaking to any parent. And, I believe, many parents fear that to think otherwise (to think that the world is not just) could potentially—if conveyed to children—break the spirit of any child. So they hold on to the American Dream, they hold on to their hope. This hope was reflected in the parents' perspectives regarding themselves, the social system they are acting on and within, and—most importantly—their children.

Discussion Questions

1. What makes the idea of meritocracy so compelling to Americans that people believe in it, even when it is contradicted by evidence all around them?
2. How would the members of your family explain their economic situation to themselves and to others? As the result of hard work and talent alone?
3. Why do you think none of the respondents talked about the role of luck in their own successes and failures?
4. Do you think that the American Dream can survive the increasing economic inequality which has is transforming American society? Why or why not?

References

Hochschild, Jennifer. 1995. *Facing Up to the American Dream: Race, Class, and the Soul of a Nation*. Princeton, NJ: Princeton University Press.———. 1981. *What's Fair? American Beliefs about Distributive Justice*. Cambridge, MA: Harvard University Press.

Schwartz, John E. 1997. *Illusions of Opportunity: the American Dream in Question*. New York: W. W. Norton.

Sennett, Richard & Cobb, Jonathan. 1972. *The Hidden Injuries of Class*. New York: W. W. Norton.

Questions to Think About

1. What is a meritocracy? Is the United States a truly meritocratic society? Why or why not?
2. What theoretical perspective do you believe the author of "The American Dream and Meritocracy" is coming from? What evidence supports this?
3. How does the American Dream of inequality justify social conditions such as poverty?
4. How can people with wealth be advantaged without knowing or understanding their advantages?

Resources

 Inequality.Org: Wealth Inequality in America: http://inequality.org/wealth-inequality-america/

 Inequality: United States Census http://www.census.gov/hhes/www/income/inequality/index.html

 Income, Education and Gender: United States S Census: https://www.census.gov/hhes/www/income/data/earnings/

 Ted Talks, Hans Rosling: Global Inequality: http://www.ted.com/talks/hans_rosling_reveals_new_insights_on_poverty?language=n

 Wealth Inequality in America: http://www.huffingtonpost.com/2013/03/04/wealth-inequality-video_n_2805811.html

SECTION III
RACIAL INEQUALITY

Introduction

Race is a social construct. Each society defines what physical traits it deems important and creates a reality that reflects this construction. The concept of race and the relative advantages or disadvantages of racial groups changes over time and varies depending on time and place. For instance, when the Irish first immigrated into the United States in the nineteenth century, they were viewed as dirty and promiscuous. "Whites" who were already in the United States felt threatened by the Irish, who were willing to work for lower wages, and accused them of "stealing" jobs. Over time this prejudice has diminished and today we hear very little about immigrants from Ireland being discriminated against.

Although presently (unlike in the past) it is illegal to discriminate against a person based on race and/or ethnicity, discrimination does still occur. Part of this continuing discrimination is due to conscious or unconscious cultural biases by individuals. Racial discrimination is also prevalent at the institutional level. Institutional discrimination is discrimination built into the institutions people use every day such as schools, housing markets, and the criminal justice system. Some examples of institutional discrimination are: 1) school funding—low-income minority schools have less funding than middle class and/or white schools, resulting in dilapidated buildings and less qualified teachers; 2) home mortgages—minorities are less likely to be offered home mortgages than whites, regardless of their qualifications, and are often given higher interest rates; and 3) steering by Realtors—Realtors often make assumptions about the "type" of neighborhood a client may want to live in. Often these assumptions are racially biased.

The essays in this section provide only a snapshot of the many discriminatory policies and practices that affect the lives of racial and/or ethnic minorities on a daily basis.

In 1995, Melvin Oliver and Thomas Shapiro published the groundbreaking book, *Black Wealth/White Wealth*. This book outlined the ways in which discriminatory housing policies contributed to the wealth gap between whites and blacks in the United States. In this selection, Oliver and Shapiro update their findings. Wealth is important because it benefits those who have it, without them ever having to think about it. When parents have wealth their children can grow up in neighborhoods with good schools, go to college without the great burden of debt, and get help with the down payment on their first home. Help buying a home is important because owning a home is a significant way for middle-class Americans to gain wealth. Property values almost always increase, leaving most middle-class wealth residing in the homes the middle class live in.

Using the theory of wealth and racial inequality, Oliver and Shapiro explore the persistence of wealth inequality between blacks and whites since 1995, the year their book was published. Although for a short time the unemployment gap was closing and blacks were slowly closing the wealth gap, this trend quickly reversed. Today the wealth gap is as large as in 1995. Redlining is no longer legal. Oliver and Shapiro argue, however, that in the mortgage market of today there are other—and less obvious—methods used to contain the wealth of blacks. Policies such as subprime loans, discriminatory lending, and the segregation penalty all work to disadvantage blacks in their quest for wealth in the housing market while at the same time advantaging whites. Whereas past discriminatory practices were legal and acknowledged, discrimination is still prevalent, if not as easily identifiable, and the ability for an individual to obtain wealth is defined by race and racialized space.

The reading "Language Oppression and Resistance: The Case of Middle Class Latinos in the United States" includes a detailed explanation of qualitative methods of conducting sociological research. Using a snowball sample of Latinos in the United States and guided by Bourdieu's theory of linguistic capital, Jose Cobas and Joe Feagin use interviews to describe the ways whites use linguistic capital to maintain their dominant status. They find that whites, regardless of their own social class, view and treat Latino Americans as a lower status group, irrespective of an individual Latino's ability to speak English or his or her social class. Cobas and Feagin found whites employed such strategies as "silencing," intended to suppress Latinos' use of Spanish, and express surprise when Latinos spoke "proper" English. They then discuss the methods Latinos in the study use to resist the demands of whites, many whom are of a lower social class than the Latinos they are denigrating.

Reading 4: Black Wealth/White Wealth: Wealth Inequality Trends

By Melvin L. Oliver and Thomas M. Shapiro

The growth and dispersion of wealth continues a trend anchored in the economic prosperity of post-World War II America. Between 1995 and 2001, the median net worth of all American families increased 39 percent, and median net financial assets grew by 60 percent. The growth of pension accounts (IRAs, Keogh plans, 401(k) plans, the accumulated value of defined contribution pension plans, and other retirement accounts) and stock holdings seems to account for much of this wealth accumulation.

While wealth grew and spread to many American families, there was little action at the bottom of the wealth spectrum as the percent of families with zero or negative net worth only dropped from 18.5 to 17.6, and those with no financial assets fell from 28.7 to 25.5.

Wealth remains highly concentrated, especially financial wealth, which excludes home equity. In 2001, the richest 5 percent of American households controlled over 67 percent of the country's financial wealth; the bottom 60 percent had 8.8 percent; and the bottom 40 percent just 1 percent.[1]

The context of wealth growth and inequality in the last decade situates our concern about racial inequality and the progress of American families, as indeed, the rich have gotten richer. The number of families with net worth of $10 million or more in 2001 quadrupled since 1980. A *New York Times* article even bemoaned how the super rich are leaving the mere rich far behind.[2] These 338,400 hyper-rich families emerged as the biggest winners in the new global economy, as new technologies spurred by tax incentives evolved, as the stock market soared, and as top executives in the corporate world received astronomical pay.

The wealthy were the biggest beneficiaries of tax policy during President George W. Bush's first term. In fact, the bulk of the 2001 tax cuts—53 percent—will go to the top 10 percent of taxpayers.[3] The tax cut share of the top 0.1 percent will amount to a 15 percent slice of the total value of the tax cut pie. Another reason that the wealthiest fare much better is that the tax cuts over the past decade have sharply lowered tax rates on income from investments, such as capital gains, interest, and dividends. While there are many reasons for the continuing wealth inequality trend, government policy has clearly abetted, encouraged, and privileged the property, capital, and income of America's wealthiest families.

What Facts Have Changed?

In 1995 when *Black Wealth/White Wealth* was published, we presented data that were in many respects a new way of gauging the economic progress of black Americans vis-à-vis white Americans. Most commentators and analysts were familiar and comfortable with income comparisons that provided a window on whether there was growing or declining racial economic inequality. But the focus on wealth, "the net value of assets (e.g., ownership of stocks, money in the bank, real estate, business ownership, etc.) less debts," created a different gestalt or perspective on racial inequality.

This gestalt had two dimensions.[4] The first is the conceptual distinction between income and assets. While income represents the flow of resources earned in a particular period, say a week, month, or year, assets are a stock of resources that are saved or invested. Income is mainly used for day-to-day necessities, while assets are special monies not normally used for food or clothing but are rather a "surplus resource available for improving life chances, providing further opportunities, securing prestige, passing status along to one's family," and securing economic security for present and future generations.[5] The second dimension is the quantitative; to what extent is there parity between blacks and whites on assets? Do blacks have access to resources that they can use to plan for their future, to enable their children to obtain a quality education, to provide for the next generation's head start, and to secure their place in the political community? For these reasons, we focused on inequality in wealth as the sine qua non indicator of material well-being. Without sufficient assets, it is difficult to lay claim to economic security in American society.

The baseline indicator of racial wealth inequality is the black-white ratio of median net worth. To what degree are blacks approaching parity with whites in terms of net worth? The change in gestalt is amply demonstrated in comparisons of black-white median income ratios to black-white median net worth ratios. For example, the 1988 data reported on in *Black Wealth/White Wealth* showed that black families earned sixty-two cents for every dollar of median income that white families earned. However, when the comparisons shift to wealth, the figure showed a remarkably deeper and disturbing level of racial inequality. For every dollar of median net worth that whites controlled, African Americans controlled only eight cents![6]

How has this landmark indicator of racial inequality changed since then? Using the most recent data available, it appears, not unsurprisingly, that the level of racial wealth inequality has not changed but has shown a stubborn persistence that makes the data presented in 1995 more relevant than ever because the pattern we discerned suggests a firmly embedded racial stratification. The most optimistic analyses suggest that the black-white median net worth ratio is 0.10, that is, blacks have control of ten cents for every dollar of net worth that whites possess.[7] However, the most pessimistic estimate indicates that the ratio is closer to seven cents on the dollar.[8] This slim range demonstrates that the level of wealth inequality has not changed appreciably since the publication of *Black Wealth/White Wealth*.[9] However, the story is far more complex.

Using 1988 data, we tabulated the racial wealth gap at $60,980.[10] By 2002 the racial wealth gap increased to $82,663, meaning the wealth of the average African American family fell further behind whites by more than $20,000 over this period. Isolating the period and dynamics of the past decade a little more closely, the racial wealth gap grew by $14,316 between 1996 and 2002. In the decade since *Black Wealth/White Wealth*, then, white wealth grew and then leveled off; black wealth grew and then declined. As a result, the overall racial wealth gap ratio persists at a dime on the dollar, and the dollar amount of the racial wealth gap grew.

Some contradictory facts and new dimensions of financial life in America have affected the persistence of the black-white racial wealth gap. They include a strong economy of the 1990s that enabled greater savings, especially in employer-based savings programs, but which has petered out recently; a stock market bust that punished some of the newest entrants into the market most severely; increasing credit card debt; a growing trend of black home ownership complemented by growing sub-prime and predatory lending directed at minority communities; and growth in the working poor due to the influx of the Temporary Assistance for Needy Families program population into the labor market. This mix of factors weaves the mosaic underlying the story of the continuing racial wealth gap in the first decade of the twenty-first century.

The Story of the Persistence of the Racial Wealth Gap

Traditionally, economists assume that wealth accumulation is the consequence of a "combination of inheritance, earnings, and savings and is enhanced by prudent consumption and investment patterns over a person's life course."[11] How these individual variables interact with the human capital attributes of family members, their education, their occupation, and their ability to begin asset accumulation at an early stage in their life course (the earlier one begins to accumulate assets, the more wealth one can accrue) moves us forward in explaining how differential accumulation occurs. But these individual factors are not the whole story.

As *Black Wealth/White Wealth* convincingly demonstrated, wealth accumulation occurs in a context where these individual attributes unfold to produce varying levels of wealth for different families and social groupings. It has been the different "opportunity structure" for savings and investment that African Americans have faced when compared with whites that has helped to structure racial inequality in wealth holding.

We developed a sociology of wealth and racial inequality in *Black Wealth/White Wealth*, which situated the study of wealth among concerns with race, class, and social inequality. This theoretical framework elucidated the social context in which wealth generation occurs and demonstrated the unique and diverse social circumstances that blacks and whites face. Three concepts we developed provided a sociologically grounded approach to understand the racial wealth gap and highlighted how the opportunity structure disadvantages blacks and contributes to massive wealth inequalities between the races. The first concept, racialization of state policy, explores how state policy has impaired the ability of most black Americans to accumulate wealth from slavery throughout American history to contemporary institutional discrimination. The "economic detour" helps us understand the relatively low level of entrepreneurship among the small scale and segmentally niched businesses of black Americans, leading to an emphasis on consumer spending as the route to economic assimilation. The third concept—the sedimentation of racial inequality—explores how the cumulative effects of the past have seemingly cemented blacks to the bottom of America's economic hierarchy in regards to wealth.

These concepts do much to show how this differential opportunity structure developed and worked to produce black wealth disadvantages. It also builds a strong case that layering wealth deprivation generation after generation has been central in not only blacks' lack of wealth but also whites' privileged position in accumulating wealth. As we noted:

> What is often not acknowledged is that the accumulation of wealth for some whites is intimately tied to the poverty of wealth for most blacks. Just as blacks have had "cumulative disadvantages," whites have had "cumulative advantages." Practically every circumstance of bias and discrimination against blacks has produced a circumstance and opportunity of positive gain for whites.[12]

The past opportunity structure that denied blacks access or full participation in wealth-building activities serves as a powerful deterrent to current black ambitions for wealth. Without an inheritance that is built on generations of steady economic success, blacks, even when they have similar human capital and class position, lag far behind their white counterparts in their quest to accumulate a healthy nest egg of assets. In *Black Wealth/White Wealth* we examined those current institutional and structural constraints that African Americans faced in the 1980s and early 1990s that curtailed and limited the ability of many African Americans to build assets. One area we focused upon was housing, the largest single element of most

American's portfolio of assets, and a major part of the wealth in most African American's asset portfolio. We identified a number of institutional constraints ranging from differential access to mortgages, higher costs of mortgages, and differential levels of equity accumulation in homes owing to persistent residential segregation.

We want to extend this mode of theorizing and analysis to the period of the 1990s and into the first decade of the twenty-first century. We attempt to formulate a compelling picture of why African Americans continue to lag so far behind whites in asset holding. Here we focus on the social context of the labor market, the stock and housing market, and growing debt.

The Rise and Decline of a Tight Labor Market and a Bull Stock Market

Black Wealth/White Wealth documented wealth data that reflected a period in the American economy characterized by relatively high unemployment rates and a stagnant economy. However, this period was followed by one of the largest and longest economic expansions in the history of the United States. From its beginning in March 1991 to its ending in November 2001, the United States endured a record expansion. Positive economic indicators that were in sharp contrast to the previous period characterized this expansion. For example, family incomes went from stagnation during the 1979 to 1993 period, where they grew only 0.7 percent over the entire time frame to an increase of 17 percent, or more than $7,000 per family, from 1993 to 2000. In terms of job growth, during the 1992 to 2000 period, the nation created more jobs than at any similar period in American history: 22.6 million, 92 percent of which were in the private sector. Moreover, in contrast to the previous period, where 1.9 million manufacturing jobs were lost, the 1992 to 2000 period saw manufacturing job growth increase by 303,000. Finally, the unemployment rate fell by 42 percent, reaching below 5 percent from July 1997 through January 2001. The 4 percent unemployment rate in 2000—the lowest in over 30 years—stands in striking contrast to an average unemployment rate of 7.1 percent for the 1980 to 1992 period.[13]

For African Americans this was a period of tight labor markets that led to greater levels of labor force participation owing to the existence of greater demand for their participation in the economy. Employers made "extra efforts … to overcome the barriers created by skill and spatial mismatch" to reach out to African American workers to fill their growing labor needs.[14] Moreover, "employers may find discrimination more costly when the economy is strong and their usually preferred type of job candidate is fully employed elsewhere."[15] In the throes of a heated and tight labor market, *Business Week* proclaimed, "With the economy continuing to expand and unemployment at its lowest point in 30 years, companies are snapping up minorities, women, seniors, and anyone else willing to work for a day's pay."[16]

African Americans, however, did not wholly benefit from this extraordinary period in American history. Black joblessness continued to be a problem. The historical ratio of two-to-one black-to-white unemployment rates persisted with black men averaging 7.1 percent compared with 3 percent for white men, while black women averaged 6.8 compared with 3.2 percent for white women in the latter half of 1999.[17] Nevertheless, those African Americans who were employed during this period saw real wage gains that could be translated into savings, investments, and an increase in net worth.

Another aspect of the expansion of the economy during the 1990s was the rapid rise in the stock market. Fueled by technology stocks and the growth of key stocks like Microsoft, Sun, Yahoo, and other new stock offerings in the technology sector, the stock market started to attract investments not only from high-income and high-wealth individuals, but also from an increasing number of middle-class families and even working-class families. This investment was facilitated by growing participation in employer-sponsored savings programs that enabled employees to make tax-deferred and/or matched contributions through payroll deductions. The ease of the transaction and the constant media and public interest in the high-flying stock market encouraged mass participation. The market rose steadily and rapidly. Beginning from a monthly average in 1992 in the low 400s, the Standard and Poor's 500 tripled in size by 1999.[18] If one were lucky enough to purchase Microsoft or Yahoo early then his or her gains would have been astronomical. For example, when Yahoo was first available as a public offering shares were sold for $1.24. By December 1999 Yahoo listed for $108.17.[19] It was the desire for these kinds of returns that fueled an overheated market and led to the description of "irrational exuberance" concerning the frenzy for the "market."[20]

African Americans, while constrained by resources, also entered into this frenzy. The decade of the 1990s was the breakthrough era for African American involvement in the stock market. Facilitated by employer savings plans and, for the first time, sought after by stock and brokerage firms, African Americans invested readily into the market. In 1996 blacks had a median value of $4,626 invested in stocks and mutual funds. At the height of the market, that value had almost doubled to $8,669. During this period African American stock market investors had closed the black-white ratio of stock market value from twenty-eight cents on the dollar to forty cents on the dollar. However, the market's plunge after 1999 sent African American portfolio values down to a median average of $3,050. This brought the black-white ratio of stock market value back in line with the 1996 level, eroding all the gains that the bull market had bestowed.[21]

African Americans did better in 401(k) and thrift savings plans, which were more likely to be diversified holdings. In 1996 African American investors held a median average of $6,939 in these instruments. With the market surging and regular savings deposits facilitated by payroll deductions, African Americans increased their value in savings or thrift plans to a median average of $10,166 in 2002. The comparison to whites is quite interesting in regard to thrift plans. Between 1996 and 2002 African Americans closed the black-white ratio slightly from 0.43 to 0.50. This is in striking contrast to the data on stock ownership.[22]

Home Ownership, New Mortgage, and Credit Markets

Over the past several years more families than ever across the United States have been able to buy homes. Home ownership rates reached 69 percent in 2004, a historic high. The main reasons for the high level of home ownership include the new mortgage market, where capital is readily available to both families and economic sectors where home ownership was always part of the American Dream—but in dream only. With home ownership comes the opportunity to accumulate wealth because the value of homes appreciates over time. Indeed, approximately two-thirds of all the wealth of America's middle class families is not in stocks, bonds, investments, or savings accounts but in the form of home equity.

Home equity is the most important wealth component for average American families, and even though home ownership rates are lower, it is even more prominent in the wealth profiles of African American families. Although housing appreciation is very sensitive to many characteristics relating to a community's demographics and profile (which realtors euphemistically call "location, location, location"), overall home ownership has been a prime source of wealth accumulation for black families. For example, for the average black home owner, homes created $6,000 more wealth between 1996 and 2002.[23] However, fundamentally racialized dynamics create and distribute housing wealth unevenly. The Federal Reserve Board kept interest rates at historically low levels for much of this period, and this fueled both demand and hastened converting home equity wealth into cash.

Black Wealth/White Wealth demonstrated the color coding of home equity, and Shapiro's 2004 book, *The Hidden Cost of Being African American*, updates the data and extends our understanding of how residential segregation affects home equity. The typical home owned by white families increased in value by $28,000 more than homes owned by blacks. Persistent residential segregation, especially in cities where most blacks live, explains this equity difference as a compelling index of bias that costs blacks dearly. This data point corroborates other recent research demonstrating that rising housing wealth depends upon a community's demographic characteristics, especially racial composition. One study concludes that homes lost at least 16 percent of their value when located in neighborhoods that are more than 10 percent black. Thus, a "segregation tax" visits black home owners by depressing home values and reducing home equity in highly segregated neighborhoods.[24] Shapiro summarizes the case: "The only prudent conclusion from these studies is that residential segregation costs African American home owners enormous amounts of money by suppressing their home equity in comparison to that of white home owners. The inescapable corollary is that residential segregation benefits white home owners with greater home equity wealth accumulation."[25] Furthermore, most African American families rent housing and thus are not positioned to accumulate housing wealth, mainly because of affordability, credit, and access issues.

The home mortgage marketplace has evolved considerably since 1990, when mortgage packages were offered at a unitary price reflecting the terms of the loan, targeting prospective home owners who met stringent credit history rules and financial criteria. As housing wealth grew and the United States mortgage market became integrated into the global market system, mortgage products proliferated and thus have changed the way American families buy homes. Underwriting standards have become more relaxed, both as financial institutions ease rules to compete in this evolving market and as federal regulations and oversight have become less stringent.[26]

Minorities are making significant inroads into all segments of the housing market. Indeed, important components feeding the general trends of increasing rates of new home construction and home value appreciation include the demographic push from new immigrants, the accomplishments of second-generation immigrants, and the success of a segment of African American families. In 2004, home ownership reached historic highs as 69 percent of American families live in a home they own. In 1995, 42.2 percent of African American families owned homes, increasing to a historic high, 49.5 percent, in 2004. This 17.3 percent increase in African American home ownership is quite remarkable, indicating striving, accomplishment, and success. The black-white home ownership gap in 1995 stood at 28.5 percent and narrowed to 26.2 percent in 2004.[27] We might expect the home ownership gap to continue closing as black home ownership starts from a considerably lower base while the higher white rate may be close to exhausting the potential of those who want to become home owners.

In 1995, access to credit for minorities was a major issue. Financial institutions responded both to criticisms regarding credit discrimination and to the newly discovered buying capacity of minorities. Increasing numbers of African American and Hispanic families gained access to credit cards throughout the 1990s: 45 percent of African American and 43 percent of Hispanic families held credit cards in 1992 and by 2001 nearly 60 percent of African American and 53 percent of Hispanic families held credit cards.[28] The irony here is that as access to credit broadened under terms highly favorable to lenders, debt became rampant and millions of families became ensnared in a debt vice.

Credit card debt nearly tripled from $238 billion in 1989 to $692 billion in 2001.[29] These figures represent family reliance on financing consumption through debt, especially expensive credit in the form of credit cards and department store charge cards. During the 1990s, the average American family experienced a 53 percent increase in credit card debt—the average family's card debt rising from $2,697 to $4,126. Credit card debt among low-income families increased 184 percent. Even high-income families became more dependent on credit cards: There was 28 percent more debt in 2001 than in 1989. The main sources of credit card debt include spiraling health care costs, lower employer coverage of health insurance, and rising housing costs amid stagnating or declining wages after 2000 and increasingly unsteady employment for many. This suggests strongly that the increasing debt is not the result of frivolous or conspicuous spending or lack of budgetary discipline; instead, deferring payment to make ends meet is becoming the American way for many to finance daily life in the new economy.

Given that a period of rising income did not lift the African American standard of living, and given the context of overall rising family debt, an examination of the racial component of credit card debt furthers our understanding of the contemporary processes associated with the continuation of the economic detour and the further sedimentation of inequality. The average credit card debt of African Americans increased 22 percent between 1992 and 2001, when it reached an average of nearly $3,000.[30] Hispanic credit card debt mirrored blacks by rising 20 percent in the same period to $3,691. As we know, the average white credit card debt was higher, reaching $4,381 in 2001. One of the most salient facts involves the magnitude and depth of African American reliance on debt. Among those holding credit cards with balances, nearly one in five African Americans earning less than $50,000 spend at least 40 percent of their income paying debt service. In other words, in every 8-hour working day these families labor 3.2 hours to pay off consumer debt. Even though black families carry smaller monthly balances, a higher percentage of their financial resources goes toward servicing debt.

The median net worth of African American families at the end of 2002 was $5,988, essentially the same as it was in 1988.[31] Again, it is not as if nothing happened since we wrote *Black Wealth/White Wealth*; indeed, African American fortunes expanded with good times and contracted with recessions and the bursting of the stock market bubble. In the last decade, the high point of African American (and Hispanic) wealth accumulation was 1999, when it registered $8,774, just before the bursting of the stock market bubble in early 2000. Between 1999 and 2002, African American wealth declined from $8,774 to $5,988, wiping out more than a decade's worth of financial gains.

Median wealth and racial wealth gap data tell us about absolute wealth accumulation and the relative positioning of African American families. Another sense of the dynamics of the last ten years concerns the dispersion of assets among African American families. In 1996, 31.9 percent of African American families owned zero net worth or—worse still—had bottom lines that put them in the red. By 1999, this figure declined to 28.2 percent but deteriorated again after the stock market burst and the beginning of the recession, by increasing to 32.3 percent in 2002. This has left more African American families in absolute asset poverty than at the time of the book's initial publication.

New Dynamics of Markets and Institutions

As we have indicated, the decade between 1995 and 2006 really is marked off by two distinct periods: African American family wealth accumulates considerably and more families move into positive wealth positions until early 2000. From 2000 through 2005, however, the financial wealth of African American families made a U-turn, both losing actual wealth and increasing the number of families with zero or negative wealth once more. Throughout the entire period, home ownership and home equity continued to rise for all segments of American families, including African Americans. An important narrative, then, involves this great expansion of financial wealth, home ownership, and housing wealth; understanding what happened to this wealth; examining the opportunities this new wealth created, especially for financial institutions looking for new markets; and importantly, the impact of these developments and new dynamics on African Americans.

Housing Wealth and Its Uses

Households cashed out $407 billion worth of equity from homes in just three years, 2002 through 2004, in the refinancing boom that began in 2001. Although such data have not been collected for very long, American families were refinancing homes at record levels, three times higher than any other period.[32] Nearly half of all mortgage debt was refinanced between 2002 and 2003, averaging $27,000 in equity per home in the early stages of the refinancing wave.[33]

As mortgage interest rates fell to record low levels during the refinance boom, and as housing continued to appreciate and result in wealth accumulation, many Americans cashed out home equity to pay down debt and finance living expenses, trading off wealth to pay off past consumption and fund new purchases.

Refinancing at lower interest rates and hence lower monthly payments is certainly a good deal for families paying off mortgages because it leaves more money in the family budget for living expenses, discretionary purchases, or savings. We need to ask the important question of how families used this bonanza. Investing in human capital through continued education or career retooling, investing in other financial instruments, building a business, home improvements, and similar choices expand opportunities, improve living standards, and may launch further social mobility. On the other hand, paying down high-interest debt may slow down temporarily the debt-driven consumption treadmill but most likely does not improve the long-term standard of living or life chances of a family, and certainly does not improve the future wealth accumulation picture. Slightly over one-half used housing wealth to cover living expenses and to pay down store and credit cards. Another 25 percent used funds for consumer expenditures such as vehicle purchases and medical expenses. Thus it appears that a majority of households used these new home equity loans to convert credit card debt and current living expenses into long-term mortgage debt.

One result is that between 1973 and 2004, home owners' equity actually fell—from 68.3 percent to 55 percent so that Americans own less of their homes today than they did in the 1970s and early 1980s. And, it is worth remembering that home equity is by far the largest source of wealth for the vast majority of American families. The intersection of wealth and race illustrates the magnified importance of home equity for African Americans and Hispanics. Among whites, home equity represented 38.5 percent of their entire wealth portfolio in 2002. In sharp contrast, home equity accounted for 63 percent of wealth among African Americans and 61 percent for Hispanics.[34]

The Dark Side of Home Ownership

Subprime lending is targeted to prospective homebuyers with blemished credit histories or with high levels of debt who otherwise would not qualify for conventional mortgage loans. A legitimate niche for these kinds of loans brings home ownership within the grasp of millions of families. These loan products are essential in expanding home ownership rates. In return for these riskier investments, financial institutions charge borrowers higher interest rates, often requiring higher processing and closing fees, and often containing special loan conditions like prepayment penalties, balloon payments, and adjustable interest rates.

The subprime market expanded greatly in the last decade as part of new, aggressive market-ing strategies among financial institutions hungrily eyeing rising home ownership and seeing promising new markets. Moreover, the mortgage finance system in the United States became well integrated into global capital markets, which offer an ever-growing array of financial prod-ucts, including subprime loans. Subprime loan originations grew fifteen-fold, from $35 billion to $530 billion between 1994 and 2004. Reflecting the increasing importance of subprime loans to the financial industry, the subprime share of mortgage loans has seen a parallel meteoric rise from less than 4 percent in 1995 to representing about 17 percent of mortgage loans in 2004.[35]

Loan terms like prepayment penalties and balloon payments increase the risk of mortgage foreclosure in subprime home loans, even after controlling for the borrower's credit score, loan terms, and varying economic conditions.[36] One study from the Center for Community Capitalism demonstrates that subprime prepayment penalties and balloon payments place Americans at substantially greater risk of losing their homes.

Delinquency (falling behind in mortgage payments) and losing one's home through foreclosure are hitting vulnerable neighborhoods hardest. Concentrated foreclosures can negatively affect the surrounding neighborhoods, threatening to undo community building and revitalization efforts achieved through decades of collaborative public-private partnerships, community organizing, and local policy efforts.

Los Angeles is a case in point.[37] In a short three-year period, 2001 to 2004, over 14,000 Los Angeles families lost their homes through foreclosure. The foreclosure rate is highest in the most vulnerable neighborhoods. In predominately minority neighborhoods (80 percent or more minority) of Los Angeles County the foreclosure rate is almost four times the rate that it is in neighborhoods where minorities are less than 20 percent of the population. In the City of Los Angeles, foreclosures occur nearly twelve times more often in predominately minority communities compared with areas that have fewer than 20 percent minorities. Los Angeles is not alone; data from Atlanta, Baltimore, Boston, Chicago, and others show that Los Angeles is part of the larger, national pattern.

A study examining pricing disparities in the mortgage market provides more context, placing the Los Angeles story in a broader pattern. Of all conventional loans to blacks, nearly 30 percent were subprime compared with only 10 percent for whites.[38] These ratios would be in closer alignment in lending markets operating with maximum efficiency and equity. Creditworthy criteria, like debt-to-income ratios, do not explain the greater propensity for African Americans to receive subprime loans. The report also discovered that subprime loans in minority communities increased with levels of racial segregation. This finding suggests an alarming new form of modern redlining that targets minority neighborhoods for subprime loans.

Using a testing methodology adapted from those that explored job discrimination, the National Community Reinvestment Coalition was able to explore how pricing disparities resulting from intensified subprime lending in minority areas occurred. Essentially, white and black testers with similar credit records and qualifications applied for preapproval for mortgages. Given similar scripts and profiles (with African Americans actually presenting better qualifications), the testing uncovered a 45 percent rate of disparate treatment based on race. The testing revealed practices that may have destructive effects on African American families and communities. These include: differences in interest rates quoted; differences in information about fees, rates, loan programs, and loan terms; and whites more often referred up to the lender's prime lending division. In *Black Wealth/White Wealth* we wrote that differences in loan rejection rates and interest rates did not result from discriminatory lending practices but from blacks bringing fewer financial assets to the mortgage table; as a result, they paid higher loan terms. Racial pricing disparities and the targeted spread of subprime lending to minority communities, however, now persuades us that minority America is experiencing a new form of redlining organized by race and geographic space.

Black Wealth/White Wealth demonstrated the power of policy, government, institutions, and history to order and maintain racial inequality. The previous sections show further the significance of financial institutions in granting access to credit and the terms of credit, and the increasing dependence on credit and debt. The basis for excluding African Americans from opportunities and creating different rules in the competition for success is no longer just who is a capable worker. Now we must add who is a worthy credit risk and on what terms. Job discrimination against individual blacks based on perceived characteristics is not the only major arena in the struggle against inequality; exclusion in terms of creditworthiness is as well.

Discussion Questions

1. What are the three sociological concepts that help us understand the racial wealth gap and highlight how opportunity structure disadvantages blacks and contributes to massive wealth inequalities between the races?
2. African Americans continue to lag behind whites in asset holdings. Discuss the effects of the social context of the labor market, the stock and housing market, and growing debt.
3. To what degree are blacks approaching parity with whites in terms of net worth?
4. How did the subprime mortgage crisis affect minority communities differently than non-minority communities? Looking ahead, discuss what long-term impact this may have on wealth accumulation among African Americans.

Notes

1. Wolff, 2004.
2. Johnson, 2005.
3. Johnson, 2005.
4. Oliver and Shapiro, p. 30
5. Oliver and Shapiro, p. 32.

6. Oliver and Shapiro, pp. 85–86.

7. Shapiro, 2004a.

8. Kochhar.

9. Federation of Consumer Services data yield a more narrowed ratio. These data are inconsistent with virtually all other data measuring wealth inequality. We are not confident with its methodology or operational definitions of wealth. See Consumer Federation of America and BET.com, 2003.

10. We adjusted the 1988 figure originally reported in the book to reflect 2002 dollars.

11. Oliver and Shapiro, p. 36.

12. Oliver and Shapiro, p. 51.

13. The National Bureau of Economic Research's Business Cycle Committee keeps track of business expansions and recessions; see http://www.nber. org/cycles/recessions.html. For a general overview of the Clinton expansion's impact on the poor, see Blank and Ellwood.

14. Bradbury, p. 14, and Holzer, Raphael, and Stoll.

15. Bradbury, p. 14.

16. Bradbury, p. 15.

17. Bradbury, p. 4.

18. Shiller. Also see http://www.irrationalexuberance.com/index.htm for historical data on the stock market.

19. See quarterly stock prices for Yahoo at http://finance.yahoo.com/q/hp?s=YHOO&a=03&b=12&c=1996&d=07&e=14&f=2005&g=m&z=66&y=66.

20. The origin of the descriptor "irrational exuberance" is found in a speech by Federal Reserve Board Chairman Alan Greenspan, 1996.

21. These data are from a survey of high-income blacks (yearly incomes of $50, 000 or more) sponsored by Ariel Mutual Funds/Charles Schwab & Co., Inc. This very valuable survey examines the financial behavior, asset value, and composition of this group of African Americans. See Black Investor Survey.

22. Black Investor Survey.

23. Kochhar, p. 18.

24. Rusk.

25. Shapiro, 2004a.

26. The exemplar for "easing" regulatory oversight and financial institution accountability was the repeal of the Glass-Steagall Act of 1933. This act was designed to protect the public from

27. between commercial banks, insurance companies, and brokerage firms, which contributed to the stock market crash of 1929. The Financial Services Modernization Act of 1999 does away with restrictions on the integration of banking, insurance, and stock trading, which has encouraged a rash of mergers leading to greater concentration in the financial sector. As a result, banks were looking for new markets and were anxious to provide new products. As part of the 1999 Act, regular oversight opportunities provided to community organizations

through the Community Reinvestment Act were relaxed considerably. Consequently, the frequency of CRA examinations was limited. See Berton and Futterman.

28. Joint Center for Housing Studies, 2005.

29. Silva and Epstein.

30. Draut and Silva.

31. Silva and Epstein.

32. This section uses SIPP data from 2002 as reported in the Pew Hispanic Center report.

33. Joint Center for Housing Studies, 2004.

34. Silva.

35. These are based on distribution of mean worth, so the figure for whites, in particular, because of the skewed distribution, looks low and vastly understates the importance of home equity in the wealth portfolios of middle-class white families (Kochhar).

36. Joint Center for Housing Studies, 2005.

37. Quercia, Stegman, and Davis.

38. Duda and Apgar.

39. National Community Reinvestment Coalition; Adams.

References

Adams, John. 1988. "Growth of U.S. Cities and Recent Trends in Urban Real Estate Values." In *Cities and Their Vital Systems*, ed., J. H. Ausubel and R. Herman. Washington, DC: National Academy Press. 108–45.

Berton, Brad, and Susan Futterman. 2003. "Community Groups see Continuing Chill on CRA, Affordable Housing Finance." http://www.housingfinance.com/ahf/articles/2002/02OctCommunityLeanding/BET.com.

Black Investor Survey. "Saving and Investing Among Higher Income African-American and White Americans," July 2005. http://www.arielmutuafunds.com//funds/2004-survey/2004%20AAIS%20FULL%20EXTERNAL.ppt.

Blank, Rebecca, and David T. Ellwood. 2002. "The Clinton Legacy for America's Poor." in *American Economic Policy in the 1990s*, Jeffrey A. Frankel and Peter R. Orszag. Cambridge, MA: MIT Press.

Bradbury, Katharine L. 2000. "Rising Tide in the Labor Market: To What Degree do Expansions Benefit the Disadvantaged?" *New England Economic Review* 4 (May/June): 3–33.

Consumer Federation of America. 2003. "More African-Americans Save and Begin to Close Wealth Gap." http://www.consumerfed.org/102903blackamsaves.pdf.

Duda, Mark, and William Apgar. 2004. Mortgage Foreclosure Trends in Los Angeles: Patterns and Policy Issues. A report prepared for the Los Angeles Neighborhood Housing Services.

Greenspan, Alan. 1996. The Challenge of Central Banking in a Democratic Society. Address to the American Enterprise Institute at the Washington Hilton Hotel, December 5, 1996.

Holzer, Harry, Steven Raphael, and Michael A. Stoll. 2003. "Employers in the Boom: How Did the hiring of Unskilled Workers Change During the 1990s?" http://www.urban.org/UploadedPDF/410780_ BoomPaper. pdf.

Johnson, David Cay. 2005. "Richest are Leaving Even the Rich Far Behind," *New York Times*, June 5.

Joint Center for Housing Studies of Harvard University. 2004. The State of the Nation's Housing. Cambridge, MA.

Joint Center for Housing Studies of Harvard University. 2005. The State of the Nation's Housing. Cambridge, MA.

Kochhar, Rakesh. 2004. *The Wealth of Hispanic Households: 1996 to 2002*. Washington, DC: Pew Hispanic Center.

National Community Reinvestment Coalition. 2005. Preapprovals and Pricing Disparities in the Mortgage Marketplace, June 2005. http://ncrc.org/pressandpubs/press_releases/documents/Preapproval_ Report_June05. pdf.

Oliver, Melvin L., and Thomas M. Shapiro. 1995. *Black Wealth/White Wealth: A New Perspective on Racial Inequality*. New York and London: Routledge.

Quercia, Roberto G., Michael A. Stegman, and Walter R. Davis. 2005. "The Impact of Predatory Loan Terms on Subprime Foreclosures." Center for Community Capitalism. http://www.kenan-flagler.unc.edu/assets/docu-ments/foreclosurepaper.pdf.

Rusk, David. 2001. *The 'Segregation Tax': The Cost of Racial Segregation of Black Homeowners*. Washington, DC: Brookings Institution Center on Urban and Metropolitan Policy.

Shapiro, Thomas M. 2004a. *The Hidden Cost of Being African American: How Wealth Perpetuates Inequality*. New York: Oxford University Press.

Shiller, Robert J. 2005. *Irrational Exuberance*. Princeton, NJ: Princeton University Press.

Silva, Javier. 2005. *A House of Cards: Financing the American Dream*. New York: Demos.

Silva, Javier, and Rebecca Epstein. 2005. *Costly Credit: African Americans and Latinos in Debt*. New York: Demos.

Wolff, Edward N. 2004. "Changes in Household Wealth in the 1980s and 1990s." In the U.S. Economics Working Paper Archive, Number 47. Annandale-on-Hudson, NY: The Levy Economics Institute.

Reading 5: Language Oppression and Resistance: The Case of Middle Class Latinos in the United States

By Jose Cobas and Joe R. Feagin

U.S. latinos have increased steadily and now constitute 13.7 percent of the population (U.S. Bureau of the Census 2004). This steady growth, "the browning of America," is viewed with alarm by many whites, who often view such immigrants as a threat to "American values" and the U.S. "core culture" (Cornelius 2002).

Language lies within that core, and the dramatic growth of U.S. latinos is viewed by many whites as a threat to the survivability of English, often termed by them "the official language of the country." As recently as 1987, most people in one national poll thought that the U.S. Constitution had already made English the official language (Crawford 1992) and thus they saw no real threat. This benign perception has changed. For example, the influential Harvard professor Samuel Huntington (2004), who has served as advisor to government officials, has articulated strong anti-latino sentiments in his stereotyped assessment of U.S. immigration. Like many prominent white officials and executives (Feagin and O'Brien 2003), Huntington worries greatly that the United States will become aggressively bilingual, with English-speaking and Spanish-speaking sectors incapable of comprehending each other's languages and values.

Our Conceptual Approach

When the first English settlers arrived in North America, they saw themselves as bringing "civilization" to the colonies. "Civilization" meant English language and culture. American Indians, viewed as "savages," constituted the serious barrier to their plans (Fischer 1989). German immigrants represented another obstacle; Benjamin Franklin established a school in Pennsylvania to educate them. Franklin feared these immigrants could "Germanize us instead of us Anglifying them" (Conklin and Lourie 1983, p. 69).

By the mid-nineteenth century the civilized-savage polarity was replaced by a racist *Weltanschauung* which played up the achievements of the "Anglo-Saxon race" against the short-comings of inferior "others." A common element in both the English-other and the white-other conceptions was that the dominant group viewed the language of the "others" with suspicion and often sought to eliminate it. In the aftermath of the 1848 Mexican–American War, the eradication of the Spanish language became an important U.S. goal. This objective was pursued in the schools of the south west (Gonzalez 1990). Efforts to squelch the Spanish and other languages persist today. In 1986 California enacted legislation making English the state's official language. Since then about two dozen states have enacted similar provisions (Navarrette 2005). Many contemporary Spanish speakers feel in their daily lives the pressure to give up their mother tongue in favor of English (Montoya 1998). One might argue that whites' attempts to prevent latinos using Spanish do not involve negative racial attitudes. Yet, this is a difficult position to sustain in light of many negative stereotypes about latinos' language and accents. In whites' stereotypical accounts, the latino speech is said to reveal low intelligence and untrustworthiness (Urciuoli 1996; Santa Ana 2002). Interference with latino speech occurs regularly, and the interlocutor is often well educated. Such acts seem to derive from strong emotions in a country which Silverstein characterizes as having a "culture of monoglot standardization" (1996, p. 284).

Pierre Bourdieu (1991) identified as socially significant a group's linguistic capital (e.g. a prestigious language dialect). The linguistic capital of Parisian French is higher than that of French in the countryside. According to Bourdieu (1977, p. 652), when individuals are in the linguistic market, the price of their speech depends on the status of the speaker. The outcome of linguistic exchange is contingent on the speaker's choice of language, such as in situations of bilingualism, when one of the languages has a lower status. A group can strive for advantage in the linguistic market in order to bring about political and material gains. One way to achieve this end is by promoting the language it commands. Yet, the efforts of a group to achieve linguistic dominance are often met with resistance (Bourdieu 1991, pp. 95–6). Although some classes, as, for example, the members of the bourgeoisie in post-Revolution France, operate from an advantageous position, the linguistic ascendancy of a class is the result of a struggle in the language market that is seldom permanently resolved. Achievement of language dominance does not necessarily mean that other languages disappear. Nonetheless, the dominant language becomes "the norm against which the (linguistic) prices of the other modes of expression … are defined" (Bourdieu 1977, p. 652). Drawing in part on these ideas, we view white efforts to delimit or suppress Spanish as a thrust to protect or enhance the reach and power of English speakers *vis-á-vis* Spanish speakers.

The mechanisms used by U.S. economic and political elites to establish English ascendancy over Spanish vary, as we will demonstrate. Language subordination of latinos in the United

States includes the idea that English is superior to Spanish (Santa Ana 2002). A second method is the denigration of Spanish-accented English. Other foreign accents are not judged in the same harsh terms:

> It is crucial to remember that not all foreign accents, but only accent linked to skin that isn't white, or which signals a third-world homeland, that evokes … negative reactions. There are no documented cases of native speakers of Swedish or Dutch or Gaelic being turned away from jobs because of communicative difficulties, although these adult speakers face the same challenge as native speakers of Spanish (Lippi-Green 1997, pp. 238–39).

Another form of language denigration is ignoring speakers of Spanish even when they have a command of English. They are ignored by some whites as groups of people not worth listening to, as if their knowledge of their mother tongue renders their message meaningless and undeserving of attention (Lippi-Green 1997, p. 201). The process of linguistic denigration of non-whites also includes another component: the expression of skepticism or surprise when people of color evidence command of standard English. It is as if non-whites' linguistic abilities were so contaminated that when they show their abilities in writing or speaking unaccented English some whites are unprepared to believe what they see or hear (Essed 1991, p. 202).

Oppressed groups typically defend themselves to the best of their ability against efforts to denigrate their languages or erect barriers against their use. Some examples are the Basque, Catalan, Occitan and Bosnian peoples (Shafir 1995; Siguan 2002; Wood 2005). Cultural groups struggle to keep their language because it is fundamental to social life and expresses the understandings of its associated culture in both overt and subtle ways (Fishman 1989, p. 470). Many latinos prefer to use Spanish because it affords them a richer form of communication. Other U.S. racial groups struggle to protect their languages (cf. Horton 1995, p. 211).

Although latinos are disadvantaged in the language market, because of the power of whites, they often resist attempts to squelch their language. When told to stop speaking Spanish on the grounds that Spanish is out of place, latinos often respond by asserting the legitimacy of their mother tongue. At a deeper level, this may be seen as a disagreement in which the white side is trying to disparage latinos' language and the latinos are making efforts to counter that image. In other instances, the latino individual persists against prohibitions on speaking Spanish through different means. In a celebrated U.S. court case, Héctor García was employed as a salesperson by Gloor Lumber and Supply, Inc., of Amarillo, Texas. Gloor Lumber allowed its employees to communicate in Spanish on the job only if there were Spanish-speaking customers. García broke company policy by speaking Spanish with latino co-workers. He was fired, sued and lost (Gonzalez 2000). García insisted on his *right* to speak Spanish.

In this article, we demonstrate a number of different techniques that are perceived by our subjects as attempts by whites to undermine the status of Spanish and Spanish speakers and discourage the language's everyday use. We also examine forms of latino resistance to this linguistic restriction and oppression.

Our Data

In this exploratory analysis of linguistic barriers and resistance, we employ new data from seventy-two in-depth interviews of mostly middle-class latinos carried out in 2003–2005 in numerous states with substantial latino populations.

For this pioneering research (the first of its kind, so far as we can tell), we intentionally chose middle-class respondents for two reasons. First, they are the ones most likely to have substantial contacts with white Americans in their daily rounds, and are thus more likely to encounter racial barriers from whites and to feel the greatest pressures to give up language and cultural heritage. Second, they are the ones who are considered, especially by the white-controlled mass media and by middle-class white Americans generally, to be the most successful members of their group—and thus to face little discrimination in what is presented as a non-racist United States. Thus, since social scientist Nathan Glazer's 1975 book, *Affirmative Discrimination*, was published, a great many U.S. scholars have argued that there is little or no racial discrimination left in U.S. society and that, in particular, middle-class people of color face no significant racial or ethnic barriers. The first extensive qualitative fieldwork on the life experiences of contemporary African Americans—conducted in the late 1980s and early 1990s—took this approach, and in this research project we have followed much of the rationale and research guidelines for that prize-winning research (Essed 1991; Feagin and Sikes 1994; Feagin, Vera, and Imani 1996).

In this innovative research we intentionally focus on those latinos generally considered middle class and economically successful, such as teachers, small business owners, office workers, and mid-level government administrators. More than 90 percent of the respondents have at least some college work, and 58 percent have completed at least a college degree. A small minority hold clerical or manual jobs. Using the qualitative methods of researchers studying everyday racial experiences (Essed 1991; Feagin and Sikes 1994), we used a carefully crafted snowball sampling design with more than two dozen different starting points in seven states to ensure diversity in the sample. Initial respondents were referred by colleagues across the country. As we proceeded, participants suggested others for interviews. Few respondents are part of the same networks as others in the sample.

The respondents are mainly from the key latino states of Arizona, California, Florida, Illinois, New Jersey, New York and Texas. Sixty percent of our respondents are Mexican-American; 18 percent are Cuban-American; 13 percent are Puerto Rican; and the remaining 9 percent are other from Latin American countries. This distribution is roughly similar to that of the U.S. latino population. Sixty-four percent of the respondents are women and 36 percent are men.[1]

Language Control Stratagems and Resistance Responses

We examine relationships between whites, the most powerful U.S. racial group, and latinos, a group that whites usually define racially as "not white" (Feagin and Dirks 2006). One reason for this focus is their central importance for the position of latinos in U.S. society. Another is that there are very few accounts in our latino interviews of other Americans of color attempting to discriminate against latino respondents on language grounds. One reason for this, we venture, is that non-latino people of color are usually not in a position to complain loudly about the Spanish language even if they wished to, because they do not have significant power in U.S. institutions.

As we observe below, even those whites not in the middle class, as much recent research has demonstrated (see Feagin and Sikes 1994), feel great power as whites to assert the privileges of whiteness versus people of color. As we will observe constantly in our accounts, Anglo whites in the upper middle, middle and working classes feel powerful over middle-class latinos. In most accounts, the white discriminators are of equal or higher socioeconomic status than those latinos targeted for discrimination.

The common goal in the language-control methods of whites is to disparage the language of latinos. The methods follow a variety of strategies. Some are aimed at latinos' use of English: asking participants to stop speaking Spanish, because "English" is the language of the land or because the white interlocutors want to know "what's going on," and ignoring latinos who speak Spanish. Other forms of control are deriding latinos' accents, raising questions about their proficiency in English when latinos demonstrate skill. Whites define latino speech as tainted in two senses. First, when latinos speak Spanish they are using a language that "does not belong" in the United States and may be saying things behind whites' backs. Second, when they speak English, their accent is inferior and does not belong. Whites see themselves as the authorities to adjudicate language use. Attempts to control latinos' language or disparage it often provoke responses from the latinos involved in the interaction or witnessing it. The discussion that follows is organized around the different types of language control and denigration stratagems.

Silencing Spanish Speakers

One language control strategy is "silencing." It is the stratagem most frequently mentioned by the respondents. Silencing is straightforward: it consists of a command from members of the white group to latinos to stop speaking Spanish. It carries the supposition that whites can interfere in the Spanish conversations of latinos to stop them from speaking Spanish.

The command is usually based on the explicit or implied assumption by the interlocutor that "We only speak English in America."

A Cuban–American attorney remembers this story from her childhood a few decades back. It shows a classic case of silencing.

> We were in [a supermarket]. … It was during the Mariel Boatlift situation … there was a whole bunch of negative media out towards Cubans "cause … many of the people that were coming over were ex-cons or what-not. … And so my mother was speaking to us in Spanish … and this [white] woman passed by my mother and said … "Speak English, you stupid Cuban!" … And then my mother turned around, and purposefully, in broken English, because she speaks pretty good English … said, "I beg your pardon?" … [The woman] repeated the statement.

The Cuban interlocutor's response is quite assertive:

> And my mother … asked her if she was a native American Indian. And when the lady responded "No… I'm Polish" … my mother responded … "Well, you're a stupid fuckin' refugee just like me. …" And, the lady, I don't know what she said, but my mother said, "Do you know why I'm here, in this country? … I'm here [which was not true] because I just came in the … [Mariel Boatlift] and the reason … was because I killed two in Cuba, [and] one more here will make no difference." … And so then [the woman] thought my mom was being serious and left there really quickly.

When she asks the white interlocutor, most likely a middle-class shopper, about her Indian ancestry, the respondent reposts by saying in essence that she and her language are as American as the white Polish woman's.

In the next account, the attempt at silencing is indirect. A white Anglo post office employee, who is probably working class or lower middle class, complains to the postmaster, a latino, that two fellow workers are speaking Spanish on the job, and asks the boss to make them stop. The postmaster refuses to comply:

> I had that situation when I was working for the post office. I had two Chicanos that were talking in Spanish. There was an Anglo carrier right in the middle and she approached me and told me that I should keep them from speaking Spanish. I said, "You know both of them are Vietnam veterans and I think that they fought for the right to talk any language they want to."

The postmaster's response attributes legitimacy to the latinos speaking any language they choose because they are veterans who fought in Vietnam and are Americans entitled to any language they please.

A latino respondent in a south-western city was trying to help a Mexican immigrant at a convenience store. Their conversation was in Spanish. As they talked, a white interlocutor interrupted and voiced his displeasure at their use of Spanish, first by the indirect means of complaining about the supposed loudness and then more directly by suggesting the immigrant should leave the country.

[This] farm worker … is Mexican. I was speaking to him [in Spanish] … and this [white] individual asked us if I had to speak so loud. "Can you guys lower your voice?" …

Were you guys talking out in the street?

No, there is a Circle K right by [work]. We were standing right by [the counter].

Did you respond to this man?

I very politely explained to him and he was shocked [at the quality of the English] when I looked at him and I said, "Pardon me sir, I am speaking to him in Spanish … because he doesn't speak English." His response then was, "maybe he should move out." I said to him … "if he moves out, then why don't you go pick the stuff out in the field?"

What did he say to that?

He just turned around and walked away.

The response from someone who may have been a fellow shopper says, in essence, that the Mexican immigrant is performing a useful function in the United States, doing necessary work that the white interlocutor and many other whites apparently are not willing to do. At the very least, the respondent appears to say, he has a right to communicate in his mother tongue.

In the next episode, a successful executive related an incident that happened when he was on vacation with his family and visiting a famous amusement park. He and his wife came to the United States at an early age, and they have an advanced English proficiency. Yet they decided to often speak to their children in Spanish while they were young, so that they would learn the Spanish language. He provided this account:

> I had a really bad experience at Disneyworld. ... My son at the time was ... three. ... He jumped the line and went straight to where there was Pluto or Mickey Mouse or something and I said, "[Son's name], come back," in Spanish and ... ran after him. And I heard behind me somebody say, "It would be a fucking spic that would cut the line." Now my wife saw who said it, and I said, "Who said that?" in English and nobody said a word. And I said [to my wife], "Point him out, I want to know who said that," and she refused. I was like, "Who was the motherfucker who said that?" I said, "Be brave enough to say it to my face because I'm going to kill you." You can see me, I'm 6'3," 275 [pounds]. Nobody volunteered. ...

> *So nobody stepped up?*

> No, no and there was a bunch of guys there, and I would have thrown down two or three of them; I wouldn't have had a problem.

The executive's response was clear, to the point, and came from the heart: his child was insulted by (probably middle-class) white visitors to this expensive theme park. He was deeply offended for his family. Clearly his strong reaction could have led to further serious consequences, yet he was willing to take this risk by responding aggressively to the ultimate racist slur for latinos.

In these accounts, whites who are attacking or discriminating vary in social status. Sometimes, they are of higher socioeconomic status than our respondents, and at other times they are of equal or lower status. Yet, all whites seem to feel the power to hurl racist commentaries at latinos who are attempting to live out normal lives.

Practices silencing Spanish speakers reveal the asymmetric statuses of the English and Spanish languages. It would be inconceivable for a latino to ask a white Anglo to stop speaking English in any latino neighborhood. Such reciprocity in action would suggest a language equality that does not exist, and latinos are well aware of this societal situation. We asked a South American respondent the following question,

> Sometimes ... I ask people I interview ... "Have you ever seen a Mexican at a grocery store turn to [white person] and say, 'Please do not speak English?'" Have you seen this happen? She laughed, "No, no!"

Despite attempts at the imposition of barriers, Spanish-speaking respondents frequently answer back, softly or aggressively, thereby insisting on their right to use their native language.

Voicing Suspicion: Fears of Spanish-Speaking Americans

In the everyday worlds of latinos, whites' language-suspicion actions differ from language silencing acts in that the latter emanate from a conviction that English is the only acceptable language in the United States. Language-suspicion actions generally involve less confrontation.

Whereas silencing actions derive from a strongly held notion about what should be the dominant language, suspicion actions are likely to reveal a notion that Spanish speakers need to be watched, that they are perfidious or sneaky (Urciuoli 1996). Silencing draws from a type of an ethnocentric discourse, one that goes back to eighteenth-century Anglo-American fears of German immigrants and their language (Feagin 1997, p. 18). The suspicion response is rooted in anti-latino stereotypes. There is a common substratum of racialized thinking: when latinos speak Spanish, they are not playing by the "right" rules as envisioned and asserted by whites.

A major difference between silencing and voicing suspicion is that some of the white interlocutors who object to Spanish on the grounds that they are excluded express, at least on the surface, a desire to be included in the interaction. This inclusion is, however, one that is seen and defined in white terms, for the conversation must be in the white person's language.

Another respondent provided an example of suspiciousness on the part of a more senior white manager who did not want her workers speaking Spanish:

Most of the coworkers and the supervisors or managers are bilingual ... but ... my manager was only unilingual. ... She does not understand ... that we were not talking about her. ... We were talking about our business ... and personal stuff, but she doesn't have to know what we were talking because we don't need for her to give us her ... point of view. If we need for her to talk we are going to ask her in English, not in Spanish. ... [She said] "I don't want you speaking Spanish" and I told her "I do not agree with you because this is not right."

And what did she say?

She said "Well, it's not right; it doesn't matter." And I said, "Yes, it does matter and you're not going to stop me from speaking my first language."

The interviewee's response is an unequivocal statement about her right to speak her first language. It resonates with the theme so frequently seen in the ripostes given by other respondents: "I'm entitled to speak my language."

A male respondent reported on a situation where he was speaking in Spanish with another latino in a bank, when a white stranger broke into their private conversation:

> On one occasion we were at a Bank of … branch. … We were talking [in Spanish] and all of a sudden this [white] lady comes and asks us [in English] what we were talking about.

What did you reply?

> We told her we were talking about our business.

Although we do not know what the white woman in this affluent setting had in mind when she interfered in the conversation, her action suggests the recurring concern of many whites that those not speaking in English may be plotting something contrary to white interests. There is no doubt that she took it for granted that she was entitled to interrupt. The latino's response is matter-of-fact and seems to convey the notion that in his mind what he and his friend were doing was legitimate.

Another respondent reported that she was hired to work at a store in a U.S. town near the Mexican border so that she could help the numerous Spanish-speaking customers who crossed from Mexico to go to the store. Yet she faced a significant problem when she tried to do her job: she could not speak to customers in Spanish if white customers were present. It seems that the store owners were less concerned with causing difficulties for their Mexican customers than with offending the white ones:

> In a store where I worked … I [saw a] lot of discrimination [against] the people that were coming from across the line [frontier] to shop here. … If I [spoke] English [to them] they'd feel discriminated because they couldn't understand me. Or if I spoke Spanish and there was an English patron shopping they'd feel that I was speaking against them or saying something that I should not be saying and I should be speaking [English]. … How could I do this when I had English speaking people and Spanish speaking people but the one I was directly addressing was Spanish speaking and a non-English speaking person? Yet I was felt made to feel that I should be speaking English because I was in America.

Even though she was upset at the unreasonable situation in which she was placed, there was little the respondent could do short of quitting her job.

Another respondent, a female manager in a public agency, was also asked if "Anglo whites ever object to your speaking Spanish at work?" She replied:

Yes. They are like, could you please speak English because we don't understand what you are saying. … Even the supervisor tells us sometimes that we should talk in English because there are some people that don't know Spanish. But you know what, I feel better speaking Spanish … because that's my primary language. There is a lady that actually, that's always complaining. There are times that … she just feels like left out of the conversation. She's like, I want to know what's going on, but there are times that she's kind of rude, so.

How do you usually respond to her?

I'm like, well, you need to learn Spanish.

The middle-class respondent asserted the legitimacy of her Spanish use in a different form by suggesting that those fellow workers, middle-class whites here, who wanted to partake in her Spanish-language conversations learn Spanish. Such a request may seem ludicrous only if one believes that English is the only language worth speaking in the United States. Even when languages have been granted official status, individuals are not forbidden to use other tongues in settings like work.

Suspicion of latinos speaking Spanish constitutes another instance of attempts on the part of whites to regulate latinos' speech. In this instance, the reason given is that whites feel that latinos are talking about them. The justification for white attempts reveals a view of Spanish speakers as sneaky and untrustworthy and the view that whites should be included in interactions with latinos on the whites' terms. Despite whites' objections, the typical latino responds by asserting his/her right to use their mother tongue.

Doubting the English Proficiency of Latinos

Since anti-latino rhetoric places such a heavy emphasis on latinos abandoning their heritage language, one would expect that when latinos ventured into the world of English they would receive encouragement from whites. This is often not the case. There is white obstinacy here: latinos speak Spanish, an inferior language, and thus they are apparently presumed to be tainted by their heritage language when they speak or write English, even when there is evidence to the contrary. In some cases, their English is assumed to be "too perfect" (cf. Essed 1991, p. 202).

One example comes from the college experience of a chicana professional. She was born in a mining town in the south west, and her English did not have the accent many whites consider undesirable. She reported on an instructor who questioned her integrity:

[A professor] in college refused to believe that I had written an essay ... because she assumed that Mexicans don't write very well and so therefore I couldn't have written this paper.

Did she tell you that?

Yes she did. ... And so she asked that I write it over again. ...

So what did you do?

I rewrote the assignment and she still didn't believe that it was my own. ... She still refused to believe that it was my handwriting or my writing because she still felt that Mexicans could not express themselves well in English. ...

Did she use those words?

Yes she did.

This woman explained that she came from a mining town where labor unions had helped Mexicans gain access to schools, so she had good English skills. The well-educated white instructor felt substantial power to impose her views: Mexicans cannot express themselves well in English. We see here an active countering response. The respondent stood up to the instructor but was unable to change her mind. Here again, we observe whites of higher social status or in more powerful positions discriminating against our latino respondents.

Another latina had a different experience. Asked whether whites have ever acted rudely after they heard her Spanish accent, she answered in the negative and discussed "left-handed compliments" she receives:

No. In fact people go out of their way to tell me that I don't have an accent.

Is that a compliment?

I think so. …

Tell me in more detail.

Well you know, they begin to ask me, well where are you from? Am I from Arizona? No I am not from Arizona. … I'm from Texas. And then their comment is that you don't have an accent. And I'm like what kind of accent are you talking about? I don't have a Texas accent, the twang. And then I'll say, no and I don't have a Spanish accent. I speak both languages. And they are like, well wow, you don't have an accent. Never fails. …

White interlocutors in her immediate environment express surprise at her apparently unaccented English. The astonishment expressed by whites is reflective of stereotypes concerning some latinos' English proficiency. In such settings, whites assume *they* have the right to determine which accented dialect of English is prized. English has many dialects, all with distinctive accents, yet most U.S. whites (unlike many European whites) are monolingual and do not view their own prized versions of English as accented.

In the next excerpt, a woman from Latin America relates her experiences with a paper she wrote. She had problems with contractions in English and had her paper checked by a campus facility that helped students. The center's staff found no mistakes. Nonetheless, the latina's highly educated white male instructor did not approve of how she used contractions, and even though he did not take off points from her grade, he made some comments to the class about foreign students:

I wrote a paper and I used some contractions and most of the time I have some problems with contractions. … I took my paper to the English writing center and nobody corrected anything. And so when I got my paper back [from the white instructor] and all the contractions were corrected and so I didn't say anything, but I took the paper back [to the writing center] and they explained to me that there was not any specific reason to have changed them. …

Did you get a bad grade on the paper?

No, but the teacher made a comment in class about foreign students and that we were in graduate school and we should write free of mistakes. … I said to myself that if I had been an American student using these words he would not have changed it. ... It was because there was nothing else to correct on the paper.

He just was looking for something to correct, that's what you are saying?

Yes.

This respondent did not confront her middle-class instructor directly, but, in going back to the writing center, she refused to accept the definition of her abilities that he attempted to impose on her and expressed her anger at the language-linked discrimination (on a similar problem for African Americans, see Essed 1991, p. 232).

Intended or not, whites' skepticism toward latinos' demonstrated proficiency in English is part of the denigration of latinos. Although it is not a direct attack on Spanish, it reflects notions of language deficiency among the mass of latinos—based, ironically, on the deviation of latino interlocutors from stereotypical expectations.

Denigrating the Accent

Another method of undervaluing latinos' English proficiency is by mocking those who have an accent whites consider undesirable. When they speak English, latinos frequently experience a close monitoring by whites, and, if some sign of a certain accent is detected, they risk ridicule. In business or government settings white customers sometimes even refuse to deal with latino personnel because their accent is "not American." Indeed, some latinos feel so self-conscious that speaking English becomes difficult (Hill 1999).

Consider this account from a highly educated latino who went to a computer store. In response to our question, "has a white Anglo ... acted abruptly after he heard your accent?" he replied:

Oh, that has happened several times. I have had *owners* of a store imitate my accent.

To your face?

In my face, yeah. I went to buy a printer ... I said, I'm here to buy a printer and the owner imitated my accent, back. ...

Did you buy the printer?

No, I did not. ... I felt that I was growing red in the face. ... And I said, "You know what, just forget it I'll buy it somewhere else," and I turned around and left.

Something as simple as buying a printer turned into a humiliating, in this case from upper-middle-class whites. Having the experience of someone powerful imitating his accent was not an isolated instance. Indeed, we see in several respondents' quotes this cumulative reality of discrimination; many forms of discrimination take place on a recurring basis in the lives of latinos. In refusing to purchase, the respondent resisted the discrimination and registered displeasure.

Another middle-class latino who works in the customer service department of a retail store gave this example:

There was one time that I answered [the telephone] at my work currently, I had this lady ... and she goes, "I don't want to talk to you, you have an accent!" I was like, "you don't want to talk to me?" she goes, "yeah, I want to talk to an American." I was like "ok, well I'm sorry you're gonna have to redial to speak to someone that you want." She goes, "well go ahead and transfer me over." I was like, "I'm sorry, I'm not going to be able to transfer you over. I have to take the call. I'm here to help you if you need anything." She goes, "well I don't understand you." And I just kept going, "well I there's anything I can do for you, I'm here." So she finally gave me her number and we went over the account and at the end she goes, "I'm really sorry that I was too rude to you at the beginning."

The white caller assumed that the individual answering the telephone could not be "an American" because she had a Spanish accent and went on to say that she wanted to deal with "an American," suggesting that the Latina could not offer the same level of service. The Latina insisted that she was able to help and the white shopper at the end gave the service representative a chance to help her.

A South American doctor, who works as a medical assistant while she attempts to validate her medical credentials in the United States, told us about her problems when dealing with patients. One in particular was very rude:

There is a white female patient who has not come out and said it, but lets me know that my accent bothers her. ... I called another patient, an elderly woman who was a little ways from me, and she did not hear me. The first patient, in a rather aggressive way, said to me, "Who is going to understand you with that accent of yours?"

What did you say?

I called the elderly patient again. ...

Do you prefer to remain quiet?

I don't like to get in trouble over things that don't matter that much.

This white patient took it upon herself to intervene where it did not concern her and used the opportunity to make a scornful comment, which served no purpose other than to demean the doctor's accent. Note again the repertoire of responses. Here the latina did not respond aggressively, but dismissed the patient's behavior and kept her professional demeanor.

For another woman, her accent was a cause of discomfort while dealing with white clerks. She replied to the question, has "a white Anglo store clerk acted abruptly after he heard your accent?" this way:

All the time. ... They tend to say, "What?" And in a rude way. ... Always it is this "What?" ... Yes, it is never "Oh, I am sorry I couldn't hear you." ... They are gesticulating ... this non-verbal behavior that is telling you ... "who are you" or "I can't understand you" or "Why are you even here?" ... you get all these messages ... [they are all] very negative.

This respondent's accent evoked unwelcoming behavior from whites who may have been of lower social status than the respondent. In many instances, as we have seen, the whites who discriminate are of equal or higher status than the respondents. In other settings, they are of lower status, yet most whites of either status seem to feel the power to discriminate in this fashion. The respondent clearly felt that the legitimacy of her status in the country was being questioned. We see here the way in which language attacks can literally crash into a person's everyday life when least expected.

Language mocking can affect a person's emotions, as the next account illustrates. The perpetrator of an attack was a dear friend who evidently thought she was just joking:

Anybody ever approach you about your accent?

Yeah, all the time, all the time. ... I had a very ... bad experience with somebody I love very much. I was in ... in nursing school and I had this friend and we're very, very close.

I mean we went through the nursing school together and we were great friends and I adored my friend, but she would always make fun of my accent. Because there's still a lot of words, I still can't say some words, a few words. She would always make fun of either the way the word sounded or whatever and I would never say anything because that's the type of person I am. I just take everything in and I don't verbalize my feelings most of the time. But that's me. So when we were graduating from the program I wrote her a letter and I told her that I loved her very much and I wanted to continue to be her friend, but that if my accent bothered her that much that it was ok with me not to be friends anymore. And that I felt very uncomfortable with the way she criticized me with my accent.

She was a non-latino?

She was Italian.

The latina's educated Italian American friend evidently did not know the pain her mocking was inflicting. Our respondent endured the pain as long as she could, but eventually decided that if taking the mocking was the price of the friendship, she could dispense with it. She was gentle, but stood up for herself.

In her interview a Mexican American with a master's degree sounded apologetic about being U.S.-born yet possibly having an "accent." She noted that some white middle-class coworkers had been supportive, but others had made fun of her:

English is my first language, so I really don't know if I have an accent, but there are sometimes where some words come out different and that does get recognized by some people that I work with. And I don't think it's an intentional making fun of [it], but it's noticeable and you know they kind of make a slight joke off of it. But I'd have to say I work around both types of people, [some] that have been really supportive despite some other people which you know they really look at you as not knowing as much [as whites].

Self-consciousness about a certain Spanish-linked accent is common among latinos (Urciuoli 1996), including those who are U.S.-born. In a related vein, Bourdieu (1991, p. 77) discusses the "self-censorship" experienced by speakers who anticipate a low price for their speech in the linguistic market. This causes a certain demeanor (tension, embarrassment) which reinforces the market's verdict.

The denigration of Spanish and Spanish accents, whether in joking or more serious commentaries, is generally insidious and thus part of the social "woodwork" in the United States. In contrast, whites rarely denigrate the many accents of fellow white English speakers in such routine and caustic ways.

Most of our respondents resist through an array of strategies. At work sometimes they refuse to go along with demands that they not speak Spanish. There are other instances, such as when they work with the public, when the targets of mocking are in no position to resist. In other circumstances, as when they are customers in a store, they can express their displeasure at the way they are being treated, such as by discontinuing their shopping.

Ignoring Spanish Speakers

Many latinos report that whites dismiss them as not being worthy of attention after hearing them speaking Spanish. Unlike silencing, deriding Spanish accents or voicing suspicion, ignoring Spanish speakers is a passive form of expressing disapproval toward the use of Spanish.

The case reported by the following interviewee occurred at a high-end resort in Arizona. She and her family went for drinks:

In the last five years have you been mistreated in restaurants by whites because of your race, ethnicity, speaking Spanish or accent?

Yeah, we went to [resort restaurant] and we tried to order some drinks, but the lady kept passing and passing and said that she would come, but never came to ask what we want to drink I think because she heard us speaking Spanish. …

And was the server, the person white?

She was white and we told her, we called her and told her if she wasn't going to take our order or what because why that discrimination? We asked her a few times to come nicely and she kept saying, "I will be back, I will be back" and so she apologized and excused herself of course 'cause if not we were going to make a problem.

Then you told her that you felt discriminated?

Yeah.

And you say "we," with whom were you at the hotel?

My mom and her husband and other friends.

And you were speaking Spanish?

Yeah.

And so the lady then came and ...?

And she kind of apologized and we said "if not we want to talk to your managers."

Did she change her attitude?

Yeah.

After repeated attempts, the respondent and family members said they felt discriminated against, and it appears that this caused the white server to change her attitude. In this case, the white person was clearly of lower social status than the latino family members, yet still felt she could discriminate in the provision of service.

Conclusion

The so-called "browning of America" has raised fears among many whites at all class levels. The reason typically given is that latinos represent a threat to the U.S. way of life, with the English language as a major symbol of that way of life. Many whites have responded in part by racializing latinos and their language and attempting to demean its importance.

Efforts at squelching Spanish at an interpersonal level take various forms: outright commands to Spanish speakers to speak English, protestations that when they speak Spanish latinos are talking about whites, skepticism about English proficiency of latinos despite evidence to the contrary, mocking latinos' "accents" and ignoring Spanish speakers. Latinos often resist these incursions into their heritage language, but their resources are usually limited when compared to those at the disposal of most of their white antagonists.

Latinos often resist this mistreatment—a formidable task in light of the white establishment's resources. Today, Spanish is ridiculed by influential whites, who often call for much stricter government control over Latin American immigrants. Ideological elements emanating from the dominant culture may mask for some latinos the structural basis of their victimization and thus interfere with their ability to see the systemic structure of their oppression, yet there are no signs of surrender to whites' anti-latino discrimination.

The xenophobic discourse aimed at latinos relies heavily on the notion that they and their culture are sounding the death knell for English culture. This white discourse is heavy in rhetoric and short on evidence. Indeed, many English-language programs for immigrants have long waiting lists. Facility in multiple languages is a valuable cultural resource for U.S. society. There is a widespread belief among our study's respondents that there should be more tolerance toward languages other than English. Asked about attempts to ban Spanish in U.S. society, one respondent's answer was typical:

I think the more languages you speak, the more culture you have, the more educated you are. We're in a global society, I mean Spanish is the number two spoken language of the Americas.

Is it ok with you to use Spanish in ballots or other official documents?

You know this is the United States and English should be the number one language but, if they are U.S. citizens and they are paying U.S. taxes, then they should have Spanish ballots.

Interestingly, not one of our seventy-two respondents argued that language tolerance should be limited only to Spanish. Not one advocated that Spanish should replace English as the language inside or outside latino communities. Analysts like Huntington (2004) accuse latinos of being a threat to democracy and the "American way of life," which for them means Anglo-Saxon ways of doing things. On close examination, this is a peculiar accusation because most latinos are accenting the virtues of language and other cultural diversity that the official U.S. ideology accents in its omnipresent "melting pot" imagery.

The struggles between latinos and whites over language do not take place on a level playing field. As Barth has put it, the interaction between the majority group and the minority group "takes place entirely within the framework of the dominant, majority group's statuses and institutions" (1969, p. 31). Given their position in the racial hierarchy of U.S. society, whites have tremendous resources at their disposal in the worlds of politics, business, finance, mass media and education. Powerful white elites control much of the normative structure (Gramsci 1988), as well as much of the dominant thinking about what is right and proper in society.

In this white-dominated milieu, latinos struggle to preserve their heritage language as best they can, but it remains a difficult task.

Discussion Questions

1. What does Pierre Bourdieu mean by the term "linguistic capital"?
2. Why did the authors avoid upper- and lower-class respondents in compiling their research? How do you think the inclusion of such respondents would have affected the results?
3. Discuss the ways in which the Spanish language is denigrated, directly and indirectly, among middle-class whites. Why, in your opinion, doesn't this discrimination generally extend to non-English speaking whites (i.e. Scandinavians or Germans)?

Notes

1. Eighty-eight percent of the interviews were done in person, the remaining 12 percent by telephone. All but two were carried out by latino interviewers, six in Spanish, the remaining ones in English.

References

Barth, Fredrik (Barth, Fredrik ed.) (1969) *Ethnic Groups and Boundaries: The Social Organization of Culture Difference* pp. 9–38. Little, Brown, Boston, MA

Bourdieu, Pierre (1977) The economics of linguistic exchanges. *Social Science Information* vol. 16:no. 6, pp. 645–668.

Bourdieu, Pierre (1991) *Language and Symbolic Power* Harvard University Press, Cambridge, MA

Lourie, Margaret A. (1983) *A Host of Tongues* The Free Press, New York

Cornelius, Wayne (Marcelo, M. Suárez-Orozco and Mariela, M. Páez eds.) (2002) *Latinos: Remaking America* pp. 165–189. University of California Press, Berkeley, CA

(1992) *Language Loyalties: A Source Book on the Official English Controversy* pp. i–ii. University of Chicago Press, Chicago

Essed, Philomena (1991) *Understanding Everyday Racism* Sage, Newbury Park, CA

Feagin, Joe R. (Perea, Juan F. ed.) (1996) *Immigrants Out! The New Nativism and the Anti-Immigrant Impulse in the United States* pp. 13–43. New York University Press, New York

Feagin, Joe R. and Dirks, Danielle (2006) Who is white.—unpublished research paper, Texas A&M University

Feagin, Joe R. and O'Brien, Eileen (2003) *White Men on Race* Beacon Press, Boston, MA

Feagin, Joe R. and Sikes, Melvin P. (1994) *Living with Racism* Beacon Press, Boston, MA

Feagin, Joe R., Vera, Hernan and Imani, Nikitah (1996) *The Agony of Education* Routledge, New York

Fischer, David Hackett (1989) *Albion's Seed: Four British Folkways in America* Oxford University Press, New York

Fishman, Joshua A. (1989) *Language and Ethnicity in Minority Sociolinguistic Perspective* Multilingual Matters, Clevedon

Glazer, Nathan (1975) *Affirmative Discrimination* Basic Books, New York

Gonzalez, Gilbert G. (1990) *Chicano Education in the Era of Segregation* The Balch Institute Press, Philadelphia, PA

Gonzalez, Juan (2000) *Harvest of Empire* Viking, New York

Gramsci, Antonio (Forgacs, David ed.) (1988) *The Antonio Gramsci Reader: Selected Writings 1916– 1935* Lawrence & Wishart, London

Jane, Hill (1999) Language, Race, and White Public Space. *American Anthropologist* Vol. 100, pp. 680–689.

Horton, John (1995) *The Politics of Language Diversity: Immigration, Resistance, and Change in Monterey Park* Temple University Press, California, Philadelphia, PA

Huntington, Samuel P. (2004) Simon & Schuster, New York

Lippi-Green, Rosina (1997) *English with an Accent: Language, Ideology, and Discrimination in the United States* Routledge, London

Montoya, Margaret E. (Delgado, Richard and Stefancic, Jean eds.) (1998) *The Latino/a Condition: A Critical Reader* pp. 574–578. New York University Press, New York

Ruben Jr, Navarrette (2005) *The San Diego Union-Tribune* p. G-3.–17 (2002) *Brown Tide Rising: Metaphors of Latinos in Contemporary American Public Discourse* University of Texas Press, Austin, TX

Shafir, Gershon (1995) *Immigrants and Nationalists: Ethnic Conflict and Accommodation in Catalonia, the Basque Country, Latvia, and Estonia* State University of New York Press, Albany, NY

Silverstein, Michael (Brenneis, Donald and Macaulay, Ronald K. S. eds.) (1996) *The Matrix of Language: Contemporary Linguistic Anthropology* pp. 284–306. Westview Press, Boulder, CO

Siguan, Miquel (2002) *Europe and the Languages*—http://www.gksdesign.com/atotos/ebooks/siguan/europe.htm

Urciuoli, Bonnie (1996) *Exposing Prejudice: Puerto Rican Experiences of Language, Race, and Class* West-view Press, Boulder, CO

U.S. Bureau of the Census (2004) *Annual Estimates of the Population by Sex, Race and Hispanic or Latino Origin for the United States: April 1, 2000 to July 1, 2003* Population Division, U.S. Census Bureau, Washington, DC–Table 3

Wood, Nicholas (2005) *New York Times* p. A4.—24

Questions to Think About

1. How are race and class social constructs?
2. What is linguistic capital? How is it used to advantage majority groups?
3. What effects will the housing crisis have on the wealth of blacks and whites moving forward?
4. What do Oliver and Shapiro mean by a "racialization of state policy?" How has this disadvantaged minorities?

Resources

See Oliver Shapito discuss "Black Weath/White Wealth":

https://video.search.yahoo.com/search/video;_ylt=A0LEVxwe1v9W95gAjS5XNyoA;_ylu=X3oDMTE-0Y3BsNzM0BGNvbG8DYmYxBHBvcwMxBHZ0aWQQjE3MjRfMQRzZWMDcGl2cw--?p=black+wealth+white+wealth&fr=mcafee&fr2=piv-web#id=2&vid=8ef106776040e455a7a64653fc86306b&action=view

In Chicago, Even Wealthy Black Families Live in Poorer Neighborhoods:

http://www.s4.brown.edu/us2010/News/inthenews.PDFs/Jul_Aug.2011/us2010news.2011.08.08.chicago-reporter.pdf

Race—The Power of an Illusion

Activities and videos about the social construction of race in the United States:

http://www.pbs.org/race/000_General/000_00-Home.htm

Hispanics and the Future of America:

http://www.ncbi.nlm.nih.gov/books/NBK19909/

United States Census. Origins of People of Hispanic descent in the United States http://www.census.gov/population/hispanic/

United States Census. Articles about Race in the United States:

http://census.gov/topics/population/race.html

Teaching Tolerance: Article on white privilege:

http://www.tolerance.org/article/racism-and-white-privilege

Pew Research Trust: Article on the US Census and definitions of race:

http://www.pewresearch.org/fact-tank/2014/03/14/u-s-census-looking-at-big-changes-in-how-it-asks-about-race-and-ethnicity/

Race and Education on Long Island: Erase Racism:

http://eraseracismny.org/our-work/education

SECTION IV
GENDER

Introduction

Unlike sex, which is biological, the concept of gender is a social construct. Each society decides what attributes to assign to different genders. These attributes are not the same in all cultures, nor are they stagnant over time. At any given time and in every culture, there can be found a distinct set of gender roles the population assumes to be "natural" and "normal." Those exhibiting behavior outside of these proscribed norms are often considered deviant. For example, in the 1800s females were told they should not become too educated because it would decrease their ability to have children and make them unmarriageable. Today, women earn over half of the college degrees awarded.

Gender role expectations are often harmful to both males and females. Less is expected of females than males because of the premise they are "weak" or "soft," which can limit what they achieve. For a male, gender norms create a feeling he needs to take more risks, not express feelings, and engage in behavior harmful to his body. Males, as well as females, who cannot—or do not—live up to these gendered expectations often experience difficulty navigating through their daily lives. The following two readings explore several problems that can arise due to gender norms.

In the reading "What's in a Name? Coverage of Senator Hillary Clinton during the 2008 Democratic Primary," Joseph E. Uscinski and Lilly J. Goren use content analysis of the transcripts of televised news reports in 2008 to understand whether the terms reporters used to reference the candidates reflected gender bias in the media. The authors use the theory of status expectations to guide their research. According to this theory, gender acts as a master status. Each person has many statuses forming a part of that individual, and there are any number of statuses a person may hold at any one point in time. For instance, a female may also be a mother, daughter, employee, and an employer. A master status is the one status that stands out and is primarily associated with an individual. For instance, Barack Obama is a son, father, and a former senator, but his master status is the president of the United States.

In this essay, the authors argue that while media strives (at least theoretically) to be unbiased, subconscious gender bias plays a part in news stories. The authors found Senator Clinton was more likely to be referred to by her first name—rather than her last name or her title—than the male candidate in the 2008 Democratic primary. This was particularly true if the reporters were male. The authors argue the first-name reference by male newscasters reflects a conscious or unconscious bias toward males. Although this treatment is possibly unintentional, the way media, particularly male newscasters, depicted Senator Clinton delegitimized her and is a form of subtle sexism. The authors assert newscasters and the public should be aware of how different genders are portrayed in media and recommend reporters use a universal language to cover both male and female candidates. They also suggest the media increase the number of female reporters, particularly for campaign reporting, because women are less biased against women than men.

The next reading in this section, "The Social Nature of Male Suicide: A New Analytical Model," examines the dire consequences of gender stereotyping for males. The World Health Organization asserts suicide is a global health issue, not just an infrequent, random occurrence. In this chapter, Coleman et. al. examine the ways socialization and gender expectations affect male suicide rates. They contend the suicide crisis disproportionally affects males because, as a result of the differences between male and female gender role socialization, when males attempt suicide they are more likely than females to use lethal methods. Consequently, in most countries suicide attempts are more likely to be successfully completed by males. Having an unsuccessful suicide attempt is viewed as weak and feminine, so males are more likely to use strategies that guarantee success. In the United States, and in other countries around the globe, the gendered social script defines men as strong and unemotional. Phrases such as "Be a man" and "Don't act like a girl" characterize men as weak if they show their feelings or are nurturing, or exhibit traits society defines as "feminine." For instance, when a male succeeds in sports or his career, it is usually attributed to his innate ability, whereas women who are successful are often viewed as lucky or individuals who have expended great effort and made significant sacrifices. Males who cannot live up to the gendered expectations of what it means to be masculine seek alternative means to escape their negative self-perception. The authors of this chapter identify the risk factors associated with suicide, such as job loss, retirement, same-sex orientation, and unemployment, among others. They argue because of gender role socialization, males are less likely to seek help for depression and other mental health issues, so there are fewer warning signs a male is contemplating suicide than there would be for women. The authors then address the individual theories of suicide such as personality disorder theory and male-depressive syndrome, and seek to develop a sociocultural theory that explores the cultural dimensions of suicide for males.

Using the escape theory of suicide and masculinity theory, the authors argue gender role socialization has a major influence on the likelihood of male suicide. In this view, males who experience gender role strain (they are not able to live up to the gendered expectations of society) may view themselves as failures and use suicide as an escape, whereas those who are successful and well liked are less likely to commit suicide. The authors call for changing the current norms of masculinity if male suicides are to be reduced.

Reading 6: What's in a Name? Coverage of Senator Hillary Clinton during the 2008 Democratic Primary

By Joseph E. Uscinski[1] and Lilly J. Goren[2]

Abstract

Throughout the 2008 Democratic primary, Senator Hillary Clinton, her supporters and advocates, feminist groups, and commentators accused the media of sexist coverage. Was Hillary Clinton treated differently in the media because of her gender? The authors attempt to answer this question by examining the forms of address that television newspeople use to refer to the Democratic primary candidates. The authors find that newspeople referred to Clinton more informally than her male competitors. This treatment stemmed from the gender of the broadcaster; males show gender bias in how they reference presidential candidates. The authors conclude with suggestions for addressing gender bias in news coverage.

Keywords

Hillary Clinton, primary election, news, gender bias

> It does seem as though the press, at least, is not as bothered by the incredible vitriol that has been engendered by the comments by people who are nothing but misogynists.
>
> Senator Hillary Clinton[1]

> The media took a very sexist approach to Senator Clinton's campaign.
>
> Howard Dean[2]

[1]University of Miami, Coral Gables, FL, USA
[2]Carroll University, Waukesha, WI, USA

Like her or not, one of the great lessons of that campaign is the continued—and accepted—role of sexism in American life, particularly in the media.

Katie Couric[3]

The troubling question is not whether race is defining this campaign, but whether sex—or to put it bluntly, sexism is.

Susan Estrich[4]

Throughout the 2008 Democratic primary season, Senator Hillary Clinton, her supporters and advocates, feminist groups, and commentators suggested she received unfair news coverage because of her gender. While media organizations discussed this during the race, the charges of "media misogyny" took hold. Subsequently, scholars found evidence indicating that Clinton was in fact covered differently than her male competitors (e.g., Miller, Peake, and Boulton 2010; Carroll 2009; Carlin and Winfrey 2009). But, was Hillary Clinton covered differently because of her gender? If Clinton was treated in a sexist way, where did this disparity emanate from?

Certainly many comments made during the primary season indicate Hillary Clinton (HRC) was treated harshly because of her gender. Table 1 provides a small sample of nationally aired remarks by well-known television newspeople; these comments suggest overt sexism because they portray HRC as a castrator, first-wife, b-word, psychotic and murderous ex-lover, and she-devil. However, these examples are anecdotal and therefore not sufficient on their own to support claims of gender bias. Simply looking at Table 1, it would be difficult to ascertain if these statements were made because she was Hillary Clinton or because she was a "she." For example, HRC endured a long history of criticism because in the minds of many, she embodies not only a stereotypical (and negative) representation of second wave feminism, partly due to her unconventional approach to the role of first lady, but also because she represents female progress in general (Burden and Mughan 1999; Gardetto 1997; Winfield 1997; M. E. Brown 1997).[5] As Candy Crowley of CNN stated in response to accusations of media sexism, "it was hard to know if these attacks were being made because she was a woman or because she was *this* woman or because, for a long time, she was the frontrunner."[6] To determine if HRC's coverage was a backlash against feminism, simply an attack on a major contender, or the resultant of sexist attitudes, we examine a more valid measure of media coverage.

Media coverage can profoundly affect election outcomes. Specifically, gender bias in coverage can disadvantage female candidates (Kittilson and Fridkin 2008; Kahn 1992, 1994b).

Table 1. Remarks about Hillary Clinton on Televised News Programming

Hillary looks at Obama "like everyone's first wife standing outside a probate court."

Mike Barincle, 23 January 2008, MSNBC's *Morning Joe*

"There's just something about [Hillary Clinton] that feels castrating, overbearing, and scary."

Tucker Carlson, 20 March 2008, MSNBC's *Tucker*

"And she had that tone of voice, where she just sounds like [covers his ears]. I can't listen to it 'cause it sounds like—it sounds like my wife saying, 'Take out the garbage.'"

Glenn Beck, 30 May 2008, ABC's *Good Morning America*

"The reason she's a U.S. senator, the reason she's a candidate for president, the reason she may be a frontrunner is her husband messed around. We keep forgetting it. She didn't win there on her merit."

Chris Matthews, 8 January 2008, MSNBC

"[Hillary Clinton] is not called a B-word because she's assertive and aggressive; she's called a B-word because she acts like one."

"She's having a catfight with America."

Marc Rudov, 10 April 2008, Fox News *Your World with Neil Cavuto*

"Well, first of all, let's be honest here, Hillary Clinton is Glenn Close in *Fatal Attraction*. She's going to keep coming back, and they're not going to stop her."

Ken Rudin of NPR, 27 April 2008, CNN's *Sunday Morning*

"I have often said, when she comes on television, I involuntarily cross my legs."

Tucker Carlson, 16 July 2007, MSNBC's *Tucker*

"She-Devil?"

Chris Matthews, 18 November 2008, NBC's *Chris Matthews Show*

Historically, female candidates receive 50 percent less coverage than their comparable male counterparts (Falk 2008b; Kahn 1994a, 1996; Kahn and Goldenberg 1991). Also, coverage of females focuses less on the substantive issues and more on physical appearance, clothing, or other traditionally "feminine" narratives (Falk 2008b; Han and Heldman 2007; Heith 2003; Aday and Devitt 2001; Devitt 1999; Kahn 1994a; Kahn and Goldenberg 1991). In the 2000 Republican primary, Elizabeth Dole received far less coverage than her status in the polls merited; 20 percent of coverage discussed her appearance while coverage of male contenders did not discuss such things (Heldman, Carroll, and Olson 2005).

Given the accusations of sexism, a history of gendered news, and the historical implications of HRC's candidacy, this article examines the terms used to reference the Democratic primary candidates to determine if sexism affected news coverage. We theorize that underlying and ingrained gender biases negatively affect people's perceptions of female presidential candidates. We expect that these subconscious biases lead broadcast journalists to reference female candidates more informally. Specifically, we hypothesize that televised newspeople will reference HRC more informally than her main male counterpart, Barack Obama (BHO), and the other male candidates in the race. Due to the tendency of males to hold sexist notions, we further hypothesize that male newspeople will refer to HRC more informally than female newspeople. We gather data from television news transcripts and correlate the use of reference terms to the gender of the newsperson and other potentially relevant factors. We conclude with suggestions for facilitating equitable news coverage for female candidates.

Theory

According to accepted theories of status expectations, gender is a master status; it is automatically processed and accounted for in social interactions (e.g., Howard and Hollander 1997). Whether one interacts with a nurse, doctor, politician, or homeless person, the stereotypes associated with gender are activated (Ridgeway 2009). American society has been shown to have gendered beliefs and a gender stratification system that devalues females and femininity (McKay 2006; Hagan 1990; Huber 1986; Blumberg 1984). The persistence of these gendered beliefs may result from a tendency to recall information based on deep-rooted stereotypes (Huddy and Terkildsen 1993b; Rothbart, Evans, and Fuler 1979). Although most people reject sexist notions when asked (Berinsky 1999), ingrained gender biases may still operate subconsciously (Rudman and Kilianski 2000; Banaji and Greenwald 1994). Thus, in a variety of situations, men are viewed as superior and more competent while women are viewed as inferior at specific tasks and in general (Foschi, Lai, and Sigerson 1994; Foschi 1989).

Gender biases are especially common among males. Studies consistently show that men are convinced of their superiority and apply a double standard when judging female competence (Paludi and Strayer 1985; Foschi, Lai, and Sigerson 1994; MacCorquodale and Jensen 1993). Males are also resistant to female leadership (Eagly and Karau 2002; Smith, Paul, and Paul 2007; Sanbonmatsu 2002).

Thus, gender bias remains a political obstacle for female candidates because people, especially men, view them as less legitimate or competent than their male competitors (Smith, Paul, and Paul 2007; Falk and Kenski 2006; Lawless 2004; Dolan 2004; Sanbonmatsu 2002, 2003; Fox and Oxley 2003; Rudman and Kilianski 2000; Huddy and Terkildsen 1993a, 1993b). While women occupy positions in lower levels of government, they have and continue to face challenges entering higher political offices (Freeman 2008; Falk 2008b; Han and Heldman 2007; Gutold 2006; Anderson and Sheeler 2005; Watson and Gordon 2003; Stivers 2002). Han and Heldman (2007) explain that successful leaders have been constructed as masculinist leaders, a position that benefits men [even minority men] and serves to generally exclude women from the highest echelons of power, and the presidency stands apart from lower offices in its hypermasculinity.

Using Reference Terms to Measure Gender Bias

A valid measure of media sexism should first be an aspect of coverage we would expect newspeople to apply similarly to candidates of both genders. This allows us to determine if a disparity in coverage between male and female candidates is attributable to the candidates' gender. Standard style guides instruct journalists to use a subject's full title and name the first time mentioned and to refer to them by last name subsequently.[7] Standard conventions of naming etiquette suggest this practice as well (e.g., Ervin-Tripp 1972; R. Brown and Ford 1961). Therefore, we would not expect that one candidate, all else equal, would be referenced more by first name or by title than another candidate. If differences in naming appear correlated with the candidates' gender, then this may indicate sexist coverage.

Second, an accurate measure of media sexism should be an aspect of media coverage that affects the audience's perception of the candidates. Coverage that is obscure or disregarded may have little influence on elections. However, if sexism shapes an aspect of media coverage that affects audience perceptions of candidates, this may hinder female success, leading to further gender disparity in representation. The names newspeople use to reference candidates paint a subtle, yet pervasive, picture of social status (R. Brown and Ford 1961). By referencing female candidates informally, newspeople infantilize the candidates and detract from their "power and legitimacy" (Han and Heldman 2007; Cowan and Kasen 1984; Slobin, Miller, and Porter 1968). Governmental titles may be especially prone to gendered use, since many positions are affiliated with one gender more than the other (Rubin 1981). Thus, gender bias may discourage the use of political titles for women. Han and Heldman (2007, 21–22) explain, "Gendered language of this sort is not consciously disrespectful, perhaps, but gender difference is not random and has the 'real world' consequence of delegitimizing knowledge, experience, and ultimately, leadership."

A series of recent experiments show that referencing a woman by first name may project an image of inferiority to the audience. In an experiment by Takiff, Sanchez, and Stewart (2001), participants read a transcript of a class session where the gender of a fictitious professor and the name used to refer to that professor (either first name or title) were manipulated. Participants, regardless of their gender, perceived the professors as having lower status when addressed by first name. Stewart et al. (2003) replicated the study and the findings were the same: use of the first name led participants to perceive the professors as having lower status.

Sebastian and Bristow (2008) investigated this phenomenon by showing participants a brief description of a fictional professor and a picture. An interactive effect between gender of the professor and form of address was found: evaluations of female professors' trustworthiness and competence were largely dependent on the name used to reference them. Male professors were not affected by naming in the same way. While these studies examine perceptions of professors, it is unlikely that the results would be different if politicians were used in their place. Therefore, informal naming practices can lead to lower evaluations of females' status and trustworthiness. Thus, naming can have a far more insidious effect than the disparaging comments in Table 1.

Historically, female presidential candidates have been referenced more casually and more often by first name than their male counterparts (Falk 2008b). For example, Victoria Clafin Woodhull (candidate in 1872), Belva Bennet Lockwood (1884), Margaret Chase Smith (1964), Shirley Chisholm (1972), Patricia Schroeder (1987), Elizabeth Dole (2000), and Carol Moseley Braun (2004) were referenced by first name an average of 5 percent of the time in newspaper articles. Their male competitors were referenced this way less than 1 percent of the time (Falk 2008b). More recently, a comparison between newspaper coverage of HRC's and BHO's announcements to run for president shows that HRC was referenced by first name 3 percent more and her title of Senator was omitted 15 percent more than it was for BHO (Falk 2008a). This is not surprising; previous studies show that female athletes, college students, professors, and lawyers are referenced by first name more than comparable males (Takiff, Sanchez, and Stewart 2001; Kissling 1999; MacCorquodale and Jensen 1993; Cowan and Kasen 1984).

The Psychology of Naming

Naming constitutes an important form of sociolinguistic etiquette, indicating deference, politeness, legitimization, and social distance (Akindele 2008; R. Brown 1965). The meanings attached to names indicate the way in which social relations operate (McDowell and Pringle 1992; Wood 1992) and elucidate underlying psychological processes and core elements of social psychology (Freud 1938; Murphy 1957; Hartman 1958). Naming is subject to a series of social rules that depend on the status of the speaker, subject, observers, and the situation; these rules comprise standard naming etiquette (e.g., R. Brown 1965). The use of a particular name is the first indicator of the speaker's perception of the subject in relation to her or his own status (Ervin-Tripp 1972). Subjects with a higher status than the speaker receive a formal title, while subjects with a lower status than the speaker are referenced more informally (e.g., Slobin, Miller, and Porter 1968). Physicians will refer to patients by first name; however, patients will refer to physicians as "Doctor." During press conferences between heads of state and reporters, the head of state refers to reporters by first name, while reporters address the head of state more formally (Rendle-Short 2007). These social interactions through language explain the connection between what individuals experience and how they define those experiences through individual and social lenses of perception. This connection is the foundational basis for many postmodern critiques that argue that the power associated with discourse, language, epistemology, and definition function to support current distributions of power in society (Foucault 1989, 2002).

While newspeople strive for objectivity, they are affected by pervasive cultural stereotypes (Braden 1996). Gender stereotypes may lead newspeople to report on and name female candidates less formally than male candidates; thus, the names used by reporters subtly suggest the operation of a gendered status system (e.g., Cowan and Kasen 1984). Even though referring to a person by a particular name rarely receives conscious scrutiny, the act of referencing is subject to a series of underlying social and psychological forces (e.g., R. Brown 1965; R. Brown and Ford 1961). Thus, analyzing reference names may capture an underlying effect that surveys or other measures may not, allowing us to determine not only the extent to which media coverage of HRC was sexist but also whether newspeople have underlying sexist notions.

Hypotheses

Given the extant literature, let us briefly restate our two primary hypotheses regarding the use of reference terms in televised news coverage of the 2008 Democratic primary.

Hypothesis 1: Newspeople will refer to HRC more informally than her male competitors.

Hypotheses 2: HRC will be referenced more informally by male newspeople than female newspeople.

To examine other factors that may affect how newspeople name the candidates, we also provide the following ancillary hypotheses. First, previous literature has shown that a candidate's coverage is partially dependent on his or her electability and standing in polls (Flowers, Haynes, and Crespin 2003; Ridout 1993; John 1989). Candidates who poll well garner better coverage than candidates who poll poorly and have little chance of winning. Therefore, we ask if the candidates' poll numbers or other measures of electability affect the way they are named.

Hypothesis 3: Poll numbers and/or perceived electability will affect how newspeople reference the candidates.

In the past thirty years, and in part because of the rise of cable television, "soft" news or "infotainment" has become part of the American news environment. Soft news is less journalistic and more entertainment oriented (Baum 2002, 2004). Because they are not *traditional* journalists and therefore less constrained by journalistic norms, we might expect the soft news personalities to reference candidates more informally. This leads us to Hypothesis 4.

Hypothesis 4: Newspeople appearing on soft news will reference the candidates less formally than newspeople appearing on hard news programming.

In recent years, the news market has become segmented, and many argue that this has led news outlets to air ideologically based programming (e.g., Hamilton 2005; Bae 1999). For example, hosts Sean Hannity and Keith Olbermann present clear ideologies that inform their programs. Given this, one might expect newspeople's ideological reputations to affect how candidates are referenced. For instance, conservative newspeople may reference HRC informally because they disapprove of her policy positions. Conversely, liberal newspeople may name her more formally because they approve of her policies and partisanship.

Hypothesis 5: Candidate naming will be dependent on the ideological reputation of the newsperson.

Finally, we examine the ideological reputation and type of station (broadcast vs. cable). A growing body of literature demonstrates that an outlet's ideological reputation influences its treatment of officials and candidates (e.g., Groeling 2008). For instance, we might expect conservative networks to name liberal candidates more informally because they disagree with their policy positions. Also, whether the station is broadcast or cable may affect the coverage given to candidates as well: broadcast network news is more traditionally journalistic while cable networks provide more soft news and commentary (e.g., Baum and Groeling 2008). These expectations motivate Hypothesis 6.

Hypothesis 6: The type of station (cable or broadcast) and ideological reputation of the station will affect how candidates are referenced.

Case Selection

The 2008 Democratic nomination race provides an ideal case for analyzing gender bias in the media. The prolonged media attention paid to HRC and BHO provides adequate data from which to draw conclusions. And given HRC's resume, the media should treat her as a major contender. HRC had spent eight years in the White House as first lady and served as second-term senator from a large state. Entering the campaign as the presumed nominee, many pundits expected HRC to win not only the nomination but also the presidency. During the nomination race, HRC garnered more votes, delegates, and state contest victories than any previous female presidential candidate. If the media referenced HRC informally, it would not be because she was inexperienced, little known, or a novelty candidate. Nor would it be due to a lack of success: she amassed 1,973 delegates and won twenty-one states. Not only can this case determine whether news-people have underlying gender biases, but it can also provide insight into what the media coverage of a general presidential election with a female candidate might look like.

Many factors contribute to media naming; therefore, it is important to examine a case where the candidates are similar. The factors that could affect newspeople's treatment of the candidates, which researchers would subsequently need to control for in a quantitative analysis, are held equal in this case. BHO and HRC share the same title: Junior Senator. Both are Ivy League educated lawyers. Both are Democrats. Each had similar poll numbers, delegates, and primary/caucus victories. They had incredibly similar stated policy preferences. As political minorities (a woman and an African American), each represented an unprecedented run. Given these similarities, we come to expect any difference in naming to be attributable to gender.

However, some objections may be raised to this study's emphasis on the use of the candidates' first name. First, HRC marketed herself using her first name on many of her stickers, lawn signs, and buttons.[8] This may have led newspeople to reference her by first name. To address this concern, we show that the names candidates use to market themselves have little effect on how newspeople reference them. Second, some might claim HRC used her first name as her "brand," somehow wanting, welcoming, or expecting to be named similarly by newspeople. However, it is highly unlikely that any former first lady and two-term senator would want reporters to reference her by first name in any official setting. The social-psychological literature on naming addresses this: while people may use their first name to appeal to certain audiences, this does not override naming etiquette by giving all people in all circumstances "permission" to use it (Ervin-Tripp 1972; R. Brown and Ford 1961; Murphy 1957). For instance, as academics, our colleagues often address us by our first name, yet we prefer that students refrain from doing so—unless we grant permission first (e.g., Little and Gelles 1975). Third, some may argue that newspeople referenced HRC by first name to differentiate her from her husband. However, due to the race's salience and the public's familiarity with the Clintons, it is hard to imagine that such differentiation was necessary.

And beyond using her first name only, newspeople could have otherwise differentiated HRC from her husband in any number of formal ways, including Hillary Clinton, Senator Clinton, or Presidential Candidate Clinton.

Method

The data are comprised of televised news stories from the three major broadcast networks, ABC, CBS, and NBC, along with the three major cable news networks, CNN, Fox News Network, and MSNBC. The transcripts were gathered from Lexis Nexus Academic Database. To narrow the search of transcripts and not select on our dependent variable of interest, we used the search terms *president* and *Democrat*. The sample was created by randomly selecting one news transcript from each news channel for each weekday.[9] The time frame of the study is 1 November 2007 through 30 May 2008. We begin in November, one year before the general election, the time that news coverage of the candidates increases. We end on May 30, the last full week that HRC was in the race.[10] The sample yielded about 600 transcripts. A mention of a candidate constitutes one observation. The data contain 1,135 observations, 560 mentions of HRC and 575 mentions of BHO, a sample large enough to draw reliable inferences.

We divide the observations into six categories.[11] The first category includes references to a candidate by first name only, in this case Hillary or Barack. The second category is for the candidate's full name, in this case Hillary Clinton or Barack Obama. We also include in this category observations in which the newsperson includes the candidates' middle or maiden name, Hussein or Rod-ham, along with the first and last name.[12] The third category includes observations in which the newsperson refers to the candidate only by their last name: Clinton or Obama. The fourth category contains observations that include the title Senator; this includes references with the full name or only the last name such as Senator Hillary Clinton or Senator Clinton. The fifth category includes observations in which the newsperson refers to the candidates by Mr. or Mrs. The final category includes observations in which the newsperson refers to the candidate by their party affiliation or with a reference to the campaign horse race. These include mentions such as Democrat Hillary Clinton, frontrunner Hillary Clinton, and chief Democratic rival Barack Obama.

We examine only the first time each candidate is mentioned in each transcript. We do this because as each candidate is mentioned subsequently, newspersons should, according to standard style guides, use a shortened version of their name. For instance, hearing a newsperson reference BHO as Senator Barack Obama repeatedly in the same short report would sound very rigid. We expect that candidates will be referred to formally in their first mention and not informally or by first name. Subsequent mentions are likely to be shorter simply for aesthetic or style purposes (Fowler 1988). Thus, informally naming a candidate during an initial reference will be dependent on factors germane to this study rather than on the length of the report.

There are 127 newspersons in the data set.[13] The data range from one mention to sixty-nine mentions per news-person with a mean of nine mentions. Twenty newspersons appear in the data set only once, while nineteen appear more than twenty times. To provide readers with some context of which newspersons comprise the data set, Table 2 provides the names and frequency of the newspersons with more than twenty mentions in the data. Chris Matthews and David Gregory appear in the data set most frequently; they specifically cover election politics for MSNBC and NBC. They are followed by Alan Colmes from the Fox News Channel's *Hannity & Colmes*.

Table 2. Newspeople with Twenty or More Appearances in the Data

Name	Station	Frequency
Chris Matthews	MSNBC	69
David Gregory	MSNBC	64
Alan Colmes	Fox News	50
Anderson Cooper	CNN	37
Andrea Mitchell	NBC/MSNBC	36
Keith Olbermann	MSNBC	34
Sean Hannity	Fox News	33
Tucker Carlson	MSNBC	32
Katie Couric	CBS	32
Harry Smith	CBS	32
Charles Gibson	ABC	31
Matt Lauer	NBC	29
Diane Sawyer	ABC	29
Dan Abrams	MSNBC	26
Wolf Blitzer	CNN	25
Bill O'Reilly	Fox News	25
Brian Williams	NBC	24
Glenn Beck	CNN	23
Campbell Brown	CNN	23

Of the 127 newspersons appearing in the data, 60 percent (76) are male while only 40 percent (51) are female. Male newspeople account for a vast majority of the observations as well, with 73 percent (832). Of the news-persons appearing in Table 3 (those newspersons with twenty or more appearances in the dataset), only four are female. Thus, the data set indicates that male newspeople reported significantly more stories about one of the two candidates (especially at the beginning of programs). This indicates that while female newspersons may be closing the disparity in on-air news jobs, females lag far behind in the amount of political coverage they provide (and in the on-air positions they hold).[14]

Table 3. Names Used to Reference Hillary Clinton and Barack Obama

Name	Hillary Clinton		Barack Obama		Difference
	n	%	n	%	%
First name only	43	8	10	2	+6***
First and last name	334	59	315	55	+4
Last name only	56	10	137	24	−14***
Senator	112	20	96	17	+3
Mrs./Mr.	1	.2	1	.2	0
Party or horse-race title	14	3	16	3	0
Total	560	100	575	101	

Statistical significance derived with difference of proportions tests. If affirmative responses were under five, a simulation was used.
***$p \le .001$.

Analysis

We now test Hypothesis 1 and ask if HRC and BHO were treated differently.

Table 3 provides the frequency and percentage of names by which the two candidates were referred. The far right column provides the difference in percentage points along with an indicator of statistical significance.[15] The terms used by newspersons to refer to the two candidates are similar: the use of the full name; the title of Senator, Mr., and Mrs.; and party/horse-race titles are statistically similar. However, HRC is referred to by her first name 8 percent of the time while BHO is referred to in this way a statistically different 2 percent. This provides support for Hypothesis 1 because HRC was referenced more informally than her main male rival.

The results of Table 3, however, provide little information about the origins of this differential in naming. These results may simply indicate a newsperson's responsiveness to the candidates' campaign "branding." To address this possibility, we examine how the media addressed two male candidates who marketed themselves by their first names. Rudy Giuliani, former mayor of New York, ran in 2008 and Lamar Alexander, former Tennessee governor and U.S. Secretary of Education, ran in 1996 and 2000. These candidates' campaign paraphernalia primarily used their first names: Rudy and Lamar (see Supplemental Materials 2 and 3 at http://prq.sagepub.com/supplemental/). Employing a similar data collection to Table 3, we find that these candidates, despite marketing themselves prominently by first name, were not referenced this way once.[16] This shows that when campaigns market a male candidate's first name, the media does not reference the candidate that way. This suggests the media's use of HRC's first name was likely due to her gender rather than her marketing strategy.

To test Hypothesis 2, that informal naming stems from *male* newspeople, Table 4 divides the HRC and BHO samples by the gender of the newsperson and shows how males and females each treated HRC in relation to BHO. Because of the disparity between male and female broadcasters on air, our data include 303 observations from females and 832 observations from males. Females referred to HRC by first name less than 1 percent of the time; males, on the other hand, referred to her by first name 11 percent of the time. Female newspersons referred to HRC with the title of Senator more often than male newspeople did: 29 percent to 16 percent, respectively; both of these differences are statistically significant. Because male newspeople referred to HRC more informally than female newspeople, the data support Hypothesis 2.[17]

Table 4. Names Used to Reference Hillary Clinton and Barack Obama by Gender of Newsperson (percentages)

	Hillary Clinton			Barack Obama		
Gender of newsperson	Female (n = 142)	Male (n = 418)	Difference	Female (n = 161)	Male (n = 414)	Difference
First name only	.7	11	−10.3***	0	2	−2
First and last name	55	61	−6	53	56	−3
Last name only	12	10	+2	16	27	−11**
Senator	29	16	+13***	26	13	+13***
Mrs./Mr.	0	.2	+.2	0	.2	−.2
Party or horse-race title	2	3	+1	6	2	+4*
Total	99	101		101	100	

Statistical significance derived with difference of proportions tests. If affirmative responses were under five, a simulation was used.
*$p \leq .05$. **$p \leq .01$. ***$p \leq .001$.

Looking at the references to BHO in Table 4, females do not address BHO by first name. Male newspersons reference BHO by Barack in 2 percent of the sample; this is significantly different than the 11 percent in which males refer to HRC as Hillary.[18] Also, female newspeople refer to HRC and BHO by Senator equally, and females are more likely than men to refer to BHO by Senator as opposed to last name only. In other words, female newspeople treat the candidates the same, while male newspeople treat the candidates differently based upon gender.

We now test Hypothesis 3, that a candidate's poll numbers or assessments of electability lead to naming. In comparing this to HRC's poll numbers, delegate counts, and victories during the time frame, we find no correlation. Supplemental Materials 4 shows the over-time distribution of Hillary mentions during the campaign. Also, we examine the other male senators who ran for the Democratic nomination in 2008. Supplemental Materials 5 provides the names used to refer to Senators Biden, Dodd, and Edwards. Of the 135 mentions of these candidates, zero were by first name only. These short-lived candidacies polled poorly and had little chance of winning even a single state, yet they were referenced more formally than the woman in the race. This demonstrates that polls, chance of winning, or other measures of electability do not affect naming.

Hypothesis 4 asks if soft news personalities will reference candidates more informally than those on hard news. While the line between hard and soft news reporting has been blurred in recent years, the majority of the data emanates from hosts, commentators, and regularly employed guest "strategists," rather than from "traditional" reporters. Of the 127 newspeople appearing in our data, about 40 percent work mainly as "traditional" reporters while 60 percent frequently provide commentary, personality, and strategy in on-air appearances. The more traditional reporters appear less frequently in the transcripts, while hosts and personalities appear more often and for longer periods. Table 5 shows the eighteen newspeople that referred to HRC and BHO by first name: all of them are "news personalities," often providing commentary rather than just traditional reporting.[19] Of the 109 newspeople who did not refer to HRC by first name only, 70 percent are "traditional" reporters. Thus, the data support Hypothesis 6, "soft" or more unscripted broadcast personalities appear to drive sexist naming practices. However, we caution readers about this finding: Previous studies have found traditional newspeople, namely newspaper reporters, whose work is very scripted and edited, treated HRC and previous female presidential candidates with the same biased naming practices (Falk 2008a, 2008b).

We now examine Hypothesis 5, that the ideology of the broadcaster affects how they name the candidates. Of the eighteen newspeople that refer to HRC by first name, five have a "liberal" reputation while five have a "conservative" reputation.[20] Twenty of the mentions stem from "liberal" newspeople (Matthews, Colmes, King, Stephanopoulos, Olbermann), while fewer, only thirteen, stem from "conservative" newspeople (Hannity, Beck, Gibson, Hume,

Table 5. Use of Clinton's and Obama's First Name by Newsperson

Newsperson	Frequency of Hillary	Frequency of Barack
Chris Matthews	13	3
Sean Hannity	6	1
Glenn Beck	3	2
Alan Colmes	3	
John Gibson	2	
Larry King	2	1
Michael Scherconish	1	2
Brit Hume	1	
Chris Cuomo	1	
Dan Abrams	1	
David Gregory	1	
Dick Morris	1	
George Stephanopoulos	1	
Harry Smith	1	
Jeanne Moos	1	
Keith Olberman	1	
Lester Holt	1	1
Matt Lauer	1	
Total	43	10

Morris). This demonstrates that gendered naming in news coverage does not stem from one ideology alone.

Readers may note that Chris Mathews drives much of the effect in Table 5 by using Hillary thirteen times. This is more than double the newsperson with the next most mentions of Hillary: Sean Hannity. Despite his reputation as a liberal, Matthews has been cited often in the blogosphere for making allegedly misogynistic comments.[21] However, even if we remove Matthews from the sample, HRC is still referred to by first name thirty times compared to BHO's seven. This is still more than four times as much and remains statistically different at the .001 level. The effect is not attributable to one fluke newsperson or to the newsperson's ideology.

We now examine Hypothesis 6 and ask if a station effect exists. Supplemental Materials 6 shows the number of first name only mentions for HRC and BHO as a percentage of total mentions from each station. The broadcast stations (ABC, CBS, NBC) mention HRC by first name 5 out of 233 times, the cable stations (CNN, Fox News, MSNBC) 38 out of 327 times. The same trend holds for BHO; the broadcast networks refer to BHO by first name 2 out of 243 times, the cable stations 8 out of 332 times. This implies that much of the less formal treatment stems from cable networks. Fox News (generally viewed as a conservative station) and MSNBC (more recently viewed as a liberal station) refer to both HRC and BHO by first name at about the same frequency. This calls into question the existence of a station effect stemming from ideological reputation. This finding seems counterintuitive, given that we expect liberal stations and commentators to be more amenable to notions of gender equality and female advancement than conservative stations and commentators.[22]

Conclusions

For the first time, a female entered the 2008 election season as the presumed frontrunner for a major party nomination. Given her prior experience and successes during the campaign, the media should have treated HRC equivalent to her male competitors. Unfortunately however, we find evidence suggesting sexism affected her coverage: HRC was named by first name four times more than her main male rival, BHO. The other male senators in the nomination race were not referenced by first name at all. This treatment was most attributable to male newspeople who appear to hold underlying sexist notions: males referred to HRC by first name 11 percent of the time; female newspeople did so less than 1 percent of the time. Males also dropped HRC's title of Senator more often than females. We buttress these findings by showing the disparity in naming does not stem from HRC's choice to market herself as Hillary or from having a politically prominent spouse of the same last name.

While many defended the media claiming that the observed disparity in the coverage of HRC and her male counterparts was due to her status in the race, her policy positions, her relationship to Former President Bill Clinton, or to the ideology of the newspeople and news stations covering her, we show that these factors played little part in her treatment. In fact, we show that sexism trumped these other factors in influencing HRC's coverage. The most acute example of this is Chris Matthews. Matthews had a history for making misogynistic comments even before the election. In line with that reputation, and despite his liberal and Democratic ideology, our data show that he treated HRC worse than all other newspeople.

During the elongated Democratic primary, the candidates were referenced hundreds of thousands of times by newspersons—this represents thousands of stories that subtly treated

HRC differently than her male competitors. The difference in naming may have been unintentional; however, with the large audiences and heightened coverage given to presidential elections, these subtle cues may have delegitimized HRC without appearing overtly sexist. Thus, this form of sexism may be more insidious because of its subtlety.

Over the past century, gender equality has attained greater acceptance; however, this evolution can be characterized by the adage "two steps forward, one step back." And the acceptance of gender equality, given our findings, seems to be more prevalent among women than among men. The media, in its role as a democratic institution, should work to alleviate gender disparities in representation by treating female and male candidates similarly (all else equal). Therefore, to provide equivalent coverage for candidates and reach the larger goal of gender equality, we advocate a "de-gendering" process (e.g., Deutsch 2007; Lorber 2005) in the news. This process involves two solutions.

First, we recommend a "universal" standard in language for all candidates (regardless of gender or demographics) with news producers and managers setting and enforcing clear policies. This would lead to news that treats candidates equally by alleviating not only the overtly sexist comments in Table 1, but also the disparity in naming. Second, sexual inequality is encouraged when men define reality through control over language (Spender 1984). Of the newspeople in our data, 60 percent are male and 73 percent of our observations come from male newspeople. Therefore, to provide females with larger voice in the language of politics, we advocate greater female representation in news programming. While women have become better represented on the news, male newspeople dominate campaign reporting, and the gendered language found in this article stems from males.[23] If gender equality is to be achieved in politics, gender disparity in news must be addressed.

The 2008 election cycle spotlighted the issue of sexism, not only because of HRC's candidacy, but also the subsequent candidacy of Governor Sarah Palin. Because of dissimilarities in the positions pursued, this study does not compare the treatment of HRC to that of Palin.[24] However, a preliminary analysis from forthcoming research indicates that not only was Palin referenced more informally than her male competitor, Joe Biden, but also that the media referenced Palin with demeaning language. For instance, newspeople referenced her as "The *woman* who wants to be vice-president," "Sara Baracuda," and "Caribou Barbie."

Attributing HRC's loss to naming alone would be difficult. The media's gendered naming practices were but one part of a hostile media environment for HRC. Beyond the gendered naming, the media covered HRC's menstrual cycle, pantsuits, laugh, and her husband's infidelity. NBC's *The Chris Matthews Show* displayed a picture of HRC with devil horns drawn on her forehead. Her male competitors were not treated this way. And whether or not the media's treatment of HRC led to her eventual defeat, we should not accept a media that treats candidates for high office differently because of their gender.

Acknowledgments

The authors would like to thank Justin Vaughn, Greg Koger, Casey Klofstad, Joe Parent, Louise Davidson-Schmich, Greg Sconzo, Nayda Verier-Taylor, the editors, and anonymous reviewers.

Declaration of Conflicting Interests

The author(s) declared no conflicts of interest with respect to the authorship and/or publication of this article.

Funding

The author(s) received no financial support for the research and/or authorship of this article.

Notes

1. Lois Romano, "Clinton Puts up a New Fight: The Candidate Confronts Sexism on the Trail and Vows to Battle on," *The Washington Post*, May 20, 2008, C01.

2. Katharine Q. Seelye and Julie Bosman, "Media Charged with Sexism in Clinton Coverage," *The New York Times*, June 13, 2008.

3. Seelye and Bosman, "Media Charged with Sexism in Clinton Coverage."

4. Susan Estrich, "The G Word," http://www.creators.com/opinion/susan-estrich/the-g-word.html.

5. The negative representation of second wave feminism often implies independent, power-seeking, angry women, who are not at all feminine but more masculine in demeanor and presentation. Susan Faludi's (1992) text, *Backlash: The Undeclared War Against American Women*, written and published before Hillary Clinton (HRC) was a nationally known individual, outlines many of the negative responses to second wave feminism that became entrenched cultural concepts.

6. Seelye and Bosman, "Media Charged with Sexism in Clinton Coverage."

7. For a brief distillation of the *AP Style Guide*, see http://cubreporters.org/AP_Style.

8. She most likely used her first name to endear herself to her supporters, distinguish her candidacy from her husband's presidency, and put forth a "soft" image (e.g., Bystrom et al. 2004). We will also note that while some of HRC's paraphernalia focused on her first name, most of it also contained her title (Senator) and her last name. Her Web site, which she marketed heavily during the last months of the primary, included her last

name (as opposed to only her first name) and was titled "HillaryClinton.com." In other words, HRC did not exclusively market herself under the name Hillary.

9. We employed a randomized counting process.

10. We concentrated on weekdays because the weekday programs generally contain the most popular and experienced newspersons and anchors, along with the largest audiences.

11. To minimize random error, two assistants coded each transcript separately. The observations from each were then compared and any disagreements were examined and corrected. The assistants disagreed on less than 1 percent of the observations; the disagreements stemmed from human error and not from bias or other reliability issues.

12. Barack Obama (BHO) was not referred to with Hussein in our sample.

13. The sample seemingly overrepresents the cable networks; however, because they are on twenty-four hours, we might expect more observations from them in a representative sample. Not all of the broadcast networks reported on the primary each day; the cable networks almost always did (see Supplemental Materials 1 at http://prq.sagepub.com/supplemental/).

14. This article was designed to sample mentions of the two major Democratic primary candidates and was not designed to sample the on-air appearances of newspeople. From these data however, we can make inferences about the amount of airtime that each gender of newsperson had.

15. The p values are based on two-tailed difference of proportions tests.

16. There are fewer observations for these candidates because their candidacies were short-lived.

17. Some may still be concerned that the HRC campaign's use of her first name drives the effects seen here. In short, if this drives the names broadcasters use, then this effect should affect both genders of newspersons equally. If newspeople of different genders do not refer to HRC and BHO similarly, then a branding effect is likely not in play. If sexism drives the names used by newspersons to refer to the two candidates, we would expect male newspeople to refer to HRC more often by first name than female newspeople—and this is what we observe here.

18. The fact that male newspersons referred to BHO as Barack does not necessarily indicate condescension—it may indicate feelings of friendship or solidarity, found to be the case with male-to-male naming interactions (McConnell-Ginet 1978; Little and Gelles 1975).

19. Eric Boehlert, 2008, "For Chris Matthews, Misogyny Pays Handsomely," http://www.alternet.org/media/82744; David Edwards and Nick Juliano, 2008, "Amid Accusations of Misogyny, Matthews Slams 'View' Hosts," http://www.rawstory.com/news/2007/Matthews_slams_View_hosts_for_questioning_0111.html; Steve Benen, "Chris Matthews' Creepy, On-Air Misogyny," http://www.thecarpetbaggerreport.com/archives/12530.html; Melissa McEwan, 2009, "Misogyny Lives on in the US Media—And It's Time Old Goats Like Hardball Host Chris Matthews Were Put Out to Pasture," http://www.guardian.co.uk/commentisfree/cifamerica/2009/jan/27/chris-matthews-hardball-msnbcmisogyny.

20. We base this general categorization on the descriptions of the newsperson found on their respective station's Web sites and on their Wikipedia entries.

21. We make this distinction based upon the reputations they have developed on the blogosphere.

22. To put this in context, nationally syndicated progressive radio hosts treated HRC and other females with similar misogynistic overtones. For instance, during the 2008 campaigns, Geraldine Ferraro was referred to as a "whore," HRC was referred to as a "big f*cking whore," and Republican vice-presidential candidate Sarah Palin was referred to as "Caribou Barbie" ("Air America Host Randi Rhodes Suspended for Calling Hillary a 'Big F*cking Whore,'" http://www.huffingtonpost.com/2008/04/03/air-america-host-randi-rh_n_94863.html; "Who Coined the Nickname Caribou Barbie?," http://www.democraticunderground.com/discuss/duboard.php?az=view_all&address=389x4266484).

23. We note that at time of submission, two of the broadcast networks now have female anchors.

24. Historically, the vice presidency has been seen as a powerless and dead-end position. As such, the job has often been depicted as more suitable for women than the presidency (Falk 2008b, 63).

References

Aday, S., and J. Devitt. 2001. Style over substance: Newspaper coverage of Elizabeth Dole's presidential bid. *Harvard Journal of Press/Politics* 6 (2): 52–73.

Akindele, Dele Feme. 2008. Sesotho address forms. *Linguistic Online* 34 (2): 3–15.

Anderson, Karrin Vasby, and Kristina Horn Sheeler. 2005. *Governing codes: Gender, metaphor, political identity.* Lanham, MD: Lexington Books.

Bae, Hyuhn-Bae. 1999. Product differentiation in cable programming: The case in the cable national all-news networks. *Journal of Media Economics* 12 (4): 265–77.

Banaji, M., and A. G. Greenwald. 1994. Implicit stereotyping and prejudice. In *The psychology of prejudice* 7, ed. M. P. Zanna and J. M. Olson, 55–76. Hillsdale, NJ: Lawrence Erlbaum.

Baum, Mathew A. 2002. Sex, lies, and war: How soft news brings foreign policy to the inattentive public. *American Political Science Review* 96 (1): 91–109.

Baum, Matthew A. 2004. Circling the wagons: Soft news and isolationism in American public opinion. *International Studies Quarterly* 48 (2): 313–38.

Baum, Matthew A., and Tim Groeling. 2008. New media and the polarization of American political discourse. *Political Communication* 25 (4): 345–65.

Berinsky, A. 1999. The two faces of public opinion. *American Journal of Political Science* 43:1209–30.

Blumberg, Rae Lesser. 1984. A general theory of gender stratification. *Sociological Theory* 2:23–101.

Braden, M. 1996. *Women politicians and the media.* Lexington, KY: University Press of Kentucky.

Brown, Mary Ellen. 1997. Feminism and cultural politics: Television audiences and Hilary Rodham Clinton. *Political Communication,* 14 (2): 255–70.

Brown, R. 1965. *Social psychology.* New York: Free Press.

Brown, R., and M. Ford. 1961. Address in American English. *Journal of Abnormal and Social Psychology* 62:375–85.

Burden, Barry C., and Anthony Mughan. 1999. Public opinion and Hillary Rodham Clinton. *Public Opinion Quarterly* 63 (2): 237–50.

Bystrom, Dianne G., Mary Christine Banwart, Linda Lee Kaid, and Terry A. Robertson. 2004. *Gender and candidate communication: VideoStyle, WebStyle, NewsStyle*. London: Routledge.

Carlin, Diana, and Kelly Winfrey. 2009. Have you come a long way, baby? Hillary Clinton, Sarah Palin, and sexism in 2008 campaign coverage. *Communication Studies* 60 (4): 326–43.

Carroll, S. J. 2009. Reflections on gender and Hillary Clinton's presidential campaign: The good, the bad, and the misogynic. *Politics & Gender* 5 (1): 1–20.

Cowan, Gloria, and Jill Kasen. 1984. Form of reference: Sex differences in letters of recommendation. *Journal of Personality and Social Psychology* 46 (3): 636–45.

Deutsch, Francine M. 2007. Undoing gender. *Gender & Society* 21 (1): 106–27.

Devitt, J. 1999. *Framing gender on the campaign trail: Women's executive leadership and the press*. Washington, DC: Women's Leadership Fund.

Dolan, K. A. 2004. *Voting for women: How the public evaluates women candidates*. Boulder, CO: Westview Press.

Eagly, A. H., and Steven J. Karau. 2002. Role congruity theory of prejudice toward female leaders. *Psychological Review* 109 (3): 573–98.

Ervin-Tripp, S. 1972. On sociolinguistic rules: Alternation of co-occurrence. In *Directions in sociolinguistics*, ed.

J. J. Gumperz and D. Hymes, 213–50. New York: Holt, Rinehart & Winston.

Falk, Erika. November 2008a. Gender bias? The press coverage of Senator Hillary Clinton's announcement to seek the White House. Paper presented at the annual meeting of the NCA 94th Annual Convention, San Diego. http://www.allacademic.com/meta/p243735_index.html

Falk, Erika. 2008b. *Women for president: Media bias in eight campaigns*. Chicago: University of Illinois Press.

Falk, Erika, and Kate Kenski. 2006. Issue saliency and gender stereotypes: Support for women as presidents in times of war and terrorism. *Social Science Quarterly* 87 (1): 1–18.

Faludi, Susan. 1992. *Backlash: The undeclared war against American women*. New York: Anchor.

Flowers, Julianne F., Audrey A. Haynes, and Michael H. Crespin. 2003. The media, the campaign, and the message. *American Journal of Political Science* 47 (2): 259–73.

Foschi, Martha. 1989. Status characteristics, standards, and attributions. In *Sociological theories in progress: New formulations*, ed. J. Berger, M. Zelditch, and B. Anderson, 58–72. Newbury Park, CA: Sage.

Foschi, Martha, Larissa Lai, and Kirsten Sigerson. 1994. Gender and double standards in the assessment of job applicants. *Social Psychology Quarterly* 57 (4): 326–39.

Foucault, Michel. 1989. *The order of things: An archaeology of the human sciences*. London: Routledge.

Foucault, Michel. 2002. *The archaeology of knowledge*. Trans. A. M. S. Smith. London: Routledge.

Fowler, C. A. 1988. Differential shortening of repeated content words produced in various communicative contexts. *Language and Speech* 31:307–19.

Fox, Richard, and Zoe Oxley. 2003. Gender stereotyping in state executive elections: Candidate selection and success. *Journal of Politics* 65 (3): 833–50.

Freeman, Jo. 2008. *We will be heard: Women's struggles for political power in the United States.* New York: Rowman & Littlefield.

Freud, S. 1938. *The basic writings of Sigmund Freud.* New York: Modern Library.

Gardetto, Darlaine C. 1997. Hillary Rodham Clinton, symbolic gender politics, and *The New York Times:* January-November 1992. *Political Communication* 14 (2): 225–40.

Groeling, Tim. 2008. Who's the fairest of them all? An empirical test for partisan bias on ABC, CBS, NBC and Fox news. *Presidential Studies Quarterly* 38 (4): 631–57.

Gutold, Nichola D. 2006. *Paving the way for madam president.* Oxford, UK: Lexington Books.

Hagan, John. 1990. The gender stratification of income inequality among lawyers. *Social Forces* 68 (3): 835–55.

Hamilton, James T. 2005. The market and the media. In *The press,* ed. G. Overholser and K. H. Jamieson, 351–70. Oxford, UK: Oxford University Press.

Han, Lori Cox, and Caroline Heldman, eds. 2007. *Rethinking madam president.* Boulder, CO: Lynne Rienner.

Hartman, A. A. 1958. Name styles in relation to personality. *Journal of General Psychology* 59:289–94.

Heith, D. J. 2003. The lipstick watch: Media coverage, gender, and presidential campaigns. In *Anticipating madam president,* ed. R. P. Watson and A. Gordon, 123–30. Boulder, CO: Lynne Rienner.

Heldman, Caroline. 2007. Cultural Barriers to female president in the United States. In *Rethinking madam president boulder,* eds. Lori Cox Han & Caroline Heldman. CO: Lynne Rienner Publishers.

Heldman, Caroline, S. J. Carroll, and S. Olson. 2005. She brought only a skirt: Print media coverage of Elizabeth Dole's bid for the Republican presidential nomination. *Political Communication* 22:315–35.

Howard, Judith A., and Jocelyn Hollander. 1997. *Gendered situations, gendered selves.* Thousand Oaks, CA: Sage.

Huber, Joan. 1986. Trends in gender stratification, 1970–1985. *Sociological Forum* 1 (3): 476–95.

Huddy, Leonie, and Nayda Terkildsen. 1993a. The consequences of gender stereotypes for women candidates at different levels and types of office. *Political Research Quarterly* 46:503–25.

Huddy, Leonie, and Nayda Terkildsen. 1993b. Gender stereotypes and the perception of male and female candidates. *American Journal of Political Science* 37 (1): 119–47.

John, Kenneth E. 1989. A report: 1980-1988 New Hampshire presidential primary polls. *Public Opinion Quarterly* 53 (4): 590–605.

Kahn, K. F. 1992. Does being male help? An investigation of the effects of candidate gender and campaign coverage on evaluations of U.S. senate candidates. *Journal of Politics* 54 (2): 497–517.

Kahn, K. F. 1994a. The distorted mirror: Press coverage of women candidates for statewide office. *Journal of Politics* 56 (1): 154–73.

Kahn, K. F. 1994b. Does gender make a difference? An experimental examination of sex stereotypes and press patterns in statewide campaigns. *American Journal of Political Science* 38 (1): 162–95.

Kahn, K. F. 1996. *The political consequences of being a woman: How stereotypes influence the conduct and consequences of political campaigns.* New York: Columbia University Press.

Kahn, K. F., and E. N. Goldenberg. 1991. Women candidates in the news: An examination of gender differences in U.S. senate campaign coverage. *Public Opinion Quarterly* 55: 180–99.

Kissling, E. A. 1999. When being female isn't feminine: Uta Pippig and the menstrual communication taboo in sports journalism. *Sociology of Sport Journal* 16 (1): 79–91.

Kittilson, Miki Caul, and Kim Fridkin. 2008. Gender, candidate portrayals and election campaigns: A comparative perspective. *Politics & Gender* 4:371–92.

Lawless, Jennifer. 2004. Women, war, and winning elections: Gender stereotyping in the post-September 11th era. *Political Research Quarterly* 57 (3): 479–89.

Little, Craig, and Richard Gelles. 1975. The social-psychological implications of form of address. *Sociometry* 38 (4): 573–86.

Lorber, J. 2005. *Breaking the bowls: Degendering and feminist change.* New York: Norton.

MacCorquodale, Patricia, and Gary Jensen. 1993. Women in the law: Partners or tokens? *Gender & Society* 7 (4): 582–93.

McConnell-Ginet, S. 1978. Address forms in sexual politics. In *Women's language and style*, ed. D. Butturff and E. L. Epstien, 23–35. Akron Press, OH: University of Akron Press.

McDowell, L., and R. Pringle, eds. 1992. *Defining women: Social institutions and gender divisions.* Cambridge, MA: Polity Press.

McKay, Steven C. 2006. Hard drives and glass ceilings: Gender stratification in high-tech production. *Gender & Society* 20 (2): 207–35.

Miller, Melissa K., Jeffrey S. Peake, and Brittany Anne Boulton. 2010. Testing the *Saturday Night Live* hypothesis: Fairness and bias in newspaper coverage of Hillary Clinton's presidential campaign. *Politics & Gender* 6:169–98.

Murphy, W. F. 1957. A note on the significance of names. *Psychoanalytic Quarterly* 26:91–106.

Paludi, Michele, and Lisa Strayer. 1985. What's in a name? Differential evaluations of performance as a function of author's name. *Sex Roles* 12:353–61.

Rendle-Short, Johanna. 2007. Catherine, you're wasting your time: Address terms within the Australian political interview. *Journal of Pragmatics* 39 (9): 1503–25.

Ridgeway, C. L. 2009. Framed before we know it: How gender shapes social interactions. *Gender & Society* 23 (2): 145–60.

Ridout, Christine F. 1993. News coverage and talk shows in the 1992 presidential campaign. *PS: Political Science and Politics* 26 (4): 712–16.

Rothbart, M., M. Evans, and S. Fulero. 1979. Confirming events: Memory processes and the maintenance of social stereotypes. *Journal of Experimental Social Psychology* 15:343–59.

Rubin, Rebecca. 1981. Ideal traits and terms of address for male and female college professors. *Journal of Personality and Social Psychology* 41 (5): 966–74.

Rudman, L. A., and S. E. Kilianski. 2000. Implicit and explicit attitudes toward female authority. *Personality and Social Psychology Bulletin* 26:1315–28.

Sanbonmatsu, K. 2002. Gender stereotypes and vote choice. *American Journal of Political Science* 46:20–34.

Sanbonmatsu, K. 2003. Political knowledge and gender stereotypes. *American Politics Research* 31 (6): 575–94.

Sebastian, Richard J., and Dennis Bristow. 2008. Formal or informal? The impact of style of dress and forms of address on business student's perceptions of professors. *Journal of Education for Business* 83 (4): 196–201.

Slobin, D. I., S. H. Miller, and L. W. Porter. 1968. Forms of address and social relations in a business organization. *Journal of Personality and Social Psychology* 8:289–93.

Smith, Jessi, David Paul, and Rachael Paul. 2007. No place for a woman: Evidence for gender bias in evaluations of presidential candidates. *Basic and Applied Social Psychology* 29 (3): 225–33.

Spender, D. 1984. Defining reality: A powerful tool. In *Language and power*, ed. C. Kramerae, M. Schultz, and W. M. O'Barr, 194–205. Beverly Hills, CA: Sage.

Stewart, Tracie L., Mathilde Berkvens, Werny Engles, and Jessica Pass. 2003. Status and likability: Can the "mindful" woman have it all? *Journal of Applied Social Psychology* 33 (10): 2040–59.

Stivers, Camilla. 2002. *Gender images in public administration: Legitimacy and the administrative state.* 2nd ed. Thousand Oaks, CA: Sage.

Takiff, Hilary A., Diana T. Sanchez, and Tracie L Stewart. 2001. What's in a name? The status implications of students' terms of address for male and female professors. *Psychology of Women Quarterly* 25:134–44.

Watson, R. P., and A. Gordon, eds. 2003. *Anticipating madame president.* Boulder, CO: Lynne Rienner.

Winfield, Betty Houchin. 1997. The making of an image: Hillary Rodham Clinton and American journalists. *Political Communication*, 14 (2): 241–53.

Wood, J. T. 1992. Telling our stories: Narratives as a basis for theorizing sexual harassment. *Journal of Applied Communication Research* 20:349–62.

Reading 7: The Social Nature of Male Suicide: A New Analytic Model

By Daniel Coleman, Mark S. Kaplan, and John T. Casey

Suicide is one of the leading causes of male mortality. In nearly every country in the world, more males than females end their life by suicide. Previous research indicates male-specific risk factors include social factors such as being unmarried, low income, and unemployment. An analytic model of male suicide is developed, proposing that the traditional male gender role creates a culturally-conditioned narrowing of perceived options and cognitive rigidity when under stress that increases male suicide risk. Suicide prevention and intervention require recognition of the role of high traditional masculinity, situating individual explanations within a broader social context. Based on this theory and the few existing empirical studies, testable hypotheses are proposed.

Keywords: suicide, men, masculinity, gender

This is what my father did, he got up, showered, shaved and dressed for work. He went downstairs and made a pot of coffee, and while it was brewing he went outside and walked the long driveway to pick up the newspaper. He left the paper folded on the kitchen table, poured a cup of coffee, carried it upstairs, and put it on my mother's table. She was still in bed, sleeping. Then he went into his study, closed the door, and shot himself.—Joan Wickersham (2008, p. 5)

Understanding male suicide requires a social lens. This paper first reviews the epidemiology of male suicide and research on risk factors for male suicide. Then an analytic model is developed that interprets male suicide as a function of male gender role extremes, and in light of Baumeister's (1990) escape theory of suicide. As Wickersham's (2008) haunting account of her father's suicide exemplifies (quoted above), many male suicides do not fit a stereotype of being visibly depressed and

---

* Portland State University.

having made previous attempts. Focus is needed on developing and testing explanatory theories of male suicide, and using this evidence to tailor prevention and intervention programming toward men. The evidence synthesized comes from many cultures, but the diversity in gender roles around the world is great, so this paper serves as a starting point for understanding gender, gender role and patterns of suicide.

Death by suicide is a strikingly a male phenomenon. More men complete suicide every year in every country in the world with one exception, China (Joiner, 2005). In the United States, men are more than four times as likely as women to complete suicide, a large effect (CDC, 2009). In Europe, the widest gap between men and women for suicide mortality is found in Greece and Ireland. In England and Wales, men are approximately three times as likely to complete suicide as women (Payne, Swami, & Stanistreet, 2008). The consistency in epidemiological data showing a male excess in suicide is impressive, but Canetto (2008) cautions that epidemiological data is missing for some developing countries, and there are cultural differences in how deaths are recorded.

Across both genders, suicide is a significant global public health problem. According to World Health Organization estimates, 10-20 million people complete suicide every year. There are wide variations between countries in terms of suicide mortality, with very low rates in some Latin American and Muslim countries, compared with high rates in Eastern Europe. Variations in the way suicide is recorded affect those comparisons, particularly in countries where suicide goes against religious beliefs, but such variations do not fully explain differences between countries (Mann et al., 2005; Payne, 2006; WHO, 2002).

Male Suicide Risk Factors and Precipitating Circumstances

The gap between women and men in suicide risk varies across the age span in many regions of the world. In Australia, for example, the widest gap between men and women in suicide deaths is found in young adults and among those aged 70 and older. Similarly, in the United States the greatest gender difference is among those aged 15-24 and those over 65. In New Zealand, men are more than three times as likely to complete suicide, but in younger age groups this increases to a four-fold risk (Payne, 2006).

There are additional gender differences in suicide methods (Payne. 2006). More men use lethal methods, including firearms, hanging and jumping. In the United States, firearms are used in nearly 60 percent of male deaths, ranging from 23 percent in Massachusetts to 66 percent in South Carolina. Methods used in suicide also vary with age. Three out of every four suicides among U.S. older adults (65+) involve firearms, compared with just over half of those aged 15-24 (Kaplan, McFarland, & Huguet, 2009).

Some risk factor studies analyzed male and female participants separately, as well as in aggregate, highlighting the divergent risks for male and female suicide. A large Danish death register study reported that males who are single, unemployed or whose income is lower than average had a heightened risk of suicide, while those same factors were not significant for women (Qin, Agerbo, & Mortensen, 2003). In a large, nationally representative study in the US, education and marital status other than married were risk factors for suicide death for men but not for women (Denney, Rogers, Krueger, & Wadsworth, 2009). The time of marital separation has been found to be a particularly vulnerable time for suicide death, with higher risk for males (Wyder, Ward & De Leo, 2009). Male attempters are more likely to be first-time attempters (Murase, Ochiai, Ueyama, Honjo, & Ohta, 2003), more likely to be underweight than average-weight (Kaplan, McFarland, Huguet, & Newsom, 2006; Carpenter, Hasin, Allison, & Faith, 2000), and more likely to be cigarette smokers and to have stressors related to low income (Zhang, McKeown, Hussey, Thompson, & Woods, 2004). Kaplan and coauthors (2006) found risk factors for suicide included male gender, physical illness and disability, psychiatric condition, and military veteran status.

There are both distal and proximal risk factors that are salient to male suicide (Hufford, 2001). Risk factors of a chronic and longstanding nature, such as alcohol dependence or psychiatric disorders, are relatively distal factors, in contrast to proximal factors that have a sudden onset and precipitate a crisis, such as an unexpected loss of job, relationship, or home (Allen, Cross, and Swanner, 2005). While substance dependence is a distal factor, acute alcohol intoxication constitutes a proximal factor that can increase the risk of both a suicide attempt and the use of lethal means (Hufford, 2001). In 17 US states, over one-quarter of male suicide decedents had a blood alcohol concentration indicative of intoxication at the time of death. Additionally, alcohol intoxication was predictive of the use of firearms after adjusting for other variables (Kaplan, McFarland and Hugeut, 2009).

Increased suicide risk is found in several male dominated occupations including police officers, the military, farmers, and physicians. These fields all have access to lethal means and a high likelihood of work related exposure to death. Police, military personnel, and farmers tend to use firearms to complete suicide, and physicians are more likely to use a medication overdose (Agerbo, Gunnell, Bond, Mortensen, & Nordentoft, 2007).

The Social Environment and Male Suicide

There has been a longstanding tension between social and individual explanations for suicide, evident as early as Durkheim's (1897/1997) pioneering sociological study of suicide. Durkheim made note of the male excess in suicide, and the majority of examples he explores were of exclusively male or male dominated segments of society such as the military. Dublin

(1962), who contributed to the development of demographic methods starting in the early 20th century, also turned his attention to suicide. Canetto (2008) points out when Dublin did attend to gender differences, it was largely informed by stereotypes about men and women. In recent decades, sociology has devoted substantial attention to the issue of suicide (Stack, 2000), but research on the social context and suicide has come from a range of disciplines.

As noted previously, men have higher risk of suicide following job loss than women. According to several reviews, being unemployed is associated with a twofold to threefold increased relative risk of death by suicide, compared with being employed. Both aggregate-level and case-control studies generally show that unemployment is positively correlated with male suicide rates in several Western countries. Based on data drawn from Danish longitudinal registers, Qin et al. (2003) demonstrated that economic stressors such as unemployment and low income increase suicide risk more in male than female subjects. The significant risk factors for men, after controlling for psychiatric admission, were unemployment, retirement, being single and sick absence. For women there were no significant risk factors other than mental illness.

The pattern of male reactivity to unemployment has been found in an impressive series of international studies. Among census-based cohorts of unemployed British and Finnish men, the suicide rates were, respectively, 1.6 and 1.9 times greater than those of the reference populations (Jin, Shah, & Svoboda, 1995). Time-series analyses also revealed strong aggregate-level correlations between unemployment and suicide among young adult males in Australia (Morrell, Taylor, & Quine, 1993). Ying and Chang (2009) showed that unemployment had a significantly positive impact on male suicide rate but mixed impacts on female suicide rate based on an analysis of panel data from G-7 industrial countries (Canada, France, Germany, Italy, Japan, UK, and US). In a Swedish study involving the impact of job loss on mortality risk, Eliason and Storrie (2009) found that the suicide mortality risk among men increased, while there was no impact on women. Men who lost their jobs were 2.15 times more likely to die by suicide four years after being displaced due to plant closures in Sweden in 1987 and 1988.

There is some evidence that the influence of unemployment varies with age. Berk, Dodd and Henry (2006) reported that the relationship between unemployment and suicide in Australia was strongest for males in the 20-34 year-old age range during the period of 1968-2002. Similarly, when the unemployment rate tripled during the Hong Kong economic crisis of the 1990s, there was a 93% increase in the rate of suicide death for males in the 30-59 year-old category (Chen, et al, 2006). It is logical that the impact of unemployment would be strongest in work and career sensitive developmental stages.

The influence of economic conditions operates at least partially independently of culture. In the US, the aggregate African-American suicide rate has been consistently markedly lower than the rate for whites. However, the gender discrepancy between African-American men and women is greater than in other groups in the US: African-American men are six times more likely to die by suicide than African-American women, and the rate for men has increased in recent decades (Joe & Kaplan, 2001). Burr, Hartman and Matteson (1999) found that African-American suicide rates were highest in geographical areas that had the greatest income disparities between whites and African-Americans. The overall lower rate of African-American suicide may stem from protective cultural factors such as strong extended family ties, but the excess in male suicide again likely reflects the influence of poverty, unemployment and racism. An additional factor may be gender role orientation within the African-American community.

The impact of historical and current poverty and social dislocation is evident also in the elevated suicide rate for Native Americans, approximately one and a half times the general population US rate. There is a male excess of suicides among Native Americans, as well, peaking with a suicide rate of two and a half times the population rate for Native American men 15-24 years of age (Olson & Wahab, 2006). These patterns appear to be similar among Aboriginal peoples in Australia (Tait & Carpenter, 2010) and Canada (Laliberte & Tousignant, 2009).

In summary, unemployment may act as a proximal stressful life event leading to suicide (Shah & Bhandarkar, 2008). Economic insecurity may be an important antecedent variable in the causal chain leading a person to attempt suicide (Jin, Shah, & Svoboda, 1995). The stress associated with unemployment can differ depending on one's options and constraints. In a later section, we argue that the traditional male gender role narrows perceived options under stressful circumstances. Given the connection of male suicidality to social influences, the dominance of individualized therapeutic models of suicidal behavior obscures critical precipitating social circumstances (Moller, 1996).

Suicide and Homophobia

There is evidence that gay and bisexual adolescent males are at greater risk for suicide attempts and completions (Cochran & Mays, 2008). Although some investigators attribute suicide risk to mental health problems, others have found that the association between suicidality and same-gender orientation in adolescence and adult men is independent of the effects of substance use and mental health diagnoses (Remafedi, 2008). Cochran and Rabinowitz's (2003) analysis of Danish data showed a six-fold increase in age-adjusted risk for completed suicide among men, but not women, who were in registered same-sex domestic partnerships when compared to married persons. Herrell et al. (1999) found that gay men were 6.5 times as likely as their fraternal cotwins to have attempted suicide and the relatively high risk was not explained by mental health or substance abuse disorders. In two large studies of students conducted in Minnesota and Massachusetts, the relative risks of attempted suicide for bisexual and gay male students were, respectively, 7.1 and 3.4 times higher than heterosexual male peers (Remafedi, 2008).

Safren and Heimberg (1999) found similar elevated rates of suicidal behavior for gay and lesbian youth, but when the increased psychosocial stress for these youth was controlled for, the group difference became much smaller. This indicates that much of the difference in suicidal ideation and behavior for sexual minority youth is due to the stress of alienation from friends and family members related to continued homophobia. In addition to the stress of homophobia of others, gay and bisexual men may struggle with internalized homophobia.

Males and Violent Means of Suicide

As noted earlier, men are more prone to use violent, highly lethal means such as guns, hanging or jumping. Eighty-percent of all suicide deaths in the U.S. involve males, and the majority of those deaths involve the use of firearms (Miller, Lippmann, Azrael, & Hemenway, 2007). Among elderly men, guns are the most common method of suicide, accounting for nearly 80% of such deaths (Kaplan et al., 2009).

The use of violent means by male attempters has been interpreted as consistent with the traditional male gender role (Canetto, 1997; Stack & Wasserman, 2009). Men are more likely to shoot themselves in the head rather than in the body, and are more likely to use rifles or shot guns to complete suicide (Stack & Wasserman, 2009). This is convergent with Canetto's (1997) summary of research on youth views of suicide and suicide attempts, where youth tended to view attempts as feminine, and suicide completion as masculine.

The male pattern of suicidality also includes impulsive attempts with lethal means, often while under the influence of drugs or alcohol, and in the absence of long term substance abuse or mental health problems. Kaplan and colleagues (2006) statistically classified decedents into those who displayed a long-term risk profile, and those who fit a short term profile. Those in the short term risk group were more likely to have been male, white, and to use firearms to complete suicide. This impulsive type of suicide is the most difficult to prevent, as warning signs are only evident in a brief window before an attempt, and attempts tend to be fatal.

Men and Suicide: Depression and Beyond

The review of risk factors indicates that men are more likely to develop suicidal behavior following major life transitions, from unemployment, and being single than women with the same stressors. The fields of suicide research and prevention have been understandably focused on the link between suicide and depression. Suicidal thoughts and behavior are by definition linked to depression by inclusion in diagnostic criteria (American Psychiatric Association, 2000), and approximately 20% of people with major depressive disorder report suicidal behavior or thoughts (Borges, et al., 2006). The majority of suicide research is conducted with clinical samples, reinforcing the link of depression and suicide.

The importance of moving beyond a depression-centered view of male suicide came into focus in one of the authors' analysis of the National Violent Death Reporting System (NVDRS) data (Kaplan, McFarland, & Huguet, 2009). This analysis used suicide death data from 16 states and included information on decedent mental health from proxy data. From the tables in the article, it can be calculated that 62% of male decedents had no mental health history or diagnosis, in contrast to 42% of female decedents. Only half as many men (16%) as women (32%) had a previous suicide attempt. The typical male suicide decedent had no history of mental health treatment and no previous suicide attempts. Given that men are less likely to seek mental health treatment, a proportion of these men probably had depression or other mental disorders. Our hypothesis is traditional masculinity would account for additional variance in suicidality beyond depression.

From this data it is clear that the majority of male suicide decedents would not have been included in a study of attempters, nor in a study based on a clinical sample. In other words, the majority of male suicide decedents are drawn from a different population than the populations on which much of our knowledge about suicide is based upon, clinical samples and previous attempters. This explains in part how the dynamics of male suicide continue to be overlooked and poorly understood.

Reframing Individual Psychopathology as a Social Problem

The gender discrepancy of rates of depression among male and female suicide decedents has been noted before, and explained as male decedents are suffering from other psychopathology: such as personality disorders, substance dependence, or an unrecognized male depressive syndrome. We review these arguments as a step toward offering an alternate, socio-cultural lens on male suicide.

The personality disorder argument to explain the non-depressed male suicide is based in studies that retrospectively diagnose decedents. A meta-analytic review of 29 studies of suicide decedents found that male decedents were more likely to fit personality disorder criteria, and female decedents mood disorder criteria (Arsenault-Lapierre, Kim & Turecki, 2004). Ernst and colleagues (2004) examined cases of suicide decedents who did not meet DSM Axis I criteria, and concluded that there was evidence of underlying psychopathology in nearly all the cases.

The male-depressive syndrome argument is partially convergent with the personality disorder explanation, as the criteria proposed for male depression overlap with personality disorder criteria. For example, Walinder and Rutz (2001) suggest a new diagnostic category of male depression that includes low stress tolerance, acting out behavior, low impulse control and substance abuse. Note that the DSM criteria for borderline and antisocial personalities include anger, impulsivity, and substance abuse. Van Praag (1996) proposed male depression as an "anxiety/aggression-driven" type, and identified the overlap with diagnostic criteria and neurotransmitter similarities of the proposed male depression diagnosis and personality disorders.

Recognizing undiagnosed personality problems and correctly identifying depressed men are essential for clinical practice. However, there are neglected social and public health explanations for male depression and suicide. The traits identified by personality disorder diagnosis, and the male depression syndrome, are also consistent with extremes of the male gender role. The emphasis on action, impulsivity, and the acceptability of anger are a part of the social norm of masculinity that sets the context for male suicide. Are these characteristics better accounted for by personality disorders, male depression, or high traditional masculinity? On one level, this is an empirical question that could be tested in a study that includes measures of all these constructs. On another level, it is a philosophical question of specifying a model and choosing variables and level of analysis.

Men and the Escape Theory of Suicide

Baumeister's (1990) escape theory of suicide, and Hufford's (2001) subsequent elaboration of it in analyzing alcohol use and suicide, provides a helpful framework for male suicide. The theory is at the individual level, but the dynamics described by escape theory reflect consequences of the dominant male gender role. Though Baumeister (1990) did not emphasize gender in his theory, he argued that depression was not a satisfying explanation for the majority of suicidal behavior, and his theory sought to explain both depressed and non-depressed suicidal acts. Stated simply, escape theory proposes that suicidal acts are more likely when an individual is emotionally distressed by a self-perception of failure and this leads to a narrowing cognitive state of limited emotion, attention, and lowered inhibition. The suicidal act is an effort to escape an intolerable view of self and the related negative affect.

This state of cognitive rigidity is particularly salient to understanding male suicide. The male gender role, with its emphasis on a high expectation of strength, providing materially for others, and the acceptability of anger and violence, provides a social script that combines with cognitive rigidity with often fatal consequences. Hufford (2001) termed the empirical evidence for cognitive constriction while intoxicated, "alcohol myopia," and argued alcohol intoxication exacerbated the dynamics identified in escape theory. We suggest that the traditional male gender role contributes its own myopia, increasing male suicide risk. In the next section we review masculinity theory, showing the connection between masculinity and the cognitive rigidity of escape theory.

Masculinity and Suicide

There is a recent tradition of literature on masculinity growing out of men's studies that dovetails with Baumeister's theory, underscoring men's limited range of options within the areas of self-identity, relationships and capacity for happiness (David & Brannon, 1976; Mahalik, 1999). Many of these theories take a developmental perspective. Pollack (2006) formulated that boys are first taught to hide their emotions between the ages of 3 and 5 through a "boy code" that rewards toughness, and relies on shame to enforce a prohibition against emotional expression or vulnerability, a condition he called "gender straitjacketing." Across the age-span, the straitjacket metaphor is a male-specific example of Baumeister's theory, where cultural gender-role expectations limit males' options when faced with stress, crisis or loss, thus increasing their risk for self-endangering or self-harming behaviors.

The traditional male gender-role, with its values of the pursuit of success, power, emotional control, fearlessness, and self-reliance (Mahalik, 1999), sets the context for male gender role strain (Levant, 1996). The feelings of inadequacy generated by not meeting gender role ideals are exacerbated by the gender role expectations themselves of avoidance of perceived weakness, unacceptability of emotions other than anger, and prohibitions against dependency or seeking help.

A small number of studies have investigated the influence of masculinity on suicide risk. Hunt, Sweeting, Keoghan and Platt (2006) found that for older participants masculinity was associated with lower suicidal thoughts, but more traditional gender role attitudes were associated with higher suicidal thoughts. The authors note a measurement limitation, that their measure of masculinity tapped participants' experience of mastery and leadership and less of the negative extremes of the traditional male gender role such as limited emotional range and difficulty seeking help. A recent analysis of the 1969 cohort of Swedish military conscripts also found higher masculinity was protective against suicide (Mansdotter, Lundin, Falkstedt, & Hemmingsson, 2009). The measure of masculinity was a crude ranking based on occupation and leisure interests from the original 1969 conscript assessments.

Despite the limitations of these studies, there likely is an association of certain dimensions of masculinity and low suicide risk in healthy and successful men. One widely used measure of gender role orientation, the Extended Personality Attributes Questionnaire (EPAQ), includes a masculine positive scale as well as a masculine negative scale (Helmreich & Spence, 1981).

Perhaps the positive and healthy parts of masculinity can be reclaimed in the social reworking of gender roles. However, it is when there is a failure to meet an expectation- job loss, relationship break-up, perceived professional failure- that the high masculine risk for suicide is exposed. This is consistent with Baumeister's (1990) escape theory process which begins with a perceived personal failure. Similarly, Mansdotter and co-authors (2009) argued that in their study, the higher rate of suicide for the low masculinity group could be contributed to by the "...stress of not meeting high masculinity ideals..." (p. 412).

A qualitative study of depressed men converges with the two quantitative studies, and reinforces some of the central arguments of this paper. Oliffe and colleagues (2010) interviewed 30 depressed men, with focused attention to suicide and masculinity. They found that men were drawn away from suicide by involvement in some masculine roles such as positive dimensions of fathering. Other men fled into masculine-associated pseudo-independence by pulling away from significant others and increasing alcohol and drug use, reporting increased suicidal thoughts. This is similar to the connection proposed between escape suicide dynamics and traditional masculinity.

Discussion

Suicide is largely a male phenomenon and has a distinct profile: male decedents are less likely to be depressed or have received mental health services, less likely to have made previous attempts, and more likely to use highly lethal means. Male suicide often follows job loss, business failure, relationship loss, or an embarrassing public disclosure. Most of the efforts to explain male suicide focus on individual and psychological explanations, such as unrecognized psychopathology or a male depressive syndrome. In their emphasis on constricted emotion, anger and impulsivity, these explanations reflect the prevailing male gender role. It is important to recognize that a group of male decedents who could be diagnosed with "male depression" are men who have grown up immersed in male socialization. As Moller (1996) stated: "...the psychosocial collage of suicide is comprised of structural conditions, of the psychological state of the individual, and of the manner in which structural or social forces converge with the personal state of the individual and define particular life situations for individuals" (p. 199). The understanding of male suicide has focused inordinate attention on individual deficits, while neglecting the power of precipitating social circumstances.

Baumeister's (1990) escape theory applies well to male suicide. Escape theory depicts the individual struggling with some injury to self-esteem, and shifting into a crisis mode where the cognitive awareness of options narrows. Hufford (2001) drew the analogy that alcohol use exacerbated this narrowing of options and cognitive rigidity, what he termed "alcohol myopia."

Higher degrees of traditional masculinity are likely a risk factor for an "escape suicide" much like acute alcohol use. We propose there may be a "masculinity myopia" that increases risk of suicide. As noted earlier, there are many cultures where we hypothesize this theory is applicable, however this hypothesis should be explored theoretically and empirically in a wide diversity of cultures.

In addition to a theoretical exploration, this paper is a call to action to take on the contribution of the traditional male gender role in suicidal behavior. The negative interpersonal and social effects of the exaggerated social norm of masculinity found in many cultures are clear: namely, an absence of empathy and emotions other than anger, misogyny, homophobia, violence and an emphasis on competition and dominance in interpersonal relationships. Part of the social influence of feminism is freeing the experience of being a woman from constricting social conceptions of femininity. Men have benefited from the reciprocal influence of changing female gender roles exerting an influence on traditional male roles, but in most of the world's societies there has not been a strong or direct focus on male gender roles.

If men are dying of an extreme of the male gender role, the implication is that male suicide prevention should be pursued through tackling those dimensions of the male gender role that increase suicide risk. At the broadest level, this suggests changing the meaning and experience of being a man from the current norm in most societies. An example of this broad view is found in Payne and co-authors' (2008) proposal that reducing suicidal behaviors will require a public health strategy that involves "...a deconstruction of the power structures that give rise to inequalities between men and women" (p. 33). Of course, power structures and social roles change slowly and haltingly, so this goal requires a long term perspective. More narrowly and immediately, public awareness and suicide prevention efforts could be tested that are tailored to the social dynamics of male suicide risk.

An example of a tailored public awareness campaign focused on mental health, not just suicide, is a recent United States Veteran's Administration campaign that centers on the phrase: "It takes the courage and strength of a warrior to ask for help" (www.realwarriors.net). This campaign attempts to work within the masculine concept of the warrior, and to paradoxically use it to increase rather than impede help-seeking behavior. We are ambivalent about working within the stereotyped gender role, and therefore reinforcing it, though we understand the immediacy of trying to break down barriers to help-seeking for veterans and active duty military.

Another example is suicide gatekeeper training, the most popular suicide prevention strategy. The most widely-used of the trainings is "Question, Persuade, Refer" (QPR; www.qprinstitute.com). The typical format of QPR is a two-hour didactic training, targeting knowledge about suicide and suicide risk factors, breaking down myths about suicide, and coaching participants to ask people at risk about suicide and get them to professional help.

QPR training involves little or no gender specific information, and centers on identifying depression and the link of depression and suicide, missing the male suicide pattern we have identified in this paper. A version of QPR could be developed that includes more information on gender differences and suicide, or could focus on male suicide for gatekeepers working in primarily male settings such as corrections or the military.

In many healthcare settings there is limited training in identifying and intervening in suicide generally, let alone male suicide. The recognition of suicidal risk among males is often limited by healthcare services that are more adapted to treating females, particularly in mental health and psychiatric settings (Rutz & Rihmer, 2007).

This paper proposes a hypothesis that male suicide is in part a function of extremes of the traditional male gender role. While we built this argument synthesizing data from a wide range of sources, the hypothesis should be directly tested. The few existing studies found that positive dimensions of masculinity such as leadership and mastery were protective against suicidal ideation and attempts. As Hunt (2006) suggested, a study is needed that includes a measure of the extreme of masculinity that includes constricted affect, inhibitions against help-seeking, and acceptability of anger and violence. Further, our theoretical perspective suggests high traditional masculinity is particularly a risk factor for men who are thwarted in efforts to maintain a masculine ideal by events such as job loss, illness or disability.

In conclusion, the epidemiology of male suicide is stark: men account for four out of five suicides in the United States, use highly lethal means, often complete suicide in their first attempt, and do not signal their risk to others through traditional symptoms of depression. The unique dynamics of male suicide merit attention in research, prevention and treatment efforts. In particular, high traditional masculinity in men experiencing psychosocial stress in work or family life, combined with easy access to lethal means, contributes to an epidemic of male suicide. We look forward to the field producing research to better understand masculinity and male suicide, developing and testing public health and clinical interventions based on this evolving understanding, and hopefully a changing social definition of men and their role in society.

References

Agerbo, E., Gunnell, D., Bond, J.P., Mortensen, P.B., & Nordentoft, M. (2007). Suicide and occupation: The impact of socioeconomic, demographic and psychiatric differences. *Psychological Medicine*, *37*, 1131–1140.

Allen, J.P., Cross, G., & Swanner, J. (2005). Suicide in the army: A review of current information. *Military Medicine*, *170*, 580–584.

American Psychiatric Association (APA). (2000). *Diagnostic and statistical manual of mental disorders*: DSM-IV-TR. Washington, DC: APA.

Arsenault-Lapierre, G., Kim, C., & Turecki, G. (2004). Psychiatric diagnoses in 3275 suicides: A meta-analysis. *BMC Psychiatry, 4,* 1–11.

Baumeister, R.F. (1990). Suicide as escape from self. *Psychological Review, 97,* 90–113.

Berk, M., Dodd, S., & Henry, M. (2006). The effect of macroeconomic variables on suicide. *Psychological Medicine, 36,* 181–189.

Borges, G., Angst, J., Nock, M.K., Ruscio, A.M., Walters, E.E., & Kessler, R.C. (2006). A risk index for 12-month suicide attempts in the National Comorbidity Survey Replication (NCSR). *Psychological Medicine, 36,* 1747–1757.

Burr, J.A., Hartman, J.T., & Matteson, D.W. (1999). Black suicide in U.S. metropolitan areas: An examination of the racial inequality and social integration-regulation hypotheses. *Social Forces 77,* 1049–1081.

Canetto, S.S. (1997). Meanings of gender and suicidal behavior during adolescence. *Suicide and Life-Threatening Beahvior, 27,* 339–351.

Canetto, S.S. (2008). Women and suicidal behavior: a cultural analysis. *American Journal of Orthopsychiatry, 78*(2), 259–266.

Carpenter, K.M., Hasin, D.S., Allison, D.B., & Faith, M.S. (2000). Relationships between obesity and DSM-IV major depressive disorder, suicide ideation, and suicide attempts: Results from a general population study. *American Journal of Public Health, 90,* 251–257.

Center for Disease Control and Prevention. (2009). *Fatal injury reports.* Retrieved October 10, 2009, from http://www.cdc.gov/ncipc/wisqars.

Chen, H., Eric, Y., Chan, C., Wincy, S., Wong, C., Paul, W., et al. (2006). Suicide in Hong Kong: A case-control psychological autopsy study. *Psychological Medicine, 36,* 815–825.

Cochran, S.D., & Mays, V.M. (2008). Prevalence of primary mental health morbidity and suicide symptoms among gay and bisexual men. In R.J. Wolitski, R. Stall, & R.O. Valdiserri (Eds.), *Unequal opportunity: Health disparities affecting gay and bisexual men in the United States* (pp. 97–120). New York: Oxford University Press.

Cochran, S.V., & Rabinowitz, F.E. (2003). Gender-sensitive recommendations for assessment and treatment of depression in men. *Professional Psychology: Research and Practice, 34,*132

140. David, D., & Brannon, R. (Eds.). (1976). *The forty-nine percent majority: The male sex role.* Reading, MA: Addison-Wesley.

Denney, J., Rogers, R., Krueger, P., & Wadsworth, T. (2009). Adult suicide mortality in the United States: Marital status, family size, socioeconomic status, and differences by sex. *Social science quarterly, 90*(5), 1167–1185.

Dublin, L. (1963). *Suicide; A sociological and statistical study.* New York: Ronald Press.

Durkheim, E. (1897/1997). *Suicide: A study in sociology* (J. Spaulding, Trans.; G. Simpson, Ed.). New York: Free Press.

Eliason, M., & Storrie, D. (2009). Does job loss shorten life? *Journal of Human Resources, 44*: 227–302.

Ernst, C., Lalovic, A., Lesage, A., Seguin, M., Tousignant, M., & Turecki, G. (2004). Suicide and no axis I psychopathology. *BMC Psychiatry, 4,* 1–5.

Herrell, R., Goldberg, J., & True, W.R. (1999). Sexual orientation and suicidality: A co-twin control study in adult men. *Archives of General Psychiatry, 56*, 867–874.

Hufford, M. R. (2001). Alcohol and suicidal behavior. *Clinical Psychology Review, 21*, 797–811.

Hunt, K., Sweeting, H., Keoghan, M., & Platt, S. (2006). Sex, gender role orientation, gender role attitudes and suicidal thoughts in three generations: A general population study. *Social Psychiatry and Psychiatric Epidemiology, 41*, 641–647.

Jin, R.L., Shah, C.P., & Svoboda, T.J. (1995). The impact of unemployment on health: A review of the evidence. *Canadian Medical Association Journal, 153*, 529–540.

Joe, S., & Kaplan, M. (2001). Suicide among African-American men. *Suicide and Life-Threatening Behavior, 31*(Suppl.), 106–121.

Joiner, T. (2005). *Why people die by suicide.* Cambridge, MA: Harvard University Press.

Kaplan, M.S., McFarland, B.H., & Huguet, N. (2009). Firearm suicide among veterans in the general population: Findings from the National Violent Death Reporting System. *The Journal of Trauma, 67*, 503–507.

Kaplan, M.S., McFarland, B.H., Huguet, N., & Newsom, J.T. (2006). Sooner versus later: Factors associated with temporal sequencing of suicide. *Suicide and Life-Threatening Behavior, 36*, 377–385.

Laliberté, A., & Tousignant, M. (2009). Alcohol and other contextual factors of suicide in four aboriginal communities of Quebec, Canada. *Crisis: The Journal of Crisis Intervention and Suicide Prevention, 30*(4), 215–221.

Lee, C., & Owens, R.G. (2002). *The psychology of men's health.* Buckingham UK: Open University Press.

Levant, R.F. (1996). The new psychology of men. *Professional Psychology: Research and Practice, 27*, 259–265.

Mahalik, J.R. (1999). Incorporating a gender role strain perspective in assessing and treating men's cognitive distortions. *Professional Psychology: Research and Practice, 30*, 333–340.

Mann, J.J., Apter, A., Bertolote, J., Beautrais, A., Currier, D., Haas, A., et al. (2005). Suicide prevention strategies: A systematic review. *Journal of the American Medical Association, 294*, 2064–2074.

Mansdotter, A., Lundin, A., Falkstedt, D., & Hemmingsson, T. (2009). The association between masculinity rank and mortality patterns: A prospective study based on the Swedish 1969 conscript cohort. *Journal of Epidemiology and Community Health, 63*, 408–413.

Miller, M., Lippmann, S.J., Azrael, D., & Hemenway, D. (2007). Household firearm ownership and rates of suicide across the 50 United States. *Journal of Trauma, Injury, and Critical Care, 62*, 1029–1035.

Moller, D.W. (1996). *Confronting death: Values, institutions and human mortality.* New York: Oxford University Press.

Moller-Leimkuhler, A.M. (2003). The gender gap in suicide and premature death or: Why are men so vulnerable? *European Archives of Psychiatry and Clinical Neuroscience, 253*, 1–8.

Morrell, S., Taylor, R., Quine, S. et al. (1993). Suicide and unemployment in Australia. *Social Science and Medicine, 36*, 749–756.

Murase, S., Ochiai, S., Ueyama, M., Honjo, S., & Ohta, T. (2003). Psychiatric features of seriously life-threatening suicide attempters: A clinical study from a general hospital in Japan. *Journal of Psychosomatic Research, 55*, 379–383.

Oliffe, J., Ogrodniczuk, J., Bottorff, J., Johnson, J., & Hoyak, K. (2010). You feel like you can't live anymore. *Social Science & Medicine.* DOI: 10.1016/j.socscimed.2010.03.057

Olson, L., & Wahab, S. (2006). American Indians and suicide. *Trauma, Violence, & Abuse, 7*(1), 19–33.

Payne, S., Swami, V., & Stanistreet, D.L. (2008). The social construction of gender and its influence on suicide: A review of the literature. *Journal of Mental Health, 5*, 23–35.

Payne, S. (2006). *The health of men and women.* Cambridge UK: Polity Press.

Pollack, W.S. (2006). The 'war' *for* boys: Hearing 'real boys'' voices, healing their pain. *Professional Research and Practice, 37*, 190–195.

Qin, P., Agerbo, E., & Mortensen, P.B. (2003). Suicide risk in relation to socioeconomic, demographic, psychiatric, and familial factors: A national register-based study of all suicides in Denmark, 1981–1997. *American Journal of Psychiatry, 160*, 765–772.

Remafedi, G. (2008). Health disparities for homosexual youth: The children left behind. In R.J. Wolitski, R. Stall, & R.O. Valdiserri (Eds.), *Unequal opportunity: Health disparities affecting gay and bisexual men in the United States* (pp. 275–302). New York: Oxford University Press.

Rutz, W., & Rihmer, Z. (2007). Suicidality in men—Practical issues, challenges, solutions. *Journal of Men's Health and Gender, 4*, 393–401.

Safren, S.A., & Heimberg, R.G. (1999). Depression, hopelessness, suicidality, and related factors in sexual minority and heterosexual adolescents. *Journal of Consulting and Clinical Psychology, 67*, 859–866.

Shah, A., & Bhandarkar, R. (2008). Cross-national study of the correlation of general population suicide rates with unemployment rates. *Psychological Reports, 103*, 793–796.

Stack, S. (2000). Suicide: A 15-year review of the sociological literature. Part I: cultural and economic factors. *Suicide & life-threatening behavior, 30*(2), 145–162.

Stack, S., & Wasserman, I. (2009). Gender and suicide risk: The role of wound site. *Suicide and Life-Threatening Behavior, 39*, 13–20.

Tait, G., & Carpenter, B. (2010). Firearm suicide in Queensland. *Journal of Sociology, 46*(1), 83–98.

van Praag, H.M. (1996). Faulty cortisol/serotonin interplay: Psychopathological and biological characterisation of a new, hypothetical depression subtype (SeCA depression). *Psychiatry Research, 65*, 143–157.

Walinder, J., & Rutz, W. (2001). Male depression and suicide. *International Clinical Psychopharmacology, 16*(Suppl. 2), S21-S24.

Wickersham, J. (2008). *The suicide index: Putting my father's death in order.* Orlando, FL: Harcourt Books.

World Health Organization (WHO). (2006). Suicide. Retrieved October 10, 2009, from http://www.who.int/topics/suicide/en.

Wyder, M., Ward, P., & De Leo, D. (2009). Separation as a suicide risk factor. *Journal of Affective Disorders, 116*(3), 208–213.

Ying, Y.H., & Chang, K. (2009). A study of suicide and socioeconomic factors. *Suicide and Life-Threatening Behaviors, 39*, 214–226.

Zhang, J., McKeown, R.E., Hussey, J.R., Thompson, S.J., & Woods, J.R. (2004). Gender differences in risk factors for attempted suicide among young adults: Findings from the third national health and nutrition examination survey. *Annals of Epidemiology, 15*, 167–174.

Questions to Think About

1. What is the role of advertising in reinforcing gender stereotypes? How does media portray males and females differently?
2. What research methods were used in the article "What's in a Name? Coverage of Senator Hillary Clinton during the 2008 Democratic Primary"? How did these methods reflect the research question posed and the theoretical perspective of the authors?
3. Why did the authors of "The Social Nature of Male Suicide" focus on males? Why are males and female suicides different?
4. For each of the readings, can the issue be addressed using another theoretical approach? If so, which one and why?
5. What are the risk factors for suicide? Why are these factors more risky for males?

Resources

Men, Masculinity, and Manhood Acts

Annual Review of Sociology

Vol. 35: 277–295 (Volume publication date August 2009)

First published online as a Review in Advance on April 6, 2009

DOI: 10.1146/annurev-soc-070308-115933

Gender Roles and Adolescents:

http://www.mamft.org/gender-roles-adolescents/

Examining Media's Socialization of Gender Roles:

http://www.huffingtonpost.com/warren-j-blumenfeld/examining-medias-socializ_b_3721982.html

Gender Stereotypes and the Perception of Male and Female Candidates

Leonie Huddy and Nayda Terkildsen

American Journal of Political Science

Vol. 37, No. 1 (February 1993), pp. 119–147

Project Implicit: Check your Implicit Bias:

https://implicit.harvard.edu/implicit/selectatest.html

SECTION V
DEVIANCE

Introduction

Every society has patterns of behavior governing the way people interact. These patterns of behavior are called norms and represent the values and beliefs of any given culture. For example, in the United States it is customary to shake a person's hand when being introduced for the first time, and to look people in the eye when speaking to them. When people fail to adhere to social norms, sanctions are imposed. Sanctions imposed for deviant behavior can range from a disapproving glance to jail time. When a deviant behavior is deemed severe enough to have formal sanctions it is labeled as a crime. The norms and rules governing behavior are—similar to the concepts of race and gender—social constructions. Each society defines what is deviant and, in turn, decides which sanctions are appropriate for each act. Sanctions, like other social constructions, change over time and place. For instance, in the United States the "thumbs up" sign usually means all is good. In other countries, such as Thailand, this gesture is viewed as childish or obscene, depending on whom you ask. Cocaine is an example of an act becoming deviant over time. In the 1800s Sigmund Freud extolled the virtues of cocaine, and cocaine extract was an ingredient in Coca-Cola. Today the possession of cocaine is illegal.

Logically, it seems people would want to follow the rules if they want to be accepted by society, but many individuals don't follow the rules all of the time. There are more theories for explaining deviance than just about any other sociological issue. Some theories of deviance overlap, and many only explain a small portion of deviant behavior. The following two readings were chosen because they both highlight several of the theories of deviance as well as identify the strengths and weaknesses of each theory.

In the first reading in this section, "The Contribution of Mainstream Theories to Female Juvenile Delinquency," Robert Agnew outlines several theoretical approaches to studying female delinquency. Most of the research in juvenile delinquency focuses on the offenses committed by males. This reading explores whether and how the mainstream theories apply to delinquent behavior committed by females. Because there is a gender gap in delinquency (males are more likely to commit most types of offenses than females), this reading also seeks to explain the reasons for the gap in offending. Agnew first describes several of the most prominent theories of delinquency such as strain theory, control theory, labeling theory, and rational choice theory. He then evaluates the theories' applicability in addressing the delinquent behavior of females. Two theories that incorporate more than one of the traditional theories are then evaluated. The first, Agnew's general theory of crime and delinquency, identifies the reasons why individuals become delinquent and then identifies why these causal factors increase delinquency—combining several theories for a more comprehensive perspective. Another integrated theory, Darrell Steffensmeier's and Allan's gendered theory of female offending, examines the way gender norms, along with the biological differences in strength and size between males and females, influence the likelihood of female delinquency.

Agnew concludes there are some causal factors for females more important than others. For females, self-control, prior delinquency, levels of supervision, associations, levels of discipline, self-image, and prior abuse are the major contributors to delinquency. Agnew, citing the reciprocal effects of these factors, then calls for comprehensive policies to reduce female delinquency. For instance, if a child is abused it may lead to a poor self-image. The child will then be more likely to associate with others who have a poor self-image, leading to drug or alcohol use to reduce the negative effects. If the associations with the delinquent peers cannot be reduced, policies may try to reduce the effects of those negative associations through programs dealing with self-image. The essay concludes with a call for future research to be more comprehensive along with including race and class differences, neighborhood effects, and longitudinal effects.

Deviance in schools is another area of interest to scholars focusing on deviance and the general public. Crime rates in the United States have declined since the 1990s and crime in schools has followed this trend. Although media portrays schools as scary, crime-ridden places, they are actually much safer than they were three decades ago. For example, in 1993 the rate for serious crimes in schools was 13 per 1,000 students. By 2000 that number had declined to 4 per 1,000.[11] Because of the real and/or perceived threat of school violence, however, schools have implemented many sanctions to deter people from committing crimes in school or to punish them when they do. Although some of the methods used may be effective, many scholars would argue increased vigilance has stigmatized poor and minority youth, unfairly labeling them and increasing the likelihood of further deviant acts.

In "The State of Public School Violence," Anthony Troy Adams describes the family, school, and community characteristics that increase the likelihood of school violence in

Michigan. Although the selection describes the state of violence in Michigan schools, similar patterns can be found throughout the country. Troy then addresses three common theories of delinquency and the criticisms of each. The final section of this reading examines methods used to control deviance in schools and the problems associated with these methods. Although there is not a solution proposed, Troy provides the framework for readers to understand why each solution has problems, and prods the reader to begin thinking about constructing his or her own solutions.

Reading 8: The Contribution of "Mainstream" Theories to the Explanation of Female Delinquency

By Robert Agnew

This chapter describes the contribution of "mainstream" theories of crime to the explanation of female delinquency and the gender gap in delinquency. Such theories include strain theory; social learning theory; control theory; labeling theory; deterrence, rational choice, and routine activities theories; Moffitt's theory of life-course persistent offending; and selected integrated theories. These theories tend to explain crime in terms of characteristics of the individual and the individual's immediate social environment. This chapter examines contributions of each theory in turn and concludes by listing the key insights from these theories.

As noted by several criminologists, most mainstream theories were developed to explain male delinquency, and most tests of these theories devote little or no attention to gender (Kruttschnitt 1996; Miller and Mullins 2006; Morash 1999; Morris 1987; Steffensmeier and Allan 1996; Steffensmeier and Broidy 2001). However, some researchers in recent years have applied these theories to the explanation of female delinquency and the gender gap in delinquency. Data suggest that the causal factors identified by these theories do apply to females and that these theories can explain much of the gender gap in delinquency (Jensen 2003; Jensen and Eve 1976; Lanctot and Le Blanc 2002; Moffitt et al. 2001; Rowe, Vazsonyi, and Flannery 1995; Simons, Miller, and Aigner 1980; Smith 1979; Smith and Paternoster 1987).

At the same time, these theories are somewhat limited in the explanations they provide. In particular, they often fail to account for the complex relationship between gender and delinquency. For example, many fail to explain why gender differences in delinquency vary by type of delinquency (e.g., why gender differences are greatest for serious violence). Also, they offer little insight into gender differences in the context or nature of particular crimes (e.g., gender differences in the motivation, victim characteristics, and level of injury for violent crimes). Further, they often fail to consider fully the varied mechanisms by which gender may influence delinquency (e.g., gender differences in socialization, social control, social position, power/resources, interactional dynamics, and opportunities). Finally, they fail to consider the ways in which gender interacts with race, class, and age to affect delinquency.

To be fair, these problems affect many feminist theories as well, but they are particularly common among mainstream theories. Clearly, a complete explanation of female delinquency will require that the insights of mainstream theories be integrated with those of feminist theories and the research on gender and crime. Describing the contributions of mainstream theories is a first step toward that integration.

The Contribution of Mainstream Theories

The examination here focuses on the best-supported version of each theory or a generic version that combines the best elements from the different versions. I briefly describe (a) the major arguments of the theory, (b) how the theory explains the gender gap in delinquency, and (c) how the theory explains female delinquency. I summarize the evidence for each theory and note areas where further research is needed.

General Strain Theory

Major Arguments

General strain theory (GST) argues that a range of strains or stressors increases the likelihood of delinquency (Agnew 1992, 2006). These strains fall into three broad groups: the failure to achieve positively valued goals (e.g., autonomy, masculine status, monetary success), the loss of positive stimuli (e.g., property, romantic partners), and the presentation of negative stimuli (e.g., verbal and physical abuse). Such strains lead to negative emotions such as anger and frustration. And individuals may cope with these strains and negative emotions through delinquency. Delinquency may be a way of reducing or escaping from strains (e.g., theft to achieve monetary goals, running away to escape from abusive parents), seeking revenge against the source of the strains or related targets, or alleviating negative emotions (e.g., through illicit drug use).

Certain strains are said to be more conducive to criminal coping than others. These strains (a) are seen as high in magnitude, (b) are seen as unjust, (c) are associated with low social control, and (d) create some incentive or pressure to engage in crime. Such strains include parental rejection; parental supervision/discipline that is erratic, excessive, or harsh; child abuse and neglect; negative secondary school experiences (e.g., low grades, negative relations with teachers); abusive peer relations (e.g., verbal and physical abuse); the failure to achieve selected goals, including thrills/excitement, autonomy, masculine status, and money; criminal victimization; residence in economically deprived communities; homelessness; and discrimination based on race/ethnicity and gender. Data suggest that these strains do increase the likelihood of delinquency, although many of these strains, such as peer abuse and discrimination, have not been well researched. Further, limited data suggest that certain of these strains increase delinquency through their effect on negative emotions such as anger (Agnew 2006).

GST also argues that some individuals are more likely than others to cope with strains through crime. Five general sets of characteristics are said to increase the likelihood of criminal coping: (a) poor coping skills and resources (e.g., poor social and problem-solving skills, the personality trait of low self-control); (b) low levels of conventional social support; (c) low social control; (d) association with criminal others and beliefs favorable to crime; and (e) exposure to situations where the costs of crime are low and the benefits are high. These factors increase the likelihood of criminal coping since they reduce the ability to cope in a legal manner, reduce the costs of crime, and increase the disposition for crime. Certain of these factors also influence the individual's perception of and sensitivity to strains. Data on whether these factors increase the likelihood of criminal coping are mixed, a fact that may reflect the difficulty of detecting interaction or conditioning effects in survey research (Agnew 2006; Mazerolle and Maahs 2000).

Explaining the Gender Gap in Delinquency

Males and females experience similar amounts of strains (Broidy and Agnew 1997). Males, however, may be more likely to engage in delinquency because they are more likely to experience strains conducive to delinquency and more likely to cope with strains through delinquency. Although the data are somewhat mixed, there is reason to believe that males are more likely to experience the following strains conducive to delinquency: harsh parental discipline; negative secondary school experiences, such as low grades and negative relations with teachers; peer abuse, with males more likely to report that their relations with peers are characterized by conflict, competition, jealousy, and imbalance; difficulty achieving several goals conducive to delinquency, such as autonomy, thrills/excitement, money, and masculine status; criminal victimization; and homelessness (Agnew 2006; Agnew and Brezina 1997; Bottcher 2001; Broidy and Agnew 1997; Cernkovich and Giordano 1979; Giordano, Cernkovich, and Pugh 1986; Hagan and McCarthy 1997; Hay 2003; McCarthy, Felmlee, and Hagan 2004; Messerschmidt 1993).

Further, females are more likely than males to experience certain strains that may inhibit other-directed delinquency. These strains include close supervision by parents and others; the burdens associated with the care of others, especially family members; problems in forming and maintaining close relationships; and pressure to conform to traditional gender roles, with such pressure increasing during adolescence (Agnew 2006; Agnew and Brezina 1997; Berger 1989; Broidy and Agnew 1997; Chesney-Lind and Shelden 2004; Gove and Herb 1974). The extent to which these gender differences in strains explain gender differences in offending is unknown. No currently available data set contains measures of delinquency and measures of all or even most of these strains. A few studies, however, provide partial support for GST. Eitle and Turner (2002), for example, found that gender differences in crime were partly explained by the higher rates of violent victimization "both experienced and witnessed" among males.

GST also suggests that males are more likely to cope with strains through other-directed crime (Agnew and Brezina 1997; Broidy 2001; Broidy and Agnew 1997; Cloward and Piven 1979; Hay 2003; Piquero and Sealock 2004; Robbers 2004). There are several reasons for this. While females are as likely as or more likely than males to respond to strains with anger, the anger of females is more often accompanied by feelings of depression, guilt, and anxiety. This may be because females are more likely to blame themselves for the strains they experience, be concerned about hurting others, and view their anger as inappropriate. The anger of males, however, is more often characterized by moral outrage. Males are more likely to blame others for the strains they experience and view their anger as an affirmation of their masculinity. The moral outrage of males is more conducive to other-directed crime than the type of anger experienced by females. (The anger of females, however, may be especially conducive to self-directed crimes and deviant acts [e.g., drug use, eating disorders] [Broidy 2001; Broidy and Agnew 1997; Obeidallah and Earls 1999].)

Males are also more likely to cope with strains through other-directed crimes because they have poorer coping skills and resources, are lower in certain types of social support, are lower in social control, are more likely to associate with other criminals, and are more likely to hold beliefs conducive to criminal coping. Cloward and Piven (1979), for example, point to those gender-related beliefs that proscribe that "women endure rather than deviate" (p. 663). In addition, males are physically larger and stronger than females, which increases their ability to engage in several types of criminal coping. However, the "sexualization and commodification of the young, female body" increases the likelihood that females will engage in selected crimes, like prostitution (Chesney-Lind 1989; Gaarder and Belknap 2002; Steffensmeier and Allan 2000).

A number of studies have examined whether males are more likely to cope with selected strains through delinquency. Most such studies find that this is the case, although some studies find that strains have comparable effects on delinquency among males and females and a few find that certain strains have larger effects on females (Agnew 2006; Agnew and Brezina 1997; Broidy 2001; Broidy and Agnew 1997; Cernkovich and Giordano 1979; Datesman, Scarpitti, and Stephenson 1975; Hay 2003; Piquero and Sealock 2004; Robbers 2004; Smith and

Paternoster 1987). More research is needed in this area, particularly research that examines a broader range of strains, that looks at different types of crime (e.g., violence versus drug use), and that more systematically examines the possible reasons for any gender differences in coping that are found.

Explaining Female Delinquency

GST explains female delinquency by arguing that many females do experience strains conducive to delinquency, such as parental rejection, harsh discipline, negative secondary school experiences, peer abuse, homelessness, a strong need for money, and criminal victimization. To illustrate, females are encouraged to focus on their appearance and are the target of massive advertising campaigns for products such as cosmetics and clothing. Many females lack the money to purchase such products and turn to shoplifting as a result (Chesney-Lind and Shelden 2004). Further, females are more likely than males to experience certain strains conducive to delinquency, including sexual abuse, gender discrimination, and, possibly, partner/dating violence and certain types of romantic disputes—such as those involving the infidelity and emotional detachment of one's partner (Agnew 2006; Bottcher 2001; Miller and White 2003).

Chesney-Lind (1989) describes the effects of sexual abuse on female delinquency, arguing that some females run away to escape from abuse at home. These females often must engage in crimes like theft and prostitution to survive on the street, and they are frequently abused by a new set of males, further increasing the strains they experience. Several studies support these arguments, suggesting that sexual abuse plays a central role in the generation of serious female offending (Acoca 1998b; Chesney-Lind and Shelden 2004; Daly 1992; Gilfus 1992; Hubbard and Pratt 2002). The effects of gender discrimination, partner abuse, and romantic disputes on offending have not been well examined, but limited quantitative and qualitative data suggest that they too increase the likelihood of crime (Bottcher 2001; Eitle 2002; Gaarder and Belknap 2002; Katz 2000; Miller and White 2003). Note that lower-class females and the members of certain racial and ethnic groups, like African Americans and Latinos, are more likely to experience most of the aforementioned strains (Chesney-Lind and Shelden 2004; Gaarder and Belknap 2002; Gilfus 1992; Miller and White 2003).

Further, some females do possess characteristics conducive to criminal coping. Among other things, criminal coping is expected to be more likely among females who are poor, are low in self-control, are low in conventional social support, associate with criminal others, hold beliefs favorable to crime, and reject traditional gender beliefs. Little research has been conducted in this area.

Social Learning Theory

Major Arguments

Social learning theory argues that individuals learn to be delinquent from others, including family members, friends, neighborhood residents, and media figures (Akers and Sellers 2004; Akers 1998). These others teach the individual to engage in delinquency in three major ways. They model delinquent behavior, which the individual then imitates, especially if the delinquency is modeled by close others and results in reinforcement. They reinforce the individual's delinquency in certain circumstances, leading the individual to anticipate further reinforcement in similar circumstances. And they teach beliefs favorable to delinquency. These beliefs do not involve the unconditional approval of all delinquent acts. Rather, individuals are typically taught that delinquency is desirable, justifiable, or excusable in certain conditions. For example, violence may be presented as a justifiable response to a broad range of provocations (Anderson 1999). Individuals are also taught certain general values conducive to delinquency, like the importance of being tough. And individuals may be taught to unconditionally approve of select, minor delinquent acts such as underage drinking, sexual intercourse, and marijuana use (Agnew 2005a).

Data provide a fair degree of support for social learning theory (Agnew 2005a; Akers and Sellers 2004; Akers 1998). Associating with delinquent peers, especially gang members, is one of the strongest predictors of delinquency. It should be noted, however, that the effect of delinquent peers is only partly explained by the mechanisms listed by social learning theory: exposure to criminal models, the reinforcement of delinquency, and beliefs favorable to delinquency (Krohn 1999; see Warr 2002 for additional mechanisms by which delinquent peers may contribute to delinquency). Having criminal parents and siblings is a relatively strong predictor of delinquency. Some data also suggest that exposure to media violence increases violent behavior, although the effect is modest in size (Agnew 2005a). Further, most data suggest that individuals who hold beliefs favorable to delinquency are more likely to engage in delinquent acts.

Explaining the Gender Gap

Social learning theorists argue that males have higher levels of delinquency than females primarily because they are more likely to associate with delinquent peers and belong to gangs. Data provide some support for this argument, with gender differences in delinquent peer association explaining a significant part of the gender gap in delinquency (Jensen 2003; Liu and Kaplan 1999; Mears, Ploeger, and Warr 1998; Moffitt et al. 2001; Moore and Hagedorn

2001; Morash 1986; Rowe, Vazsonyi, and Flannery 1995; Warr 2002). Males are said to be more likely to associate with delinquent peers because they are subject to less parental supervision, are less often confined to the home, are more attracted to delinquent peers because of their values and individual traits, and are less likely to be excluded from delinquent peer groups because of their greater physical strength and other factors (Steffensmeier 1983). Further, most studies suggest that delinquent peers have a larger effect on delinquency among males than females, perhaps because females are more constrained by their moral beliefs and are higher in self-control (Crosnoe, Erickson, and Dornbusch 2002; Elliott, Huizinga, and Ageton 1985; Johnson 1979; Mears, Ploeger, and Warr 1998; Moffitt et al. 2001; Piquero et al. 2005; Simpson and Elis 1995; Smith 1979; Warr 2002).

Related to the studies mentioned, a few recent studies suggest that all-female peer groups are less conducive to delinquency than mixed-gender or all-male peer groups (Bottcher 1995, 2001; Giordano, Cernkovich, and Pugh 1986; McCarthy, Felmlee, and Hagan 2004). Female peers provide less pressure, reinforcement, and models for delinquency than do male peers. Also, female peers may be less likely to abuse one another and more likely to function as sources of support.

Social learning theorists also explain the gender gap in delinquency by arguing that males are more likely to hold beliefs favorable to delinquency. Data provide some support for this argument (Jensen 2003; Liu and Kaplan 1999; Mears, Ploeger, and Warr 1998). For example, Heimer and De Coster (1999) found that males were more likely to agree with statements such as "It is alright to beat up another person if he/she called you a dirty name" and "It is alright to beat up another person if he/she started the fight."

Further, social learning theorists argue that males are more likely to be taught identities that are conducive to delinquency. In particular, male identities are said to emphasize competitiveness, independence, risk-taking, and strength. Female identities are said to emphasize concern for others, dependence, caution, passivity, and submissiveness. Research on the relationship between gender identities and delinquency has produced mixed results, for reasons that are not entirely clear (Bottcher 1995, 2001; Chesney-Lind and Shelden 2004; Costello and Mederer 2003; Giordano and Cernkovich 1979; Heimer 1995, 1996; Heimer and De Coster 1999; Jensen 2003; Norland, Wessel, and Shover 1981; Shover et al. 1979). Some researchers suggest, however, that gender-linked identities may be related to crime when one focuses on those aspects of identity most directly relevant to crime. Jensen (2003), for example, found that males were somewhat more likely to view themselves as tough, mean, unforgiving, and prone to trouble; while females were more likely to view themselves as nice, prone to avoid trouble, caring about others, and forgiving. These differences in identity partly explained gender differences in delinquency. (It should be noted that some evidence suggests that delinquent beliefs and gender identities may differ by class and race/ethnicity, although more research is needed in this area before definitive conclusions can be drawn [Bottcher 2001; Heimer and De Coster 1999; Simpson and Elis 1995].)

Explaining Female Delinquency

According to social learning theory, some females are more likely than others to engage in delinquency because they are more likely to associate with others who provide exposure to delinquent models, reinforce delinquent behavior, and teach beliefs favorable to delinquency. Also, some females are more likely to be taught identities favorable to delinquency.

Association with delinquent peers and gang members is a critical variable, with one recent meta-analysis suggesting that such association, along with a prior history of antisocial behavior, is the strongest predictor of female delinquency (Elliott, Huizinga, and Ageton 1985; Heimer 1996; Hubbard and Pratt 2002; Jensen 2003; Johnson 1979; Laundra, Kieger, and Bahr 2002; Liu and Kaplan 1999; Moore and Hagedorn 2001; Piquero et al. 2005; Smith and Paternoster 1987; Warr 2002). Several factors increase the likelihood of delinquent peer association in females, including poor parental supervision, sexual abuse by family members, running away from home, poverty, school problems, early puberty, limited prospects for the future, and residence in economically deprived communities (Acoca 1998b; Chesney-Lind and Shelden 2004; Elliott, Huizinga, and Ageton 1985; Joe and Chesney-Lind 1999; Moffitt et al. 2001; Morash 1986).

In addition, research suggests that females are more likely to engage in delinquency if they associate with older males, including romantic partners, and are part of mixed-sex or all-male peer groups (Agnew and Brezina 1997; Bottcher 2001; Giordano 1978; Giordano and Cernkovich 1979; Haynie et al. 2005; Heimer and De Coster 1999; McCarthy, Felmlee, and Hagan 2004; Moffitt et al. 2001; Warr 2002). Further, data suggest that females are more likely to engage in delinquency if they have criminal parents or siblings, hold beliefs favorable to delinquency, and, possibly, have identities emphasizing "masculine" traits such as toughness and meanness (Heimer 1996; Heimer and De Coster 1999; Jensen 2003; Johnson 1979; Lanctot and Le Blanc 2002; Laundra, Kieger, and Bahr 2002; Miller 2002a; Shover et al. 1979; Steffensmeier and Broidy 2001).

Control Theory

Major Arguments

Control theorists do not ask why individuals engage in delinquency, but rather why they conform. According to control theorists, delinquency requires no special explanation. It is frequently the easiest or most expedient way for individuals to satisfy their needs and desires. What requires explanation, then, is conformity. Control theorists contend that people conform because of the controls or restraints to which they are subject (Agnew 2005a; Gottfredson and Hirschi 1990; Hirschi 1969; Sampson and Laub 1993). These controls are of three types.

The first is external control. Here individuals conform because they fear they will be sanctioned by others if they do not. These others include parents, friends, school officials, neighbors, and police. External control is enhanced to the extent that these others set clear rules that forbid delinquency and related behaviors, monitor the individual's behavior, and consistently sanction rule violations in a meaningful but not overly harsh manner.

The second type of control involves the individual's "stake in conformity." Some individuals are less likely to engage in delinquency because they have a lot to lose through delinquent acts. In particular, they have strong emotional bonds to conventional others, like parents and teachers, that may be jeopardized by delinquency. And they have a large investment in conventional activities, like getting an education. Individuals who are doing well in school, devote more time to homework, and anticipate obtaining a good education and job are less likely to engage in delinquency because it might jeopardize their accomplishments and future plans.

The third type of control is internal control, which refers to the individual's ability to restrain him- or herself from responding to temptations and provocations with delinquency. Internal control is partly a function of the individual's beliefs regarding delinquency. Some individuals have been taught to condemn delinquency and are less likely to engage in delinquency as a result. Other individuals, however, have an amoral orientation toward delinquency (control theorists contend that few individuals are deliberately taught beliefs favorable to delinquency). And internal control is partly a function of several related personality traits that influence the individual's ability to exercise self-restraint. Those traits conducive to delinquency include impulsivity, a preference for immediate versus delayed rewards, a preference for risky activities, high activity levels, little ambition or motivation, and an irritable disposition. Individuals with these traits are said to be low in self-control.

Explaining the Gender Gap

Control theorists argue that males have higher rates of offending than females because they are lower in the three major types of control (Costello and Mederer 2003; Gottfredson and Hirschi 1990; Heimer and De Coster 1999; McCarthy, Felmlee, and Hagan 2004; Shover et al. 1979). Males are subject to less external control; most notably, they are less well supervised by parents and less strongly tied to the household than females. Also, males are less likely to be sanctioned by parents, peers, and others for aggressive and delinquent behavior. Males are less strongly attached to conventional others such as parents and teachers. Males do less well at school, spend less time on homework, and dislike school more. Males are less likely to condemn crime. And males are lower in self-control. These gender differences in control are explained in several ways, including the greater desire of parents and others to regulate the sexual behavior of females (reflecting the double standard for sexual behavior). Also, some researchers have said that females need to show more concern for others and exercise greater self-control since they are the primary caregivers in society (Bottcher 1995; Costello and Mederer 2003).

Some criminologists also argue that certain control variables have a stronger effect on delinquency among females or males. Most notably, emotional bonds to others are said to have a stronger effect among females, since females attach greater importance to establishing and maintaining close relationships with others. School performance, however, is said to have a stronger effect among males, given their greater concern with achievement (Canter 1982a; Heimer and De Coster 1999; Rankin 1980).

Data provide a fair degree of support for control theory explanations of the gender gap. Most studies suggest that male adolescents are less well supervised by parents, are less strongly tied to the household through chores and family-care responsibilities, are less constrained from crime by peers, have lower grades in school, like school less, are less likely to condemn crime, and are much lower in self-control (Bottcher 1995, 2001; Canter 1982a; Cernkovich and Giordano 1987, 1992; Chesney-Lind and Shelden 2004; Costello and Mederer 2003; Crosnoe, Erickson, and Dornbusch 2002; Hagan and McCarthy 1997; Hagan, Simpson, and Gillis 1979; Jensen and Eve 1976; LaGrange and Silverman 1999; McCarthy, Felmlee, and Hagan 2004; Moffitt et al. 2001; Richards and Tittle 1981; Rowe, Vazsonyi, and Flannery 1995; Simons, Miller, and Aigner 1980; Singer and Levine 1988; Smith and Paternoster 1987; Thornberry et al. 1991). These gender differences in levels of control, particularly self-control, explain a significant portion of the gender gap in delinquency. Less evidence exists for the proposition that males have weaker emotional bonds to conventional others. Data on whether certain types of control have stronger effects on delinquency among males or females are somewhat mixed (Canter 1982a; Cernkovich and Giordano 1987, 1992; Heimer and De Coster 1999; Johnson 1979; Krohn and Massey 1980; Kruttschnitt 1996; Laundra, Kieger, and Bahr 2002; Rankin 1980; Smith and Paternoster 1987). Most studies suggest that the different types of control generally have similar effects among males and females, although a meta-analysis of studies about control types and gender effects would be quite useful.

Explaining Female Delinquency

Some females are more likely to be delinquent than others because they are lower in the forms of control described earlier. That is, they are lower in parental supervision, are less tied to their homes and families, are weakly bonded to conventional others such as parents and teachers, do poorly in school, spend little time on homework, are in peer groups in which the constraints against delinquency are lower (e.g., delinquent peer groups, mixed-gender or all-male groups), do not condemn crime, and are low in self-control. Data suggest that these types of control affect female as well as male delinquency (Elliott, Huizinga, and Ageton 1985; Fleming et al. 2002; Friedman and Rosenbaum 1988; Heimer 1995; Hubbard and Pratt 2002; Huebner and Betts 2002; Jensen and Eve 1976; Johnson 1979; Krohn and Massey 1980; LaGrange and Silverman 1999; Lanctot and Le Blanc 2002; Mason and Windle 2002; Smith 1979; Smith and Paternoster 1987). It should be noted, however, that certain types of control have a stronger effect on delinquency than others, with some data suggesting that parental supervision, the nature of peer relations, and self-control are among the more important predictors of delinquency (Agnew 2005a).

Labeling Theory

Major Arguments

Labeling theory focuses on the reaction to delinquency, both the formal reaction by the juvenile justice system and the informal reaction by parents, friends, teachers, and community residents. The key insight of labeling theory is that others often react to the individual's delinquency in ways that increase the likelihood of further delinquency (Agnew 2005b; Braithwaite 1989; Cullen and Agnew 2003; Heimer and Matsueda 1994; Matsueda 1992; Schur 1984; Sherman 1993). In particular, others often treat individuals who are labeled delinquent in a harsh and rejecting manner. Among other things, labeled individuals may be severely punished by parents, school officials, and the justice system. They may be viewed with suspicion and mistrust. They may be denied certain opportunities; for example, their schooling may be interrupted and their future educational and occupational plans may be jeopardized. And conventional others may be reluctant to associate with them.

These reactions increase the likelihood of delinquency for four reasons. First, they increase the labeled individual's strain, since the individual is subject to much negative treatment by others. Second, they reduce the individual's level of control, since bonds to conventional others such as parents and teachers are weakened. Also, the individual's stake in conformity is threatened. Third, they foster the social learning of crime. Labeled individuals often associate with other delinquents, since conventional others do not want to associate with them. Finally, labeled individuals may eventually come to see themselves as delinquents and act in accord with this self-image.

The evidence on labeling theory is mixed. Data suggest that labeling by parents and teachers may increase the likelihood of further delinquency, partly by affecting the juvenile's relations with others and self-concept (Adams and Evans 1996; Matsueda 1992; Triplett and Jarjoura 1994). And several studies find that individuals who are arrested or officially sanctioned by the justice system are more likely than comparable individuals to engage in subsequent delinquency, although not all studies find this (Agnew 2005b; Huizinga et al. 2003; Stewart et al. 2002b). Part of the reason for these mixed findings may be that some labeled individuals are more subject to the harsh and rejecting reactions described than others. Also, some individuals may be more likely than others to respond to this reaction with crime. Recent work on labeling theory has focused on these issues, with some attention being devoted to the ways in which gender influences the labeling process and the response to labeling.

Explaining the Gender Gap

Labeling theorists argue that males are more likely than females to be labeled delinquents, because of the cultural stereotype of males as troublemakers and the fact that males engage in more delinquency (Gove and Herb 1974). Males are also more likely to be treated in a harsh and rejecting manner by others once they are labeled, because they are viewed as more threatening and are less likely to have close ties to others (Braithwaite 1989). Further, males are more likely to respond to this harsh and rejecting treatment with crime for the same reasons they are more likely to respond to strains in general with crime. A major exception to these arguments, however, is said to involve status offenses, especially those linked to sexual behavior or the possibility of sexual behavior. Female status offenders are said to be more likely to be labeled delinquent and treated in a harsh and rejecting manner because of the sexual double standard, with sexual behavior on the part of female adolescents being more strongly condemned (Bartusch and Matsueda 1996; Chesney-Lind and Shelden 2004).

Research provides some support for these arguments. Males are more likely to be informally labeled as delinquents/troublemakers by others such as parents and teachers, primarily because they are more likely to engage in delinquency (Adams and Evans 1996; Bartusch and Matsueda 1996; Giordano et al. 1999; Liu and Kaplan 1999; Simons, Miller, and Aigner 1980). Males are also more likely to be falsely labeled as delinquents, although some females are falsely labeled as well (Bartusch and Matsueda 1996). Among females, false accusations are most common against the poor, African Americans, and those from broken homes. It is important to note, however, that Bartusch and Matsueda (1996) found that females are more likely than males to be labeled delinquent by parents and others for *a given delinquent act*, but *not* for a given status offense (Liu and Kaplan 1999; Schur 1984). Bartusch and Matsueda (1996) speculate that this may occur because "female offending is inconsistent with gender-specific expectations and readily violates parents' stereotypical conceptions of delinquency as a male enterprise" (p. 154). Related to this, Hagan, Simpson, and Gillis

(1979) present data to the effect that women are more often the objects of informal social control.

Bartusch and Matsueda further found that being labeled a rule violator by parents increases the likelihood that juveniles will label themselves as rule violators, which in turn increases the likelihood of delinquency (see also Jensen 2003). This effect was stronger for males than females. In addition, they found that being labeled a rule violator by parents has a direct effect on delinquency among males, but not among females. Bartusch and Matsueda speculated that labeling by parents may be more likely to act as a deterrent to females, who are more concerned with maintaining a positive image and a positive relationship with others. Also, as Braithwaite (1989) suggests, labeled females may be less subject to harsh and rejecting reactions from others, given their closer ties to conventional others. Rather, labeled females may be more subject to "reintegrative shaming." Further, labeled females may be more responsive to such shaming. In this area, Jensen and Erickson (1978) found that females were more concerned than males about the negative consequences of labeling (Heimer 1996).

In summary, data suggest that males are more likely than females to be negatively labeled by parents and others, because of their higher levels of delinquency and, possibly, increased susceptibility to false labeling (although females may be more likely to be labeled for a given delinquent act). This labeling leads to delinquent self-concepts among both males and females, although males are more likely to have delinquent self-concepts since they are more often labeled (Jensen 2003). Further, labeling may be more likely to lead to delinquency among males. These gender differences in informal labeling explain a significant part of the gender gap in delinquency.

Several studies have examined official labeling, with most attempting to determine whether gender influences the likelihood of arrest, court referral, court processing, and sanctioning. The data here are mixed, but there is reason to believe that in some jurisdictions females who commit status offenses and selected minor crimes may be treated more severely than males. This may be especially true for poor females and the members of certain minority groups (for overviews, see Chesney-Lind and Shelden 2004; and MacDonald and Chesney-Lind 2001). A few studies have examined the impact of official labeling on future life changes. These studies suggest that such labeling typically has a negative effect on both males and females, although there are some gender differences in effects. Both males and females report negative educational consequences, but males also report negative occupational consequences (Moffitt et al. 2001; Tanner, Davies, and O'Grady 1999). Those few studies that have examined the effect of official labeling on future offending typically do not report results separately by gender. Clearly, more research is needed on the likelihood and impact of both informal and formal labeling on males and females.

Explaining Female Delinquency

Labeling theory argues that some females are more delinquent than others because they have been informally labeled as delinquents by parents, teachers, and others; they have been formally labeled by the juvenile justice system (i.e., they have been arrested, detained, formally or informally processed by the court, and sanctioned); or both. Delinquency should be more likely among those who have been severely labeled by a broad range of individuals and groups (e.g., treated in the harsh and rejecting manner described earlier, severely sanctioned by the juvenile justice system). Related to this, delinquency should be more likely among those females who see themselves as delinquents, troublemakers, and the like. As suggested, there is some support for these arguments.

Deterrence, Rational Choice, Routine Activities Theories

Major Arguments

Deterrence, rational choice, and routine activities theories differ from one another in important ways (Agnew 2005a; Cornish and Clarke 1986; Cullen and Agnew 2003; Felson 2002; Miethe and Meier 1994; Piquero and Tibbetts 2002). But these theories are all based on the idea that individuals consider somewhat the costs and benefits of crime and choose to engage in crime if they believe it is to their advantage. Deterrence theorists focus on the legal costs of crime and argue that individuals are more likely to engage in crime when they believe that the certainty and severity of official sanctions are low. Rational choice theorists focus on a broad range of costs and benefits. The benefits of crime may be both monetary and nonmonetary (e.g., thrills, social approval), and the costs may be both legal and nonlegal (e.g., disapproval from parents, guilt). Rational choice theorists do *not* argue that individuals carefully consider all of the potential costs and benefits of crime. Rather, individuals are said to give at least some consideration to certain of the costs and benefits, even though this consideration may be hurried and based on incomplete or inaccurate information. Crime is said to be more likely when benefits are seen as outweighing costs.

The data provide some support for these arguments. Individuals are more likely to engage in crime when (a) the perceived certainty and, to a lesser extent, severity of official sanction are low; (b) the perceived likelihood and severity of informal sanction are low; (c) the anticipated moral costs of crime, such as guilt and shame, are low; and (d) the anticipated pleasure associated with crime is high (Agnew 2005a, 2005b; Cullen and Agnew 2003; Piquero and Tibbetts 2002). Rational choice theorists have discussed those factors that influence the perceived costs and benefits of crime, and they draw heavily on the theories described in this area. For example, the perceived costs and benefits of crime are said to be influenced by such things as the individual's level of monetary strain, parental supervision, moral beliefs, self-control, and association with delinquent peers. The costs and benefits of crime are also influenced by a range of situational factors, most of which are specific to particular types of crime. For example, individuals contemplating burglary are likely to conclude that the costs of burglary are low if they encounter an isolated, unguarded home with easy entry.

The routine activities perspective is also built on the idea that offenders take into account the potential costs and benefits of crime. This perspective focuses on the factors that influence the calculation of costs and benefits, and its core idea is that crime is most likely when motivated offenders encounter attractive targets for crime in the absence of capable guardians (Felson 2002). The characteristics of attractive targets vary somewhat by type of crime. For property crimes, attractive targets are visible, accessible, easy to move, and valuable. The term "capable guardians" refers to individuals who might intervene if a crime occurs, like parents, teachers, community residents, and police. The likelihood that motivated offenders will encounter attractive targets for crime in the absence of capable guardians is said to be a function of the routine activities in which people engage; that is, what people do, who they do it with, when they do it, and where they do it.

One major finding to emerge from the research on routine activities is that juveniles are more likely to engage in crime if they spend a lot of time engaged in unstructured, unsupervised activities with peers (Osgood et al. 1996). The costs of crime are likely to be seen as lower in such situations, because capable guardians are absent and peers often lower the perceived costs of crime. In particular, peers may help neutralize the moral costs of crime, provide assistance in committing crimes, and foster a sense of power through the "strength in numbers." The benefits of crime are also likely to be seen as higher in such situations. Individuals are more likely to encounter attractive targets for crime when engaged in unstructured, unsupervised activities with peers. Also, peers frequently reinforce crime, often with social approval.

Explaining the Gender Gap

These theories would argue that males are more likely to engage in crime than females because they are more likely to view the costs of crime as low and the benefits as high (Blackwell and Eschholz 2002; Braithwaite 1989; Costello and Mederer 2003; Richards and Tittle 1981). Several reasons explain why males are more likely to view the costs of crime as low, most of which are related to the theories described earlier in this chapter. Males are not as well supervised as females, so their crimes are less likely to be detected. If detected, male crimes are less likely to be sanctioned by certain others, such as peers. This is mainly because crime is viewed as more appropriate for males, but is also related to such things as the greater physical strength of males. Males have less to lose through crime, since crime is more compatible with male roles and identities. Males are more likely to hold beliefs favorable to crime, thereby lowering the moral costs of crime. Males are lower in self-control, so they give less thought to the possibility of sanctions or the harm that their crimes might cause others. Males spend more time in unstructured, unsupervised activities with peers, which lowers the costs of crime for the reasons indicated. And males are more likely to belong to delinquent peer groups and to engage in crime themselves. This teaches males that the likelihood of sanction for crime is low, since they frequently commit crimes without sanction and see their friends do the same.

Males are also more likely than females to view the benefits of crime as high. This partly stems from the fact that males are lower in self-control, so they are more likely to enjoy engaging in risky and aggressive activities like crime. And it partly stems from the fact that the routine activities of males expose them to more attractive opportunities for crime. Males, in particular, are given more freedom to explore the public sphere, where they might encounter attractive targets for crime. Females, by contrast, are more often involved in conventional activities associated with the home, family, and school, like chores, the care of siblings, homework, and interacting with parents. More freedom allows males to spend more time associating with other males, especially in unsupervised, unstructured settings. Reinforcement for crime is more likely in such circumstances.

Some data support these arguments (Blackwell and Eschholz 2002; Cernkovich and Giordano 1992; Heimer 1996; Jensen and Erickson 1978; McCarthy and Hagan 1999, 2005; Richards and Tittle 1981; Singer and Levine 1988; Smith and Paternoster 1987; Tibbetts and Herz 1996). Males perceive the certainty and severity of official sanctions as lower than females perceive them. Some studies also suggest that the perceived certainty/severity of sanctions may have a larger effect on delinquency among females, although not all studies find this (Cernkovich and Giordano 1992; Smith and Paternoster 1987). Males are less concerned about the reactions of parents and others to their crimes. Males are less concerned about the moral costs of crime, like the guilt and shame that might result from crime. And limited data also suggest that males are more likely to estimate the expected pleasure from crime as high (Hagan, Simpson, and Gillis 1979; Tibbetts and Herz 1996). Such factors explain a substantial portion of the gender gap in crime.

The reasons for gender differences in these factors are still being examined, but evidence supports many of the aforementioned arguments. Most notably, males have more opportunities for crime since they are away from home more often; interact with more people; have greater access to cars; and spend more time in unstructured, unsupervised activities with peers (Bottcher 1995, 2001; Costello and Mederer 2003; LaGrange and Silverman 1999). While males generally have more opportunities for crime than females, the greater sexual interest in young females creates opportunities for crimes like prostitution. Females may also have much opportunity to engage in crimes involving family violence, including partner violence and petty theft (Chesney-Lind and Shelden 2004; Steffensmeier and Allan 2000).

Explaining Female Delinquency

Not surprisingly, these theories would predict that some females are more likely to engage in crime than other females because they are more likely to estimate the costs of crime as low and the benefits as high. Limited data suggest that estimates of the costs and benefits of crime influence female as well as male delinquency (Piquero and Paternoster 1998; Smith 1979; Smith and Paternoster 1987). Females likely differ in their estimates of the costs and benefits of crime because they differ in such factors as level of supervision; moral beliefs; self-control; time spent in unstructured, unsupervised activities with peers; association with delinquent peers; and prior delinquency (see previous section). For example, some females are more likely to spend unstructured, unsupervised time with peers than others. This is especially true of females who run away from home and spend a lot of time on the "street" (Hagan and McCarthy 1997).

Moffitt's Theory of Life-Course Persistent Offending

Major Arguments

All of the theories discussed focus on the effect of the social environment on delinquency. Moffitt's (1993) theory of life-course persistent offending has played a major role in introducing biological factors and individual characteristics into mainstream criminology. Moffitt's theory states that there are two major types of offenders: life-course persistent and adolescence-limited. Life-course persistent offenders tend to offend at relatively high rates over much of their lives. They commit both minor and serious crimes and, although they comprise only about 5 percent of the population, they account for a majority of all serious crimes. Adolescence-limited offenders limit their offending largely to the adolescent years and they commit primarily minor offenses. The large majority of people are said to be adolescence-limited offenders. Another 10 percent or so of all people are said to refrain from offending. Data provide some support for this typology, with most studies finding evidence for both life-course persistent and adolescence-limited offenders (D'Unger et al. 1998; Moffitt et al. 2001; Piquero and Tibbetts 2002).

Moffitt argues that the causes of life-course persistent and adolescence-limited offending differ. The causes of adolescence-limited offending are said to be largely social in nature. As juveniles enter adolescence, they physically resemble adults but lack many of the privileges of adults, like the right to stay out late, drink alcohol, and engage in sexual relations. They notice, however, that their delinquent peers engage in these activities. As a consequence, they are attracted to these peers and come to mimic certain of their delinquent behaviors. There has not been much research on this explanation, although some data are compatible with it (Piquero and Brezina 2001). The causes of life-course persistent offending, however, are biological, psychological, and sociological in nature.

Life-course persistent offenders tend to possess a set of individual characteristics that are conducive to crime, with perhaps the most notable of these characteristics being the major personality traits of low constraint and negative emotionality. Individuals low in constraint are impulsive, like risky activities, and have little concern for moral norms and values. Individuals high in negative emotionality are easily upset, have trouble coping with stressors, tend to blame their problems on others, and have an aggressive disposition. (Note: these traits overlap a great deal with low self-control.) These traits form early in life and are fairly stable over time. Individuals with these traits are more likely to respond to temptations and provocations with crime, thereby partly explaining their high rates of offending over the life course. Individuals with these traits are also more likely to impact their environment in ways that increase the likelihood of crime. In particular, individuals with these traits are not pleasant people, and they often elicit negative reactions from others, like parents, teachers, and peers. Parents, for example, may come to reject children with these traits; may treat them in a harsh, abusive manner; or may do both. Also, individuals with these traits often select themselves into environments conducive to crime, like delinquent peer groups, bad jobs, and bad marriages. These environmental effects also help explain high rates of offending over the life course.

The traits of low constraint and negative emotionality are in part biologically based. They are inherited from parents to some degree, and they may also result from certain biological harms, like mothers' drug use during pregnancy, birth complications, head injuries, and exposure to toxic substances like lead. The ways in which such biological factors influence these traits are still being investigated, but there are several promising leads (Fishbein 2001; Moffitt 1993; Rowe 2002). These traits are also influenced by environmental factors, particularly economic disadvantage and family problems. Unfortunately, individuals with a biological predisposition for these traits are frequently exposed to these environmental factors. Among other things, parents who genetically transmit these traits are more likely to be poor and to engage in poor parenting practices (since they are low in constraint and high in negative emotionality). Also, biological harms of the type just described are more common in disadvantaged environments and troubled families.

Data provide some support for Moffitt's theory (Moffitt et al. 2001). Life-course persistent offenders are more likely to show evidence of a biological predisposition for crime, they are more likely to possess the personality traits of low constraint and negative emotionality, and these traits have social consequences that increase the likelihood of crime.

Explaining the Gender Gap

Data suggest that males are much more likely than females to be life-course persistent offenders (Broidy et al. 2003b; D'Unger, Land, and McCall 2002; Moffitt et al. 2001). This is because males are more likely to experience those biological and environmental factors that contribute to low constraint and negative emotionality (Udry 2000). Research does indicate that males are lower in constraint and higher in negative emotionality, and this fact explains a good part of the gender difference in offending, especially serious offending (Hagan, Simpson, and Gillis 1979; Moffitt et al. 2001).

Gender differences in adolescence-limited offending are much less pronounced. Females, like males, often experience a gap between their biological maturity and the privileges granted to them. So females frequently engage in adolescence-limited offending. This is especially true of females who reach puberty at an early age and are in environments where they are regularly exposed to older male adolescents and delinquent peer groups (Caspi et al. 1993; Haynie 2003; Moffitt et al. 2001). These facts help explain why gender differences in minor offending are much smaller than differences in serious offending.

Explaining Female Offending

While life-course persistent offending is much more common among males than females, a very small percentage of females become life-course persistent offenders. And data suggest that the causes of such offending are similar for males and females (Moffitt et al. 2001). Such offenders should be a high priority for intervention, given their high rates of offending, including serious offending (Daly 1992).

Integrated Theories

A good number of theories have been reviewed up to this point, including strain; social learning; control; labeling; deterrence, rational choice, and routine activities; and Moffitt's theories. Several criminologists have attempted to combine some of these theories in an effort to develop more complete explanations of delinquency (Barak 1998; Messner, Krohn, and Liska 1989; Tittle 1995). Some of the more popular integrated theories include those of Catalano and Hawkins (1996); Elliott, Ageton, and Canter (1979); Thornberry (1987); Braithwaite (1989); Cullen (1994); Tittle (1995); and Colvin (2000). It is not possible to review these theories in this brief chapter. As a consequence, I focus on two recent integrated theories. The first, Agnew's (2005b) general theory of crime and delinquency, draws quite heavily on the integrated theories just listed. The second, Steffensmeier and Allan's (1996, 2000) gendered theory of female offending, draws on both mainstream and feminist theories to explain the gender gap in crime and the causes and nature of female offending.

Agnew's General Theory of Crime and Delinquency (AGTCD)

AGTCD begins with the recognition that many of the theories listed earlier examine the same or similar causal forces. For example, most of these theories argue that erratic and harsh parental discipline increases the likelihood of delinquency. Where these theories most differ from one another is in specifying the reasons *why* these causal forces increase delinquency. For example, strain theory states that harsh/erratic discipline increases delinquency by making juveniles angry; social learning theory states that such discipline models aggressive behavior; and control theory states that such discipline reduces control—including direct control, the emotional bond to parents, and internal control. AGTCD argues that all of these theories are correct. In particular, AGTCD identifies a core set of causal factors and argues that these factors increase delinquency for reasons related to all or most of the leading crime theories.

Four major sets of factors are said to increase the likelihood of delinquency: high irritability and low constraint; poor parenting practices; negative school experiences; and peer delinquency. Adolescents high in irritability and low in constraint are easily upset, blame others for their problems, are impulsive, like risky behavior, care little about others, and hold beliefs favorable to crime. Adolescents high in poor parenting practices are weakly bonded to parents, poorly supervised, subject to harsh or abusive discipline, and have criminal parents and siblings. Adolescents high in negative school experiences dislike school, do poorly in school, spend little time on homework, have low educational and occupational goals, are poorly supervised and disciplined by teachers, and do not get along with teachers. And adolescents high in peer delinquency have close friends who engage in delinquency; spend much time in unsupervised, unstructured activities with their friends; and experience much peer conflict and abuse.

Each of these factors increases strain, fosters the social learning of crime, and reduces control. It is for these reasons that the factors increase delinquency. Further, these factors influence one another. Individuals low in constraint and high in negative emotionality, for example, are more likely to experience poor parenting practices, dislike and do poorly in school, and associate with delinquent peers. To give another example, individuals who experience poor parenting are more likely to be low in constraint and high in negative emotionality, do poorly in school, and associate with delinquent peers. Further, these factors interact with one another in their effect on delinquency. Poor parenting practices, for example, are more likely to lead to delinquency among those who are high in peer delinquency. Finally, engaging in crime, especially crime that is detected by others, can increase the likelihood of subsequent crime for several reasons. Among other things, engaging in crime can contribute to irritability and low constraint, poor parenting practices, and peer delinquency. This is more likely in some conditions than others, however (Agnew 2005b).

Explaining the Gender Gap

AGTCD states that the individual's standing on the four sets of factors affecting delinquency is influenced by a range of factors, particularly the individual's age, gender, socioeconomic status, the socioeconomic status of the individual's community, and race/ethnicity in certain cases (although the effect of race/ethnicity is due largely to its correlation with socioeconomic status). Females are said to score lower on the four factors than males, and that is the primary reason for the gender gap in offending. In particular, females are less likely to be irritable and low in constraint, to experience certain types of poor parenting practices, to have negative school experiences, and to be high in peer delinquency (see previous and Agnew 2005b). Gender differences in irritability/low constraint and peer delinquency are said to be especially important in explaining the gender gap in delinquency.

Explaining Female Delinquency

According to AGTCD, some females are more likely than others to engage in delinquency because they score higher on those four sets of factors that contribute to delinquency. Females who are from poor families and live in poor communities are more likely to fall into this category.

Steffensmeier and Allan's Gendered Theory of Female Offending (SAGTFO)

SAGTFO examines the ways in which gender influences the level and impact of the causal forces identified in many of the aforementioned theories. The theory begins by pointing to the importance of the "organization of gender" and sex differences in biological factors.

The organization of gender refers to gender differences in norms, moral development, and social control. With respect to norms, females are supposed to care for others, especially family members; be subservient to the key males in their lives; act in a weak, submissive manner; and attend to their physical appearance, while protecting their "sexual virtue." With respect to moral development, females are socialized to care for others and be concerned about the maintenance of relationships, while men are socialized to be more independent and competitive. And, with respect to social control, female behavior is more closely monitored and female misbehavior is more likely to be sanctioned. As indicated here, these differences strongly influence gender differences in the motivation for and constraints against crime.

SAGTFO identifies two major sets of sex differences in biological factors. The first involves differences in physical strength, which help account for the much lower rates of violence and certain other types of serious crime by females. The second involves reproductive-sexual differences, along with norms regarding appropriate sexual behavior for males and females. Such differences provide females with greater opportunities for prostitution and reduce their need to commit serious property crimes. These sexual and strength differences also increase the likelihood that females will align themselves with males for protection.

These two sets of factors restrict female opportunities for crime. Females are more often confined to the home and involved in the care of others. Related to this, females are less often involved with delinquent others or engaged in unstructured, unsupervised activities with peers. According to Steffensmeier and Allan (1996), these factors also reduce the motivation for crime among females by "contributing to gender differences in tastes for risk, likelihood of shame and embarrassment, self-control, and assessment of costs versus rewards of crime." Further, opportunities and motivation influence one another: "being able tends to make one more willing, just as being willing increases the prospects for being able" (Steffensmeier and Allan 1996, p. 478).

Finally, gender organization, sex differences in biological factors, and motivations influence the "context of offending," including the circumstances and the nature of the criminal act (e.g., the setting, victim, extent of injury, purpose of the offense). So, for example, females who commit violent crimes are more likely than males to target people they know, are less likely to use weapons, and are less likely to seriously injure their victims.

SAGTFO has not received a formal test, but it helps integrate the gender research with much of the mainstream literature on the causes of crime. Also, the theory provides one model for constructing an integrated theory that combines mainstream and feminist theories. We might, however, expand on SAGTFO by drawing on more recent developments in both feminist and mainstream theories, more explicitly listing the key causes of delinquency, and more fully describing how they affect one another and work together to impact delinquency.

Conclusions

The mainstream theories of delinquency reviewed here have much to say about the causes of female (and male) delinquency and the gender gap in delinquency. A good many causes were listed, but, as indicated, there is reason to believe that some causes may be more important than others. The integrated theories describe certain relationships between these causes and, in the case of Steffensmeier and Allan, describe certain ways in which gender impacts these causes. This concluding section summarizes the major points from the review in terms of a number of "take home points." Such points should be considered by those seeking to develop an integrated theory of female delinquency and to control female delinquency.

Take-Home Points

1. The causes of female delinquency likely include a range of individual characteristics, family factors, school factors, peer factors, perceptions of the costs and benefits of crime, strains or stressors, and a prior history of delinquency. Some of these causes appear to have relatively large, *direct* effects on female delinquency, including low self-control (or low constraint/negative emotionality), parental rejection, poor parental supervision, harsh/erratic discipline, association with delinquent others, time spent in unstructured/unsupervised activities with peers, prior delinquency, delinquent self-image, sexual abuse, and other criminal victimization. These causes should occupy a central place in any integrated theory of female delinquency, and they should be given high priority in efforts to control female delinquency.

2. These causes likely affect delinquency for several reasons. They may lead to negative emotions, such as anger, which create a disposition for delinquency. They may reduce the costs of delinquency. They may foster the impression that delinquency is an appropriate or desirable response in certain situations. And they may lead individuals to believe that they are the type of person who engages in delinquency. It is important to note that, while it is sometimes not possible to alter a cause of delinquency, it may be possible to alter the reason why a cause impacts delinquency. To illustrate, it is not possible to erase a prior history of victimization, but it may be possible to address the anger and depression that such victimization has produced.

3. Most of these causes likely have reciprocal effects on one another. These reciprocal effects are important because they highlight the importance of comprehensive efforts to control delinquency. For example, trying to reduce delinquent peer associations will be quite difficult unless one also addresses those individual characteristics and family problems that help maintain such associations. Further, the causes may sometimes interact with one another in their effect on delinquency. For example, association with delinquent peers is more likely to lead to delinquency among those low in self-control (Wright et al. 2001). Knowledge of such interaction effects also has important policy implications. For example, such knowledge may allow us to reduce the

negative effects of delinquent peer association in those situations where it is difficult to reduce contact with delinquent peers.

Mainstream theories, then, have much to say about the causes of female delinquency. Much is still to be learned, however. In particular, there is a strong need for research that (a) considers a broad range of causes, (b) is longitudinal, (c) includes a good portion of serious offenders, (d) analyzes males separately from females, (e) explores reciprocal and interactive effects, and (f) takes into account possible class and racial/ethnic differences in causal effects (Cernkovich and Giordano 1992; Chesney-Lind and Shelden 2004; Giordano 1978; Heimer 1995; Simpson and Elis 1995; Simpson and Gibbs 2005). In addition, we need research that examines the ways in which the larger social environment, such as the community in which people reside, impacts the causes of delinquency described in this chapter. Further, mainstream theories need to be better integrated with feminist theories and research to provide more complete information on the mechanisms by which gender influences the level and sometimes the effect of the aforementioned causes on delinquency.

Reading 9: The State of Public School Violence

A Quandary

By Anthony Troy Adams

A spate of shootings throughout the United States has permanently marred the public's perception about schools as safe and secure places where students learn and teachers teach. An example of this is the April 20, 1999, high school massacre that occurred in Littleton, Colorado. That incident of senseless killing left 12 students and one teacher dead and 21 other students directly injured by their assailants, Eric David Harris and Dylon Bennett Klebold. Another instance of youth violence occurred on the schoolyard March 24, 1998, in Jonesboro, Arkansas. Thirteen-year-old Mitchell Johnson and 11-year-old Andrew Golden opened fire on their classmates killing Natalie Brooks, Stephanie Johnson, Brittany Varner, Paige Ann Herring, and Shannon Wright, their teacher who was pregnant at the time. The gunshot blasts also seriously wounded one other teacher and ten students.

Despite these tragedies, violence in the nation's public schools appears to be on the wane. The Centers for Disease Control and Prevention reports that violence-related behaviors in school settings actually decreased during the 12-year period from 1991 to 2003. The 2007 CDC Youth Risk Behavior Surveillance report notes countrywide, 5.5% of students did not attend school on at least one day within 30 days because they felt unsafe going to and from school or unsafe at school. The findings of the survey indicated greater absenteeism from school among black (6.6%) and Hispanic (9.6%) than white (4%) students because of safety concerns. The fear of violence on school grounds is very prevalent as 18% of students had carried a weapon (e.g., a gun, knife, or club), with higher percentages of males (28.5%) than females (7.5%) students carrying weapons. Additionally, when examining the trends by gender and race/ethnicity, a higher percent of white males (30.3%) in contrast to black males (24.6%) or Hispanic males (28.2%) and larger numbers of black females (10%) and Hispanic females (9%) than white females (6.1%) (Centers for Disease Control and Prevention, 2008).

This chapter has a sixfold purpose: (1) to deconstruct school violence by examining popular conceptualizations of the phenomenon and incorporating a comprehensive view; (2) to present recent statistics on the prevalence of school violence in Michigan; (3) to explore indicators of factors linked to school violence; (4) to describe traditional theories of deviance related to school violence, critiquing them in terms of their utility for explaining school violence; (5) to examine how schools manage school violence, focusing on the relationship of school violence to exclusionary disciplinary techniques (i.e., suspension and expulsion), the medicalization of discipline, school uniform and zero-tolerance policies, and the deleterious effect of various managerial responses to violence and discipline; and (6) to describe the status of African American youth in Michigan. The last of these purposes is intended to elicit dialogue among parents, teachers and aspiring educators, administrators, researchers, policymakers, and concerned individuals. The chapter closes with several policy recommendations that can serve as a baseline for stimulating further conversation on the topic of school violence.

Deconstructing School Violence

School violence is often conceptualized as a generic or umbrella term. It includes many other social constructs. For example, school disturbance, indiscipline among youth, misbehavior, and asocial behavior are frequently associated with school violence (Adams, 2000; Crews & Counts, 1997). In recent years, however, the term has grown in popularity. This is partly due to the media frenzy that typically accompanies coverage of feature stories. The public's lack of a critical understanding about school violence exacerbates the oftentimes wild coverage in the news. I employ a two-pronged definition of school violence. First, school violence involves any act that harms or has the potential to harm students in or around school buildings. Such acts may include, but are not limited to, emotional and physical threats, bullying, assaults (including those of a domestic nature), rape, homicide, and possession of firearms or other deadly weapons.

Second, I widen the aperture on school violence by incorporating what Epp and Watkinson (1997) call *systemic violence*. Systemic violence is broad-based. It transcends victims and perpetrators; it considers school culture vis-à-vis the organization, leadership, and pedagogy. According to Epp and Watkinson, "Systemic violence is any institutionalized practice or procedure that adversely impacts on disadvantaged individuals or groups by burdening them psychologically, mentally, culturally, spiritually, economically, or physically. It is perpetrated by those with power, entitlement, and privilege against those with less" (1997, 5). This definition closely parallels Freire's (1970) philosophy of education, which asserts that any situation in which people are prevented from learning is one of violence.

Prevalence of School Violence in Michigan

Findings from the *School Safety Practices Report* (2001–2) include the following statistics about Michigan's public school districts:

- The rates of juvenile crime in Michigan's schools are drastically lower than the rates of juvenile crime within the state generally.
- Incidents involving physical assault, drugs or narcotics, and non-firearm-related incidents together accounted for 58 percent of all reported expulsions.
- Out of the approximately 1.7 million students enrolled in Michigan's public schools, 1,588 students (one-tenth of 1 percent) have a record of expulsion.
- Compared to other ethnic groups, African American students received a greater percentage of long-term (180 days or more) expulsions. African American students were expelled at higher rates than their prevalence in the general student population would predict.
- African American male expulsions represent 66.3 percent of all African American students expelled.
- African American students represent 19.5 percent of the Michigan public school student population but nearly two-fifths (39 percent) of all students expelled.

What Are the Indicators of Factors Linked to School Violence?

Minogue, Kingery, and Murphy (1999) list eight factors linked to school violence. These factors include (1) community characteristics, (2) family characteristics, (3) school climate, (4) substance abuse, (5) student engagement at school, (6) occurrences that instigate violence, (7) attitudes favoring violence, and (8) weapon possession at school or on campus grounds. The categories are not discrete. For instance, an act of violence may occur both because of school climate and because of family characteristics, making it difficult to disentangle a complex web of influences. As factor (1) indicates, community (structural features) factors are correlates of school violence as well (Adams, 1993; Cooley, Turner, & Beidel, 1995; Elliot, 1996; Farrell, Danish, & Howard, 1992; Farrell & Bruce, 1997; Gottfredson & Gottfredson, 1985; Hellman, 1986; National Institute of Education, 1978; Needleman et al., 1996). The effects of unemployment and under-employment of adults and youth, involvement of youth in violence, drug trafficking, gangs, and the proliferation of community blight (e.g., abandoned, boarded-up, and unoccupied dwelling units) may also affect the levels of violence occurring inside schools (Williams, Stiffman, & O'Neal, 1998). Schools tend to be mirror images of the neighborhoods and communities that engulf them. Community characteristics are also likely to affect the school organization in many unfavorable ways (e.g., unemployment, community-crime, normlessness, etc.).

Family risk and community factors may be linked to school violence (Bennett-Johnson, 2004). Family dynamics may also differentially affect school violence. For example, Dryfoos

(1990) and Burton and Owen (1990) maintain that the absence of a parent, family poverty, parents' education, family approaches to handling conflict, parental and/or family involvement in their offspring's education, and parental substance abuse and past or present criminal activity can affect school violence. Family structure is a likely antecedent of school violence.

School climate is widely accepted as a correlate of school violence. The literature on the impact of school climate on violence in schools is comprehensive, spanning nearly three decades (Adams, 1993; Fitzpatrick & Boldizar, 1993; Gottfredson, 1986; Gottfredson & Gottfredson, 1985; Grossnickle, Bialk, & Panagiotaros, 1993; Hill, 1997; Jenkins, 1997; Moles, 1990; Toby, 1983; Walsh, 1995; Welsh, 2000). The availability school security and surveillance technology, whether consistent and fair application of school rules is practiced, the types of penalties, adherence to procedural due process, accurate reporting of school infractions, and sufficient training and staff have all been identified as potentially influencing school violence. Whether students perceive that academic excellence is encouraged, and that diversity is promoted and embraced, may also be related to the level of school violence (National Institute of Education, 1978).

Mounting evidence suggests that substance abuse in schools may intensify the level of school violence (Allen et al., 1997; Farrell, Danish, & Howard, 1992). Widespread substance abuse and corollary drug trafficking in the neighborhoods surrounding a school can increase the level of violence on schoolyards. Drug trafficking in schools and the local neighborhood environment may be associated with any number of drug-related permutations, including turf battles between gangs, competition for "customers," and physical violence both on and off campus. Substance abuse and drug trafficking are likely precursors to schools marred by violence.

A number of empirical studies suggest that student engagement, or lack thereof, contributes to school violence (Hanish & Guerra, 2000; Noonan, 2005; McNeely and Falci, 2004). Schools that promote academic excellence, have a diverse curriculum, and offer significant numbers of Advanced Placement courses have been found to experience less school violence than those schools that do not (Gottfredson & Gottfredson, 1985; McDermott, 1980). More broadly, this suggests that schools where unequal educational opportunities are prevalent; there is a greater likelihood for disobedience and violence (Lawrence, 1998; Polk, 1982; Jencks et al., 1972). Students that have greater "access" to educational opportunities in schools, including Advanced Placement courses, state-of-the-art facilities and equipment, extracurricular and extramural activities, and the resources to attract sought-after teachers and staff, may experience less school violence. An unexpected outcome, or latent function, of schools offering extensive extracurricular activities (e.g., band, sports, drama, and student government) is that fewer students are likely to feel alienated or disconnected. These activities can serve as social buffers. Extracurricular and extramural activities may discourage students from asocial behaviors and reduce the potential for school violence (Gottfredson & Gottfredson, 1985; Noonan, 2005).

The research on bullying has increased sharply. Students' experiences of being hassled, shoved, insulted, disrespected ("dissed"), annoyed, bullied, teased, bossed around, dared, talked about, called names, or disliked can also lead to school violence (Berman et al., 1996; Durant, Pendergrast, & Cadenhead, 1994; Espelage & Swearer, 2003). The extent to which students feel alienated, isolated, or polarized is an additional factor that can lead to school disorganization and school violence.

Some school cultures promote violence; other school cultures mitigate violence. A school's level of violence is, in part, a function of its uniqueness. We know that school cultures vary. No two school cultures are identical. School cultures differ according to the percentage of minority and nonminority students, socioeconomic status, and values and beliefs. Prevailing student attitudes can affect the level of school violence. Attitudinal factors that may be related to violence are students' admiration for peers who are well-versed at fighting and using weapons as well as their beliefs that students should defend themselves when confronted (and conversely that avoidance of conflict is cowardice). Fighting impresses some students. Some believe that instigation by others makes fighting inevitable. Such belief orientations, confounded by the influences of peers or intimate playgroups (reference groups), school culture, and family have an impact on the social organization of schools. These factors in turn heighten the potential for school violence. Social organizations and prevailing attitudes that glorify violence are almost certain to fuel emotions and spark violence.

Lastly, the availability of weapons in and around schools is another factor related to school violence. Potential weapons are ubiquitous. Knifes, guns, brass knuckles, clubs and bats, bricks and boards, scissors, explosives, razor blades, and school-related tools or equipment have been confiscated from students accused of assault on school campuses (Callahan & Rivara, 1992; Clough, 1994; Shapiro et al., 1998). The availability of makeshift weapons and the proliferation of firearms in public schools is a growing concern (Callahan & Rivara, 1992; Clough, 1994; Durant, Pendergrast, & Cadenhead, 1994; Durant et al., 1997). Although detection and surveillance equipment are widely used, more deliberate planning measures are called for. Careful thought must go into developing ways to identify and confiscate weapons before they can be brought into school buildings while guaranteeing students' right to privacy. Moreover, developing ways to deter students from using school-related tools or equipment (e.g., rulers, pencils, lab equipment, etc.) as weapons should be a reigning priority.

Traditional Theories Explaining School Violence

Three sociological theories of deviance are examined in this section. First, Merton's (1938) strain theory posits that a mismatch exists between culturally defined goals (e.g., material success, wealth, higher education, etc.) and culturally defined means for achieving those goals (e.g., quality schooling and education, Protestant work ethic, etc.). For instance, youths may embezzle, steal, sell illicit drugs, or cheat on examinations to achieve culturally prescribed goals of success (e.g., expensive watches, designer clothing, performing well in school, etc.). Strain theory predicts that some individuals will not conform to society's conventional goals, but instead they will achieve culturally defined goals by inventing ways to attain those goals. Students, for example, who break into school lockers and sell items to purchase trendy athletic apparel often do so to impress their peers. Expensive clothing provides some students with a modicum or "illusion" of success. Students on the fringes may feel equal to their middle-class schoolmates because they too have designer shoes, boots, and garments and accessories.

Behavioral theorist Edwin Sutherland's (1974) differential association theory posits that deviance is a by-product of social interaction. Sutherland asserts that delinquency and other misbehaviors are learned and reinforced through group acceptance and validation. Unacceptable forms of behavior may become the norm. Particularly for youth that internalize belief systems that run counter to socially acceptable forms of behavior, certain deviant acts become acceptable when youths are in the company of those who condone asocial behavior.

Hirschi's (1969) social control theory provides an alternative lens to examine school violence. According Hirschi, some deviance is tempting, but the risk of being caught, sanctioned, or punished keeps most people in check. For those with nothing to lose, however, deviance is attractive. They are more likely to violate rules. Social control theory is predicated upon the idea that *attachment, opportunity, involvement,* and *beliefs* determine the likelihood of deviance. Strong familial, work group, or organizational attachment coupled with strong beliefs in conventional morality and respect for authority figures encourages conformity. Moreover, it also creates situations that lead to access to legitimate opportunities.

What are the Criticisms of Traditional Theories of School Violence?

Strain, differential association, and control theories have several limitations. The predictive power of strain theory is delimited. It assumes that youths, in general, and Black youth more specifically, live out their daily experiences concerned about their future and long-term aspirations. Moreover, strain theory assumes that students of color are cognizant of culturally defined goals. Youth aspirations are strongly influenced by parents, family, peers, schools, reference groups, media, and cultural (as well as subcultural) variation. Peer and media influences are like juggernauts. They represent a vexing problem for educators, and there is no clear causal connection between youth aspirations and school violence.

Differential association theory offers limited predictive power too. It predicts that deviance is the result of "negative" intimate social interaction among playmates. Notwithstanding the potential for peer influences, many factors provide social buffers and discourage student involvement in school violence. Social buffers, such as consistent adult supervision, extended family involvement, participation in extracurricular activities, and exposure to positive role models have been shown to reduce youths' propensity for violence. Some youths may join youth gangs regardless of the presence of these factors in their lives. They may participate in some illegal activities (e.g., smoking marijuana, drinking under the legal age) but abstain from others (e.g., criminal involvement, including auto theft, grand larceny, etc.).

Control theory is a distant cousin of strain theory. Control theory combines a number of the ideas about the causes of deviant behavior expressed in strain theory. For that reason it too has several limitations. First, control theory does not significantly enhance our understanding of deviant behavior beyond differential association theory's contribution. It is an amalgamation. Second, it operates from the presumption that weak attachment, limited access to legitimate opportunities and involvement, and lack of beliefs consistent with conventional morality are precursors to social deviance. Control theory thus fails to acknowledge the effects of familial, socioeconomic, cultural, and structural antecedents on deviance. The various concepts associated with control theory (e.g., attachment, opportunity, etc.) have been difficult to test empirically.

Public School Attempts to Manage Violence

This section explores several instruments of social control. Social control refers to any method used to regulate, suppress, subdue, or restrict group behavior. High school codes of conduct are an example. They spell out in detailed terms appropriate forms of deportment. Codes of conduct also articulate school norms and the penalties associated with rule violation (e.g., student-to-teacher insubordination results in a suspension of not more than five concurrent days). Public schools often have elaborate codes of conduct. Exclusionary techniques, including suspensions and expulsions, are two mechanisms public schools use to manage disruptive behavior.

Suspensions come in three forms. In-school, short-term, and long-term suspensions are used to deter and regulate student misbehavior. With in-school suspensions students are supervised by adults or certified staff, and a reasonable amount of instruction may take place. Importantly, students remain in school under the supervision of adults. Short-term suspensions (typically one to five days) and long-term suspensions (which vary in length according to school district and state laws) are used to reduce the number of nonthreatening behaviors (e.g., quarrelsome students, insubordination). Short-term suspensions are handled by principals and assistant principals. They may or may not require procedural due process proceedings. That depends on the gravity of the offense (e.g., whether there is a perceived threat or danger to other students).

Out-of-school suspensions are less desirable for several reasons. First, students who are disciplined using out-of-school suspensions are generally unsupervised by adults. This can increase their opportunity for delinquent behavior and crime (Adams, 1994). Second, suspended students may befriend youth who are predisposed to delinquent or criminal activity. Third, students may engage in risk-taking behaviors while suspended, including drug, alcohol, and substance abuse. Fourth, out-of-school suspension can derail students from the educative process, and increase the odds of dropping out (DeRidder, 1990). Finally, long-term suspension may undermine students' respect for authority, leading them to behave in ways that increase the chances of their removal from school. Concerns have been raised about over escalating rates of exclusionary disciplinary practices in America's schools (Adams, 2000, 144–46).

Expulsion is another social control apparatus used by schools. Only local school boards have the authority to expel students. Expulsion is the permanent denial and deprivation of schooling, typically for a period of not more than one year. African American and Hispanic male students are significantly more likely to be expelled and suspended from public schools (Skiba, Nardo, & Peterson, 2000).

The medicalization of discipline has become another mechanism through which schools manage violence. Over the last 50 years, the influence of psychiatry and medicine has led to the medicalization of discipline. Students' moral and legal deviance has been transformed from adolescent indiscretions into a medical predisposition (Macionis, 2006). As a result, youths are not blamed for misbehaving, nor are their parents accused of poor parenting skills. Instead, students misbehave because they have a "medical" problem. Attention Deficit Disorder (ADD) and Attention Deficit Hyperactive Disorder (ADHD) are two frequently diagnosed disorders among school-aged children. Both illnesses have medically recognizable symptoms (American Psychiatric Association, 1994). Methylphenidate and amphetamine stimulants have become the most widely used treatments for ADD and ADHD, which are characterized by some or all of the following symptoms:

- Difficulty with selective attention
- Poor impulse control
- Inability to maintain appropriate task-related activities
- Difficulty with organization of cognitive tasks
- Failure to recognize and respond to social cues
- Poor ability to follow directions or instructions
- Easy distraction by extraneous stimuli

Several dilemmas accompany the medicalization of discipline. First, African American and Hispanic males are more likely to be diagnosed as having either ADD or ADHD (MacMillian & Reschly, 1998). Students diagnosed with these conditions are often treated differently by their teachers (e.g., low expectations, increased disciplinary referrals). Second, because the diagnostics for assessing ADD and ADHD lack precision, many children are misdiagnosed. Overdiagnosis is a critical problem as well. The above-mentioned symptoms are ubiquitous in the general population. They can be easily masked by individual emotional and psychological duress, familial dysfunctions (e.g., physical abuse, inadequate childcare), and structural antecedents (e.g., poverty, nutritional deficiencies). To state the point alternatively, there is great potential for false-positive diagnoses.

According to Pfuhl and Henry (1993), the medicalization of discipline enhances public schools' administrative efficiency at the expense of due process. School administrators can do a tap dance around students' constitutional guarantees. They can recommend that disruptive students be seen by medical personnel. Subsequently these students are evaluated by school psychologists, social workers, or other professionals. These professionals have the legitimate authority to label disruptive students (e.g., ADD, ADHD, learning disabled, etc.). As a result of these labeling practices, students may be segregated or excluded from the educative process. "Medical discipline" is a clear example of how students can be deprived of fundamental guarantees of life and liberty, protected by the Fourteenth Amendment. Procedural due process is often ignored. It ensures that students have the right to *notification* (and official transcripts), access to *counsel*, and an opportunity to *confront their accuser*. Schools, in short, can control misbehaving youths by justifying therapeutic interventions while they deny students their constitutional rights.

The use of pharmaceutical treatments, including methylphenidate and amphetamine stimulants for attention disorders, has increased exponentially in recent decades. Two indicators provide evidence of this surge: the United States Drug Enforcement Agency's aggregate production quotas (APQ) for all Schedule I and II controlled substances, and the Food and Drug Administration's sales and inventory data on the amounts of these substances used for legitimate medical and research purposes. As Woodworth states:

> The methylphenidate quota has increased from 1,768 kilograms in 1990 at which time there were 2 bulk manufacturers and 4 dosage-form manufacturers. This year [1999], the APQ is 14,957 kilograms with 6 bulk manufacturers and 19 dosage form manufacturers. Prior to 1991, domestic sales reported by manufacturers of methylphenidate remained stable at approximately 2,000 kilograms per year. By 1999, domestic sales increased nearly 500 percent. (2000, 2)

Nationwide, the average methylphenidate quota was 3,082 grams per 100,000 people in 1999. Methylphenidate treatment for ADD and ADHD is widespread in the state of Michigan, which ranked third in its use of the drug, distributing 4,848 grams per 100,000 people. Table 1 offers a geographical perspective on the distribution of methylphenidate nationwide. It provides a list of the top 10 methylphenidate-using states for 1999 (U.S. Drug Enforcement Administration, 2000).

The increase in the production and use of methylphenidate is more compelling when compared to worldwide usage. According to a report of the United Nations International Narcotics Control Board (1999), the United States produces and consumes about 85% of the world's production of methylphenidate. The vast majority of all U.S. prescriptions for methylphenidate are written for children diagnosed with ADHD. More than 50% of those prescriptions are written by pediatricians. Boys are four times more likely to be prescribed stimulant medication.

Table 1. Top Ten States for Methylphenidate Use, 1999

Rank	State	Grams Per 100K
1	New Hampshire	5,524
2	Vermont	5,005
3	**Michigan**	**4,848**
4	Iowa	4,638
5	Delaware	4,439
6	Massachusetts	4,318
7	South Dakota	4,235
8	Virginia	4,207
9	Minnesota	3,941
10	Maryland	3,935

Source: U.S. Drug Enforcement Administration, 2000.

Given the disturbingly high levels of methylphenidate production in the United States and the many lingering questions surrounding its use, one wonders how many African American students are being senselessly subjected to stimulant treatment for ADD and ADHD. Worse still, how many are suffering from methylphenidate's noted side effects, including stomach pains, appetite loss, seizures, severe headaches, agitation, aggression, and possible carcinogenic exposure? Children by their very nature are energetic, hyperactive, reactive to stimuli, and impulsive. When and why did we as a society decide that they needed to be "medicated" to be educated?

Public school uniform policies are another managerial approach aimed at reducing school violence. The first districtwide public school uniform policy was implemented in the Long Beach (California) Unified School District (LBUSD) in 1994. The LBUSD policy was institutionalized to reduce peer competition and strife associated with students' wearing or lacking name-brand clothing. It was pegged as a "cure-all" for many of the problems plaguing public schools. In the 10 years following the first implementation of the LBUSD policy, approximately one-quarter of the nation's public schools—mostly elementary schools and disproportionately those schools serving poor and minority students—were enforcing some kind of standardized school uniform policy (Brunsma, 2006). Are school uniform policies inversely correlated with school violence?

The empirical evidence linking school uniform policies and school violence is inconclusive. A great deal of media attention and public debate surrounded the publication of Stanley's (1996) study on the impact of the Long Beach Unified School District's school uniform policy. Although inconclusive, the study maintained that students' behavioral problems and gang-related activities decreased following implementation of the standardized uniform policy; however, very few published accounts since have tested theories, used rigorous methodologies, or collected sound empirical evidence to test the worth of Stanley's assertion. Indeed, the literature on school uniform policies is fraught with methodological problems.

Much of the discussion about such policies stems from anecdotal statements, news articles, and policy reports; while the bulk of the research examining the relationship between school uniform policies and school violence emanates from doctoral dissertations. From 1994 to 2004, twenty-five dissertations examined the issue of school uniforms. Brunsma (2006) contends that these dissertations vary widely in quality and depth. Some are largely descriptive; others use multivariate approaches to account for "between-group" variation linking the effects of school uniform policies to attendance, disciplinary referrals, and classroom environments (Burke, 1993; Hughes, 2006). Many of the dissertations relied upon small and nonrandomized samples. Sampling errors are plentiful with small samples, and many of the studies were cross-sectional. To confound matters, many of these studies were not subjected to the scrutiny of the peer review process. More research on the impact of school uniform policies on school violence is needed. The school uniforms literature has failed to develop and test theories, impose strict methodological adherence, and feed further discourse.

The literature on school uniform policy and its outcomes also suffers from conceptual and methodological problems. First, the very notion of conceptualizing school uniforms is a murky proposition. Researchers have not reached consensus on what exactly constitutes a school "uniform," and for this reason conceptual clarity remains tentative. School uniform policies can be placed on a continuum. They can range from uniforms that require polo shirts, navy pants, and solid-colored shoes to the more restrictive policies that require sport jackets adorned with iconic symbols. These uniforms are reminiscent of those worn by students attending elite boarding schools. In fact, Fossen (2002) distinguishes between distinctive uniforms that identify the wearer as a group member (e.g., uniforms bearing school-specific iconography) and uniforms that are nonrestrictive dress (e.g., not bearing school-specific iconography); he latter he called common or standard dress. Hughes (2006) uses a bifurcated framework to distinguish uniform types, describing casual uniform policies as *modes of dress*. He labels as *formal* those dress policies that require students to purchase uniforms from uniform companies.

Another method that educators employ in curbing school violence is zero-tolerance policies. These stringent conduct codes have been adopted by urban school districts as a means to manage and deter violence. Historically, zero-tolerance policies evolved from federal drug enforcement terminology in the 1980s. The intent of school districts that deploy zero-tolerance policies is to send a message. This school response makes it loud and clear that certain behaviors will not be tolerated. Zero-tolerance policies are fraught with problems. For instance, there is no causal link between zero-tolerance policies and violence reduction (Skiba & Peterson, 1999). Second, numerous civil rights controversies have arisen because of the broadness of many zero-tolerance policies (Skiba & Peterson, 1999). Third, significant numbers of African American and Hispanic students have been suspended or expelled from school for relatively minor offenses. Fourth, low-income students are overrepresented in suspension and expulsion statistics. Racial disproportionality persists, even after controlling for social class. It is the author's opinion that zero-tolerance policies have the deleterious effect of derailing large numbers of already marginalized students from the educational process. This further undermines students' respect for authority figures and deprives them of education they so desperately need. Zero-tolerance approaches have also been shown to lead to the indiscriminate use of suspension and expulsion (Essex, 2001; Skiba and Leone, 2001; Skiba & Peterson, 1999; Civil Rights Project & Advancement Project, 2000), and no evidence confirms that suspension and expulsion change students' behaviors or have additional school safety benefits.

References

Adams, A. T. (1993). Violence in public secondary schools: The contributions of community structure and school factors. *Journal of Applied Sociology, 10,* 75–98.

Adams, A. T. (1994). The economic determinants of high school punishments: A travesty of justice. Paper presented at the annual meeting of the Eastern Sociological Society, Baltimore, March.

Adams, A. T. (2000). The status of school discipline and violence. *Annals of the Academy of Political and Social Science, 567,* 140–56.

Allen, T. J., Moller, F. G., Rhodes, H. M., & Cherek, D. R. (1997). Subjects with a history of drug dependence are more aggressive than subjects with no drug use history. *Drug and Alcohol Dependence, 46,* 95–103.

American Psychiatric Association. (1994). Diagnostic criteria from DSM-IV. Washington, D.C.: The Association.

Bennett-Johnson, E. (2004). The root of school violence: Causes and recommendations for a plan of action. *College Student Journal, 38*(2). Retrieved September 7, 2008 from http://findarticles.com/p/articles/mi_m0FCR/is_2_38/ai_n6130139.

Berman, S., Kurtines, W. M., Silverman, W., & Serafini, L. (1996). The impact of exposure to crime and violence on urban youth. *American Journal of Orthopsychiatry, 66*(3), 329–36.

Breuer, N., Lowry, R., Barrios, L., Simon, T., and Eaton D. (2005). Violence-related behaviors among high school students—United States, 1991–2003. *Journal of School Health, 75*(3), 81–85.

Brunsma, D. L. (2006). *Uniforms in public schools: A decade of research and debate.* Lanham, MD: Rowman & Littlefield Education.

Burke, N. D. (1993). *Restructuring gang clothing in the public schools. Education Law Report,* 513 (April), 391–404. Laramie: University of Wyoming College of Law.

Burton, D. L. & Owen, S. M. (1990). The relationship between trauma, family dysfunction, and the psychopathology in male juvenile offenders. Doctoral dissertation, Fuller Theological Seminary, Pasadena, CA.

Callahan, C. M. & Rivara, F. P. (1992). Urban high school youth and handguns: A school-based survey. *Journal of the American Medical Association, 267*(22), 3038–42.

Centers for Disease Control and Prevention (2008, June 6). *Youth risk behavior surveillance—United States, 2007.* Atlanta, GA: Centers for Disease Control and Prevention (CDC), U.S. Department of Health and Human Services.

Children's Defense Fund. (1975). *School suspensions: Are they helping children?* Cambridge, MA: Washington Research Project.

Civil Rights Project & Advancement Project. (2000). *Opportunities suspended: The devastating consequences of zero tolerance and school discipline policies.* Cambridge: Civil Rights Project, Harvard University.

Clough, J. B. (1994). Attitudes toward guns and violence. In L. L. Dahlberg, S. B. Toal, & C. B. Behrens (Eds.), *Measuring violence-related attitudes, beliefs, and behaviors among youths: A compendium of assessment tools,* 40–43. Atlanta: Centers for Disease Control and Prevention.

Cooley, M. R., Turner, S. M., & Beidel, D. C. (1995). Assessing community violence: The children's report of exposure to violence. *Journal of the American Academy of Child and Adolescent Psychiatry, 34*(2), 201–8.

Crews, G. A. & Counts, M. R. (1997). *The evolution of school disturbance in America: Colonial times to modern day.* Westport, CT: Praeger.

DeRidder, L. M. (1990). How suspension and expulsion contribute to dropping out. *Educational Horizons,* 153–57.

Dryfoos, J. (1990). *Adolescents at risk: Prevalence and prevention.* New York: Oxford University Press.

Durant, R. H. (1996). Intentions to use violence among young adolescents. *Pediatrics, 98*(6), 1104–8.

Durant, R. H., Kahn, J., Beckford, P. H., & Woods, E. R. (1997). The association of weapon carrying and fighting on school property and other health risk and problem behaviors among high school students. *Archives of Pediatric Adolescent Medicine, 151,* 360–66.

Durant, R. H., Pendergrast, R. A., & Cadenhead, C. (1994). Exposure to violence and victimization and fighting behavior by urban Black adolescents. *Journal of Adolescent Health, 15,* 311–18.

Elliot, D. S. (1996). The effects of neighborhood disadvantage on adolescent development. *Journal of Research in Crime and Delinquency, 33*(4), 389–426.

Epp, J. R. & Watkinson, A. M. (1997). *Systemic violence in education: Promise broken.* Albany: State University of New York Press.

Espelage, D. L. & Swearer, S. M. (2003). Research on school bullying and victimization: What have we learned and where do we go from here? *School Psychology Review, 32*(3), 365–83.

Essex, N. L. (2001). The limits of zero tolerance. *Principal Leadership, 1*(8), 5–7.

Farrell, A. & Bruce, S. E. (1997). Impact of exposure to community violence on violent behavior and emotional distress among urban adolescents. *Journal of Clinical Psychology, 26*(1), 2–14.

Farrell, A., Danish, S. J., and Howard, C. W. (1992). Risk factors for drug use in urban adolescents: Identification and cross-validation. *American Journal of Community Psychology, 20*(3), 263–86.

Fitzpatrick, K. M. & Boldizar, J. P. (1993). The prevalence and consequences of exposure to violence among African American youth. *Journal of the American Academy of Child and Adolescent Psychiatry, 32*(2), 424–30.

Fossen, L. L. A. (2002). School uniforms and sense of school as a community: Perceptions of belonging, safety, and caring relationships in urban school settings. Doctoral dissertation, University of Houston.

Freire, P. (M. B. Ramos, transl.). (1970). *Pedagogy of the oppressed.* New York: Seabury Press.

Gottfredson, D. C. (1986). An empirical test of school-based environmental and individual interventions to reduce the risk of delinquent behavior. *Criminology, 24,* 705–31.

Gottfredson, G. & Gottfredson, D. (1985). *Victimization in schools.* New York: Plenum Press.

Grossnickle, D. R., Bialk, T. J., & and Panagiotaros, B. C. (1993). The school discipline climate survey: Toward a safe, orderly learning environment. *NASSP Bulletin, 77,* 60–69.

Hanish, L. D. & Guerra, N. G. (2000). Children who get victimized at school: What is known? what can be done? *Professional School Counseling, 4*(2), 113–19.

Hellman, D. A. (1986). The pattern of violence in urban public schools: The influence of school and community. *Journal of Research in Crime and Delinquency, 23,* 102–27.

Hill, S. C. (1997). School-related violence: A secondary analysis of the youth risk behavior survey data (1993 and 1995). Doctoral dissertation, Southern Illinois University at Carbondale.

Hirschi, T. (1969). *Causes of delinquency.* Berkeley: University of California Press.

Holzer, H. J., Edelman, P., & Offner, P. (2006). *Reconnecting disadvantaged young men.* Washington, DC: Urban Institute Press.

Hughes, E. (2006). Effects of mandated school uniforms on student attendance, discipline referrals, and classroom environment. In D. L. Brunsma (Ed.), *Uniforms in public schools: A decade of research and debate.* Lanham, MD: Rowman & Littlefield Education.

Jencks, C., Smith, M., Acland, H., Bane, M. J., Cohen, D., Ginits, M., Heyns, B., and Michelson, S. (1972). *Inequality: A reassessment of the effect of family and schooling in America.* New York: Basic Books.

Jenkins, P. H. (1997). School delinquency and the school social bond. *Journal of Research in Crime and Delinquency, 34,* 337–67.

Lawrence, R. (1998). *School crime and juvenile justice.* New York: Oxford University Press.

Macionis, J. J. (2006). *Society: The basics.* Upper Saddle River, NJ: Pearson Prentice Hall.

MacMillian, D. L. & Reschly, D. J. (1998). Overrepresentation of minority students: The case for greater specificity or reconsideration of the variables examined. *Journal of Special Education, 32*(1), 15–24.

McDermott, J. (1980). High anxiety: Fear of crime in secondary schools. *Contemporary Education, 52,* 3–8.

McNeely, C. & Falci, C. (2004). School connectedness and the transition into and out of health-risk behavior among adolescents: A comparison of social belonging and teacher support. *Journal of School Health, 74*(7), 284–92.

Merton, R. (1938). Social structure and anomie. *American Sociological Review, 3*(6), 672–82.

Minogue, N., Kingery, P., & Murphy, L. (1999). *Approaches to assessing violence among youth.* Washington, DC: Hamilton Fish National Institute on School and Community Violence.

Moles, O. C. (1990). *Student discipline strategies.* Albany: State University of New York Press.

National Institute of Education. (1978). *Violent schools—safe schools: The safe school study report to Congress.* Washington, DC: U.S. Government Printing Office.

Needleman, H. L., Riess, J. A., Tobin, M. J., Biesecker, G. E., & Greenhouse, J. B. (1996). Bone lead levels and delinquent behavior. *Journal of the American Academy of Medicine, 275*(5), 363–69.

Noonan, J. (2005). School climate and the safe school: Seven contributing factors. Safety in the schools. *Educational Horizons, 83*(1), 61–65. Pfuhl, E. H. & Henry, S. (1993). *The deviance process.* New York: Aldine de Gruyter.

Polk, K. (1982). Curriculum tracking and delinquency: Some observations. *American Sociological Review, 47,* 282–84.

School safety practices report. (2001–2). Lansing: Michigan Department of Education.

Shapiro, J. P., Dorman, R. L., Welker, C., & Clough, J. B. (1998). Youth attitudes towards guns and violence: Relations with sex, age, ethnic group, and firearm exposure. *Journal of Clinical Child Psychology, 27*(1), 98–108.

Skiba, R. J. & Leone, P. (2001). Zero tolerance and school security measures: a failed experiment. In T.J. Johnson, J.E. Boyden, & W. Pittz (Eds), *Racial profiling and punishment in U.S. schools*, 34–38. Oakland, CA: Applied Research Center.

Skiba, R. J., Nardo, A. C., & Peterson, R. (2000). *The color of discipline: Source of racial and gender disproportionality in school punishment.* Bloomington: Indiana Education Policy Center.

Skiba, R. J. & Peterson, R. (1999). The dark side of zero-tolerance: Can punishment lead to safe schools? *Phi Delta Kappan, 80*(5), 372–82.

Stanley, M. S. (1996). School uniforms and safety. *Education and Urban Society, 28*(4), 424–35.

Sutherland, E. H. (1974). *Criminology* (9th ed.). Philadelphia: Lippincott.

Toby, J. (1983). Violence in school. In M. Tonry & N. Morris (Eds.), *Crime and justice: An annual review of research*, vol. 4, 1–47. Chicago: University of Chicago Press.

United Nations International Narcotics Control Board. (1999), *Narcotics control board releases report on worldwide use of controlled drugs*. INCB Annual Report Embargo, February, Release No. 2.

U.S. Drug Enforcement Administration (2000). Www.house.gov/ed_workforce/hearings/106th/ecyf/ritalin51600/woodworth.htm.

Walsh, M. (1995). The relationship of exposure to community violence with posttraumatic stress disorder and expression of anger in adolescents. Doctoral dissertation, Fordham University.

Welsh, W. N. (2000). The effects of school climate on school disorder. *Annals of the American Academy of Political and Social Science*, (January), 88–107.

Williams, J. H., Stiffman, A. R., & O'Neal, J. L. (1998). Violence among urban African American youths: An analysis of environmental and behavioral risk factors. *Social Work Research, 22*, 3–13.

Woodworth, T. (2000). *Statement of Terrance Woodworth, Deputy Director Office of Diversion Control, Drug Enforcement Administration, before the Committee on Education and the Workforce Subcommittee on Early Childhood, Youth Families*. http://www.house.gov/ed_worforcehearings/106th/ecyf/ritalin51600/woodworth.htm.

Questions to Think About

1. What are the limits of current theories of deviance in describing the reasons for public school violence?
2. How do zero tolerance policies and dress codes affect school discipline?
3. Which theory best describes female juvenile delinquency? Why?
4. Why is one policy not necessarily enough for reducing female juvenile delinquency? What other factors should policymakers take into account?

Resources

 Centers for Disease Control—School violence fact sheet and other useful information: http://www.cdc.gov/violenceprevention/youthviolence/schoolviolence/data_stats.html

 National School Safety Center:
http://www.schoolsafety.us/

 PBS: The Big Picture: Crime and punishment in South Carolina:
http://www.pbs.org/video/1592647999/

 Immigrants and Crime: Shows differences in perspectives on immigrant crime:
http://www.pbs.org/video/2365526647/

 Office of Juvenile Justice: Girls at Risk:
www.ojjdp.gov/programs/girlsatrisk.html

 Office of Juvenile Justice: Causes and Correlates of Girls' Delinquency:
http://www.ojjdp.gov/publications/PubAbstract.asp?pubi=248352

SECTION VI
EDUCATION

Introduction

Although education and schooling are often assumed to mean the same thing, they are actually two different concepts. Anyone can be educated, even if a person never attended school. Parents teach their children how to take care of themselves, work on cars, farm, clean house, take care of animals, and a host of other important activities. Schooling, on the other hand, is the formalized mechanism of educating individuals. Today, we assume that to be educated students need to attend their local school or a private school. Students "graduate" from high school after attending the institution for twelve years. They then go out into the workforce or continue their formal education by attending college or a trade school. Most people think of this structure as "normal" and "natural" but in actuality schooling is a social construction. Society has defined, over time, what it means to be educated. For instance, in the 1800s and early 1900s students were expected to miss a lot of school when they were needed to work on the family farm. During this time, most people did not complete high school. In 1950, only 34 percent of adults age twenty-five and older had completed high school. By 2000 that number had increased to 80 percent.[12] As the need for more educated workers grew, the norms of society changed as well. Today it is difficult for anyone to get any job without at least a high school education, and increasingly higher education is becoming the norm rather than something only the very intelligent take on. Over time, the concept of schooling and what it means to be "educated" has changed.

In "Modern Mass Education," Stephen Sanderson traces the history of mass education from a conflict perspective. Unlike the structural-functional argument that asserts educational systems change to meet the needs of the society, Sanderson contends education systems benefit those who are well off. In this view, there is inequality even in those systems that seek to promote equality.

In the essay "Social Class, the Commodification of Education, and Space Through a Rural Lens," Michael Corbett uses three examples of schools to show

how the concept of "school" can have a different meaning depending on the spatial context. Using Marx's notion of commodification, or assigning a monetary value to a concept that should not be compared in this way, he maintains judging the "quality" of a school in quantitative terms (i.e., test scores) does not tell the whole story. The school environment reflects far more than test scores, such as the differences in the capital of the parents and the location. Corbin asserts this commodification is not appropriate for education and social class works in different ways depending on the space. A spatial perspective, he argues, is necessary for understanding educational systems.

Reading 10: Modern Mass Education

By Stephen K. Sanderson

One of the most striking features of the modern world is the enormous role that education has come to play in the lives of most individuals. Within the past century and a half, education has been transformed from a tiny social institution that had little relevance to the lives of most individuals into a large-scale, mass institution with a huge impact on most peoples' lives. This has been especially true in the rich democracies, but it is also true to a significant extent in less-developed countries. We can get a better appreciation of this by looking at what education was like in preindustrial societies.

Education in Historical Perspective

Randall Collins (1977) has pointed to three basic types of education found throughout the world's societies: education in practical skills, education for status-group membership, and bureaucratic education. *Practical-skill education* is designed to impart certain technical skills and capacities deemed to be important in performing occupational or other activities. In large-scale agrarian societies, scribes or specialists in record keeping needed to learn basic literacy and numeracy skills, and architects and engineers who designed and built monuments had to spend considerable time learning their crafts. Preindustrial forms of practical-skill education were often based on a master-apprentice form of teaching, but sometimes there were also schools providing more formal instruction. In ancient Mesopotamia and Egypt, for example, specialized schools were established to train children for careers as scribes (Collins 1977). Practical-skill education is also found in modern industrial societies, but not in the manner in which most people think. Much of primary education is practical-skill education, where literacy and numeracy are taught, but of course there are courses in geography, civics, history, science, and the like. These subjects provide practical skills, but in a more indirect and abstract form. They are considered to be important for a person to become a well-informed modern citizen.

Status-group education is conducted for the purpose of symbolizing and reinforcing the prestige and privilege of elite groups in highly stratified societies. It is generally designed to be impractical in any technical sense and is often given over to the learning and discussion of esoteric bodies of knowledge. It has been widely found in agrarian and industrial societies. As Collins (1977: 9–11) comments,

> In historical perspective, education has been used more often for organizing status groups than for other purposes. Since the defining locus of status-group activity is leisure and consumption, status-group education has been sharply distinguished from practical education by the exclusion of materially productive skills. Because status groups have used a common culture as a mark of group membership, status-group education has taken the form of a club and has included much ceremony to demonstrate group solidarity and to publicly distinguish members from nonmembers. This club aspect characterized the activities of Chinese gentlemen who met for genteel conversation and poetry writing, as well as the periodic festivals put on for the Greek public by students, an elite sector of the population.

> Status-group education, then, has been ceremonial, aesthetic, and detached from practical activities. Its rituals rarely have dramatized rankings within the group; formal grades, competitive examinations, and degrees usually have been absent. . . . The main distinctions have been between insiders and outsiders, not among members of the group. Frequently, there have been no formal attendance requirements, and the absence of formal degrees has reflected the fact that acquisition of the status group's culture is the object of education. . . .

> . . . In China, the first educated men were diviners or sages, who read oracles for the court and probably passed their skills along through apprenticeship. . . . [In later eras the] leisure pursuits of Chinese gentlemen . . . centered on poetry writing and painting; the prestigious form of sociability was the "literary gathering" where literature was read and discussed. . . .

> . . . In India, from the beginnings of literacy, education was closely associated with status-group prestige. Brahmin priests monopolized knowledge of the Vedic traditions and thereby helped not only to close off entry to their caste but also to legitimate the caste system. . . .

> Similarly, in the Heian court of early Japanese civilization (AD 1000), men and women courtiers developed an elaborate culture of poetry writing and art appreciation and even produced the first great Japanese works of prose fiction, largely through informal

family education. In the Islamic world, education developed from religious training in the holy scriptures and laws to a form of culture that, in the cosmopolitan cities of prosperous periods, provided entertainment and status for the wealthy. . . .

In Europe, informal education as the basis of status emulation was most prominent during the Renaissance, especially in the wealthy commercial cities of Italy, but also in Germany, the Netherlands, France, and England. Poetry writing and allusions to the classics were marks of prestige in every day social life.

Bureaucratic education is created by governments to serve either or both of two purposes: the recruitment of individuals to governmental or other positions and the socialization of the masses in order to win their political compliance. This type of education has generally placed great emphasis on examinations, attendance requirements, grades, and degrees. It has been common in several of the great historic civilizations, especially in those with centralized bureaucratic states. In classical China, for example, an elaborate form of bureaucratic education existed, the core of which was its examination system. Rigorous examinations had to be passed in order to gain entry to the important positions in the government bureaucracy. The higher the position, the more elaborate the series of examinations a candidate had to pass. Usually only a tiny fraction of degree candidates was allowed to pass each examination (Collins 1977).

Bureaucratic education has also characterized more contemporary societies. The creation of modern school systems clearly had a great deal to do with the emergence and consolidation of strong bureaucratic states in Europe (Collins 1977). As Collins (1977: 19) notes, "The militarily expansive and rigidly bureaucratized Prussian state led the way in the seventeenth and eighteenth centuries in building a public school system at the elementary and university levels and in drawing state officials from among holders of university degrees."

These different types of education are frequently combined in the same society. Agrarian societies, for example, often combined all three types, although one might very well have been emphasized over the others. Modern industrial societies have educational systems that are primarily combinations of status-group and bureaucratic education, with the bureaucratic element taking priority and increasingly gaining the upper hand. Although such systems also teach practical skills, this is largely at lower educational levels.

The Emergence and Expansion of Mass Education

Modern systems of formal education arose mainly during the nineteenth century and became consolidated in the twentieth. With a single exception, public primary education did not exist before the nineteenth century. Table 10.1 sketches out the development of primary education in the Western world and Japan. The first Western society to introduce compulsory primary education was Germany (Prussia), which did so in 1763, followed by Denmark (1814), Sweden (1842), Norway (1848), Italy (1859), Switzerland (1874), England and Wales (1880), France (1882), the Netherlands (1900), and Belgium (1914) (Flora 1983; Johansen, Collins, and Johnson 1986). In the United States, the first state to establish compulsory education was Massachusetts, in 1852; by 1900 thirty-two states had established it (Flora 1983). Japan first began compulsory education in 1872 (Hane 1992). By the end of the nineteenth century, compulsory primary education had become well established throughout the Western world (Benavot and Riddle 1988).

Table 10.1 The Development of Primary Education in Industrial Societies

Country	Date	Timing of Introduction of Compulsory Education
United States	1852–1900	First law establishing compulsory schooling passed by state of Massachusetts in 1852; compulsory schooling established in thirty-two states by 1900
Belgium	1914	Eight years of compulsory schooling introduced (ages six to fourteen)
Denmark	1814	Seven years of compulsory schooling introduced three days a week (ages seven to fourteen)
	1849	Compulsory schooling extended to six days a week
France	1882	Seven years of compulsory schooling introduced (ages six to thirteen)
	1936	Compulsory schooling extended to eight years (ages six to fourteen)
Germany	1763	In Prussia, seven to eight years of compulsory schooling introduced (ages six to thirteen or fourteen)
	1871	In German Empire, eight years of compulsory schooling introduced (ages six to fourteen)
Italy	1859	In Kingdom of Sardinia, two to four years of compulsory education introduced (ages six to eight or ten)
	1877	Compulsory schooling extended to all regions of united Italy
	1904	Compulsory schooling extended to six years (ages six to twelve)
	1923	Compulsory schooling extended to eight years (ages six to fourteen)
Netherlands	1900	Six years of compulsory schooling introduced (ages seven to thirteen)
	1920	Compulsory schooling extended to seven years (ages seven to fourteen)
	1942	Compulsory schooling extended to eight years (ages seven to fifteen)
Norway	1848	Seven years of compulsory schooling introduced (ages seven to fourteen)
Sweden	1842	Compulsory schooling introduced for undefined period
	1878	Length of compulsory schooling fixed at six years (ages seven to thirteen)

Country	Date	Timing of Introduction of Compulsory Education
Switzerland	1874	Compulsory schooling introduced (with age of entry and length of time varying by canton)
England and Wales	1880	Eight years of compulsory schooling introduced (ages five to thirteen)
	1918	Length of compulsory schooling extended to nine years (ages five to fourteen)
Japan	1872	Eight years of compulsory schooling introduced (but frequently not enforced)
	1879	Period of compulsory schooling set at four years, with each school year lasting four months
	1880	Period of compulsory schooling reduced to three years, but school year extended to thirtytwo weeks
	1900	Period of compulsory schooling extended to four years

Sources: Flora (1983: 561–623); Johansen, Collins, and Johnson (1986: 230); Hane (1992: 102–104).

Table 10.2 shows primary school enrollment figures for eighteen representative countries for the period between 1870 and 2008. As can be seen, primary enrollment figures were already high in most industrial countries by 1870, and primary education had become universal by 1976. In the less-developed countries, by contrast, primary enrollments were extremely low in 1870 and were in most instances still low in 1940. However, by 1976 enrollments had skyrocketed, and a number of countries had achieved nearly universal primary education by this time. Primary education had obviously become a major part of the lives of all youngsters in industrial countries and most youngsters in the less-developed world.

Table 10.2 Worldwide Primary Enrollments, 1870–2008

Country	1870	1940	1976	2008
Developed countries				
United States	72	91	90	93
Canada	75	100	98	99
Australia	70	89	100	97
Italy	29	59	100	99
Netherlands	59	70	99	99
Belgium	63	63	100	99
Switzerland	76	70	92	99
Denmark	58	67	100	96
Japan	20	61	100	100

Country	1870	1940	1976	2008
Less-developed countries				
Mexico	16	38	100	100
Argentina	21	58	100	98
Colombia	6	26	100	94
China	—	12	100	99
India	2	12	83	96
Ceylon (Sri Lanka)	7	54	84	99
Egypt	—	25	65	95
Ghana	—	10	69	77
Nigeria	—	10	48	63

Notes: Figures represent enrollment as a percentage of persons ages five to fourteen. Some figures exceed 100 percent because of a tendency to overestimate enrollments in some countries. These have been reset to 100. Sources: Benavot and Riddle (1988); UNESCO (1999, 2010).

Secondary education lagged considerably behind. In fact, it was irrelevant to the lives of most people in Western societies until well into the twentieth century. As late as 1910, when primary school enrollments were very high, enrollment of the relevant age cohort in secondary schools was a mere 4 percent in Britain, only 11 percent in the United States, and only 12 percent in Japan (Collins 1979; Dore 1976). However, by 1960 secondary education had expanded dramatically, as Table 10.3 indicates. More than half of the relevant age cohort was enrolled in a secondary school in all of the developed countries shown in the table, and in the United States and Japan, enrollment reached three-quarters or more. By 2008 secondary education was essentially universal in the developed world. Predictably, enrollment figures were very low in the less-developed world in 1960. But between 1960 and 1976, enrollments underwent major expansion, and expansion was even more dramatic between 1976 and 2008. Today many less-developed countries are approaching universal secondary education.

Table 10.3 Worldwide Secondary Enrollments, 1960–2008

Country	1960	1976	2008
Developed countries			
United States	86	85	94
Canada	46	90	100
Australia	51	—	100
Italy	34	71	100
Netherlands	58	89	100

Country	1960	1976	2008
Belgium	69	83	100
Switzerland	26	90	96
Denmark	65	96	100
Japan	74	92	100
Less-developed countries			
Mexico	11	34	90
Argentina	23	56	85
Colombia	12	39	91
China	21	57	76
India	20	29	57
Sri Lanka	27	49	100
Egypt	16	39	—
Ghana	5	36	55
Nigeria	4	7	30

Note: Figures represent enrollments as a percentage of the relevant age cohort.
Sources: World Bank (1984); UNESCO (1999, 2010).

Enrollments in tertiary education have, of course, been the last to expand.[1] As Table 10.4 shows, as late as 1960 an average of only 13 percent of the relevant age cohort was enrolled in a tertiary institution in the nine industrial countries in the table, and the corresponding figure was a mere 4 percent for the less-developed countries. But then things exploded, especially in the industrialized world. By 1976 the nine rich democracies in the table had achieved an average enrollment of 30 percent, and by 2008, it had more than doubled to 68 percent. There was expansion as well in the less-developed world, although enrollments remained very low in 1976 and were at best modest in 2008.

Table 10.4 Worldwide Tertiary Enrollments, 1960–2008

Country	1960	1976	2008
Developed countries			
United States	32	55	83
Canada	16	48	80
Australia	13	24	77
Italy	7	26	67

---

* Tertiary education is all postsecondary education: two- and four-year colleges, universities, and the various types of technical schools.

Country	1960	1976	2008
Netherlands	13	26	61
Belgium	9	23	63
Switzerland	7	14	49
Denmark	10	30	80
Japan	10	27	58
Less-developed countries			
Mexico	3	10	27
Argentina	11	27	68
Colombia	2	7	35
China	—	1	23
India	3	5	13
Sri Lanka	1	1	—
Egypt	5	13	28
Ghana	—	1	6
Nigeria	—	1	—

Note: Figures represent enrollments as a percentage of the relevant age cohort.
Sources: World Bank (1992); UNESCO (1999, 2010).

In the late 1970s, John Meyer, Francisco Ramirez, Richard Rubinson, and John Boli-Bennett (1977) spoke of a "world educational revolution" in the period between 1950 and 1970. They were certainly correct, and yet the real revolution was to come in the next three decades. If we step back and look at the world as a whole in 2008 (at all countries, not just the ones shown in the tables), we find that almost everyone is attending a primary school, four out of five are attending a secondary institution, and one in three is enrolled in a tertiary institution (two in three in the rich democracies). Educational explosion indeed. Is the end in sight? Probably not.

Explaining Educational Expansion

What accounts for mass education? Why did it get started, and why has it expanded so enormously? It is almost universally understood by ordinary citizens and political and economic leaders that advanced education is essential to providing the knowledge people must have in order to perform the increasingly demanding work of societies that are undergoing rapid technological change. Schools teach important knowledge and skills, and students must spend longer and longer periods passing through the educational system in order to acquire them (Clark 1962; Trow 1966). In this view, which is often called *the human capital* or *technocratic theory*, the expansion of education over the past century or so is a consequence of the changing needs of an industrial society, particularly the new requirements brought about by technological and economic change.

However, many social scientists have grown skeptical of this theory. In his critique of the received wisdom, Randall Collins (1979) poses two critical questions: "Are better-educated employees more productive than less-educated ones?" and "Are job skills learned in school or elsewhere?" His answer to the first question is no; to the second, elsewhere. Regarding the first question, he points to a major study (Berg 1971), which shows that better-educated employees are typically not more productive than less educated ones, and in some cases they are even less productive. In terms of the second question, Collins sets forth evidence indicating that most of what students learn in schools has little or no relevance to the acquisition of job skills and that most such skills are acquired much more quickly and easily on the job (cf. D. Brown 1995).

Think of many of the subjects students study in today's colleges and universities: English literature, philosophy, sociology, psychology, foreign languages (including dead languages), history, and natural and physical sciences. These subjects are almost totally unnecessary for doing the vast majority of the jobs that people do. Mathematics beyond a fairly basic level is also of little use. Of course, if you want to become a research scientist, you need science. If you want to become an engineer, you need high-level mathematics and physics. Computer science courses are very useful for careers in that field. But most people are not going to be research scientists, engineers, or computer scientists. Most of what students actually learn in college is neither necessary nor useful in performing the jobs they will actually end up in. And the majority of students eventually come to this conclusion themselves.

Another line of argument sees mass education as an essential ingredient in *nation building* (Meyer et al. 1977; Meyer, Tyack, Nagel, and Gordon 1979; Boli, Ramirez, and Meyer 1985). The proponents of this theory contend that an adequate explanation must account for the following features of modern mass education:

- Mass education is intended to be universal, standardized, and highly rationalized. It applies to everyone in the same fashion, cutting across the class, ethnic, racial, religious, and gender cleavages of a society.
- Mass education is highly institutionalized at a world level. It is extraordinarily similar in very different societies throughout the world, and different educational systems have become increasingly similar over time.
- Mass education is specifically directed toward the socialization of the individual as the primary social unit. This is seen, for example, in the extent

to which educational rituals celebrate individual choice and responsibility rather than the embeddedness of individuals in such corporate groups as social classes, castes, or extended families.

The nation-building theory proposes that mass education arose in the modern world as a mechanism for the intensive socialization of the individual in the values and aspirations of the modern, rational nation-state. To build such a state means creating the modern citizen. Modern citizens have to be loyal and committed to the state, and they must be sufficiently knowledgeable about political life to participate in and help maintain it. This is particularly so where democracy is the prevailing mode of government. If people are going to vote, they need to understand what is at stake in order to cast their votes intelligently.

Advocates of this theory have in more recent years argued that the rapid expansion of education, especially secondary and tertiary education, throughout the world in the past sixty years has been part of a new "world culture" (Shofer and Meyer 2005). It has become almost universally accepted, they claim, that the world's less-developed societies recognize that to become modern, developed nations, they must build educational systems that closely resemble those of the societies that are already highly developed—the rich democracies.

A third theory has been offered by Collins in his book *The Credential Society* (1979). Collins focuses on the American educational system and why it has become one of the world's largest and most comprehensive systems, but the most important part of his theory can be extended to other modern educational systems. Collins begins with the assumption that regardless of how educational systems get started, in time they come to be viewed by those who pursue education as establishing a set of *credentials* that can provide access to certain desired occupational positions. Education thus becomes an arena in which people compete for economic success. But as more and more people obtain educational credentials, an unexpected and unwanted thing happens: these credentials decline in value. Drawing an analogy to monetary inflation, Collins calls this process *credential inflation*. Just as money inflates when there is more of it in circulation, educational credentials inflate when people possess more of them. Credential inflation in the educational sphere means that the same amount of education no longer "purchases" what it once did. One must acquire more of it just to keep even in the struggle for economic success.

Collins argues that this is exactly what has been happening in the American educational system over the past century. The struggle over education has caused continual credential inflation, resulting in the massive expansion of the educational system (and educational requirements for jobs) over time. Since it now takes a college degree to obtain a job that could have been obtained with a high school diploma fifty years ago, a greater number of young people are going to college. Most of them go not because of a desire for learning, Collins insists, but because they seek credentials that they hope will pay off in economic success.

Ronald Dore (1976) has developed a similar argument that he believes applies well beyond the bounds of the United States. What Collins calls *credentialism*—the process whereby education is devoted to the pursuit of educational certificates for their occupational value rather than to learning for its own sake—Dore refers to by the term *qualificationism*. Contemporary nations have become infected with what Dore calls "the diploma disease," a type of vicious circle in which individuals become preoccupied with the acquisition of diplomas or degrees because employers increasingly emphasize them in job requirements. The two sides feed off each other, and educational certificates inflate as a result.

It is possible to use the nation-building and credential-inflation theories together. The creation of universal primary education corresponded closely in time to the formation of modern nation-states, and thus the nation-building theorists may well be correct to say that mass education was created to form the modern citizen. However, this theory cannot really explain why education has expanded so much at all levels, especially the tertiary level, in the past sixty years. To say that this is a product of a newly emergent "world culture" begs the question of why such a culture would develop in the first place. Collins argues that a world educational culture is a result of people's recognition of the credential value of education and increasing amounts of it. And the United States led the way. In Collins's (2002: 45) words, "The dynamics of credential inflation in the expansionary U.S. higher educational market created this culture."

Who is responsible for credential inflation? Just about everyone: educators, students, and, not to be overlooked, employers. Primary education has never had that much credential value, but once secondary education was established, its credential value was quickly established. The earliest public high schools in the United States were not highly credentialized (see below), but that was soon to change. Everyone seems to accept the myth—and, indeed, that is what it is—that education teaches skills that are necessary for the jobs that people do. Educators promote this idea, and would-be students and their parents uncritically accept it. Then employers get into the act. Not only do they accept the myth, but when assessing a pool of applicants, the possession of a degree can be used as a convenient screening device. If there are, say, twenty-five applicants for a particular job but only ten of them have received high school diplomas, an employer can decide to keep only the high school graduates in the pool. The selection process is that much easier and takes up less of the employer's valuable time. A spiral is set in motion that is difficult to stop because all of the parties are an integral part of the process. And so education continues to expand to higher and higher levels.

And status-group considerations may also be involved. A good example is the education of nurses. Traditionally nurses went through three years of training in nursing schools that were usually affiliated with hospitals. They were given both classroom instruction and clinical training. Much of what they learned came from sustained contact with patients. But in the 1970s the process was changed. Nursing education was incorporated into the universities with students earning BSN (Bachelor of Science in Nursing) degrees. They spent much more time in the classroom and less in clinical training. And now they took courses in English literature, philosophy, anthropology, and numerous other subjects bearing no relationship at all to the quality of nursing care they would provide. But the status of the nursing profession was enhanced, or at least so it was assumed.

Credentialism and Its Consequences

Highly credentialized educational systems have a number of consequences, most of them negative. These may be identified as (1) overeducation, (2) ritualized learning, (3) reduced educational quality, and (4) credential crises.

Overeducation: Credentialism, at one point or another, will always lead to "overeducation." This does not mean that people have become too knowledgeable for their own good. It means that, because the number of jobs requiring a certain type of degree does not expand as fast as the number of people possessing the degree, many degree holders will be unable to obtain the kind of job they had been preparing themselves for. In the United States the overeducation problem had begun to appear in the 1970s or perhaps even earlier (Berg 1971; Freeman 1976). Overeducated degree holders have two options. One is to take jobs for which they have more education than is required. This is problematic, however, because it produces high levels of frustration and a sense that one has squandered resources attaining a degree that cannot be properly used. The other option is to set one's sights even higher and go on to obtain still more education in hopes of achieving the type of job originally sought. But this can also be problematic because it requires yet further investment of resources and more years spent in school. Some people choose the first option, others the second. As more and more people choose the second, the process of credential inflation is further intensified, leading to even more overeducation in the future.

Overeducation occurs not just in undergraduate education but in graduate education as well. It has reached critical proportions in graduate schools in such countries as the United States and Japan. In the United States there is now a huge overproduction of PhDs in many fields. Students finishing their degrees confront a job market that is saturated with applicants for positions in colleges and universities. In most of the social sciences and the humanities, the academic world is the main outlet for employment. A single position may draw several hundred applicants. Many students don't get jobs, or they don't get full-time jobs that can lead to tenure. They are often lucky to get even part-time adjunct jobs that pay very little, provide no benefits, and in some cases may last only a year or two. Obtaining a PhD often requires eight years of hard work, considerable financial investment, and a vow of poverty for that length of time. Moreover, many university administrators now pressure departments to admit more and more graduate students, meaning that they are forced to admit applicants who are not really qualified to earn graduate degrees, PhDs in particular. Professors have to hold these students' hands, coax them along, and hope they improve enough to finish their degrees. Many do not, because they either drop out or are asked to leave the program.

In Japan the situation may actually be worse. Not only is there an overproduction of PhDs, but the bad economic situation that Japan has been experiencing for some twenty years means that few jobs are available. Even outstanding students from top universities often have difficulty finding jobs. Like US students, they end up in part-time temporary positions that pay very little and provide no benefits or job security.

Many of these PhDs are actually PhDs in name only. Students who hold them would have had no chance fifty years ago of receiving this highest of all academic degrees. It is only because standards for the PhD, as for all degrees, have been substantially lowered that many students manage to attain them. When weak PhDs become professors in some colleges and universities, standards drop even further because weak PhDs will almost invariably be both poor teachers and poor scholars. They will churn out even weaker PhDs.

Ritualized learning: Dore has said that when credentialism gains the upper hand in an educational system, examinations begin to dominate the curriculum, learning becomes ritualized, curiosity and creativity are deemphasized, and students not only fail to develop an interest in what they are learning but even lose concern for its relevance. Education becomes oriented around passing examinations and receiving chits rather than expanding minds and developing educated persons (Labaree 1997). Classrooms become sterile places characterized by pervasive boredom. And the later a society begins to establish an educational system, the more credentialized it becomes and the more ritualized its learning.

Because Japan was a relatively late developer among contemporary industrial societies, it has created one of the most credentialized educational systems in the industrialized world (Dore 1976). As Dore remarks, almost from the very beginning of its industrialization, Japan was building credentialism into its career preparation. Even as early as 1910, many Japanese business firms were attempting to recruit only university graduates. University degrees were also becoming increasingly necessary at this time for entry into the technical professions and government administration.

Japan has undergone enormous educational expansion throughout the twentieth century. In 1918 private colleges were given the right to call themselves universities, and two decades later twenty-six such universities had been established. At the same time there were also nineteen state universities and two municipal universities (Dore 1976). By 1960 the total number of institutions of higher education (*daigaku*) had exploded to 525 (245 four-year *daigaku* and 280 two-year *daigaku*) (Kitamura 1991). By 1997 there were over 3 million students enrolled in 1,174 *daigaku* (576 four-year *daigaku* and 598 two-year *daigaku*) (McVeigh 2002). This obviously represents an extremely high rate of educational expansion, with apparently no end in sight.

But this tells only part of the story. A look at the nature and content of Japan's educational system reveals the great extent to which it is a highly qualification-oriented system. There is enormous pressure on students in primary and secondary schools to achieve high grades so that they can get into the best universities. Many students spend most of their after-school time studying, often until late each night. Parents, especially the notorious "education mamas," drive their children relentlessly. As if this were not enough, many students enroll in the famous *juku*, or "cram schools," which are designed to give them extra preparation for the examinations on which they must achieve high marks in order to get into the university of their choice (Frost 1991). And the examinations themselves put an emphasis on rote learning, stressing largely the memorization of facts that most Westerners would consider to be very trivial (Frost 1991).

This whole process is referred to by the Japanese as "examination hell," and it is a process they dislike and constantly complain about. As Peter Frost (1991: 291–292) has said,

> At least since the 1920s there have been repeated complaints in the Japanese press that examination hell has prevented Japanese students from having a healthy childhood, has blunted intellectual curiosity, has discouraged females from applying to universities, has overlooked less academic leadership skills, and has encouraged those students who finally do get admitted to do almost no academic work while in college.

This last point may appear startling: *it has encouraged those students who finally do get admitted to do almost no academic work while in college*! Yes, that statement does read correctly. *Daigaku* are variously described as "playgrounds," "kindergartens for adults," "resorts," "Disneylands," and "Mickey Mouse universities." Academic standards are very low, and some professors are urged to pass students even if all they do is attend class (McVeigh 2002).

In terms of widespread popular conceptions of the nature and role of higher education, the Japanese system appears to make no sense whatsoever. But from the perspective of educational credentialism, it is fully comprehensible. What it shows virtually beyond doubt is that Japanese education is a system of highly ritualized learning, the content of which is essentially irrelevant. The fact that much of what Japanese students learn consists of trivial facts learned by rote, as well as that Japanese university students often need to do little real academic work, demonstrates that Japanese education is purely an occupational recruitment or filtering device that has little to do with the acquisition of valuable knowledge. What is important is not that students acquire what they "need to know" in order to perform certain jobs but that they can survive an extremely competitive and psychologically stressful process. And that surely is the hallmark of credential-oriented education.

Reduced educational quality: When an educational institution wishes to enroll only a small number of those who apply for admission, it can be highly selective and maintain rigorous academic standards. Consider the American high school 150 years ago. David Labaree (1997) tells a fascinating story of how things worked in Philadelphia's Central High School in the nineteenth century. Compared with today's high schools, Central was focused overwhelmingly on academic excellence and was rigorous almost beyond belief. Enrollment in a high school in this period was voluntary, and one had to apply for admission. Central rejected most applicants, and thus competition for admission was intense. Central regarded only a minority of its students as worthy of receiving a diploma; in its first eight decades, only 27 percent of Central's students actually graduated, and many of these were required to repeat one or more terms. Most students dropped out: at the end of their first year, 37 percent had dropped out; after the second year, 61 percent had left; and after the third year, 72 percent were gone. The courses required of students were those generally considered most difficult: foreign languages, science, and mathematics. Labaree (1997: 79) notes that "students entering school in 1871, for example, had to take six yearlong units of science, four units each of mathematics, English, history, and drawing, three units of classical languages, [and] two and a half units of a modern language." And just as students were selected on the basis of extremely high standards, so were faculty. Over half of Central's faculty were former Central students who had succeeded in meeting Central's extremely demanding standards.

But when the demand for education is great and institutions are forced to accept large numbers of applicants, the kinds of standards characteristic of Philadelphia's Central High School can no longer be maintained. Randall Collins (1979) points out that as American education expanded, educational institutions were forced to make major changes in their curricula and in their overall character in order to appeal to an increasingly mass clientele. The most prominent changes involved the watering down of the classical liberal arts curriculum and the introduction of a host of extracurricular activities. The transformation of the high school into a mass institution, for instance, was accompanied by the so-called progressive movement in education. Two of progressivism's major innovations were the introduction of athletics and other extracurricular activities and the attempt "to substitute a rather vague 'life-adjustment' training for the classical curriculum" (Collins 1979: 115–116).

Similar changes occurred when colleges and universities started to be attended by a larger clientele, most of whom were seeking educational credentials rather than intellectual stimulation. As Collins (1979: 124–125) remarks,

The main appeal of the revitalized university for large groups of students was not the training it offered but the social experience of attending it. The older elite was being perpetuated in a new, more easy-going form.... Through football games colleges for the first time became prominent in the public eye, and alumni and state legislators found renewed loyalty to their schools. At the same time, fraternities and sororities became widespread, and with them came college traditions of drinking, parties, parades, dances, and "school spirit." It is little exaggeration to say that the replacement of the pious, unreformed college by the sociable culture of the university was crucial in the growth of enrollments, or that football rather than science was the salvation of American higher education.

... The rise of the undergraduate culture indicates first of all that college education had come to be treated as consumption by the new industrial upper classes, although it also attracted growing numbers of the intellectually oriented and those seeking careers in teaching. College attendance had become an interlude of fun in the lives of upper-class and upper-middle-class young Americans....

... [An attempt] to put training back as the central function of the college was a failure. Students did not want to disturb the rituals of freshman and sophomore class rivalries, junior dances, and senior privileges. . . . Most students found the essence of college education to be the enjoyable and status-conferring rituals and social life of college rather than the content of classroom learning.

Credential crises: Educational credentials can inflate only so much. Eventually a saturation point is reached. Either credential requirements reach their logical limits or the pursuit of degrees becomes prohibitively expensive—or both. In the United States, the first has not yet happened, but how far away is it? The second clearly *has* happened. In recent decades the costs of education have risen astronomically, even to absurd proportions. To send one's child to an elite institution may cost the parents $50,000 a year or more. (In 2012, the $60,000 barrier was crossed by the elite Sarah Lawrence University.) Even sending a son or daughter to an average institution could cost $20,000 a year or more. Is it worth it? For some parents, especially the relatively wealthy, it is. But for others, the costs are becoming simply too much to bear. What will these costs be in ten years, or in twenty or thirty?

Another mark of a credential crisis is the appearance of numerous "diploma mills." These have always existed in the United States, but they have become much more numerous in the past few decades. I refer to the for-profit institutions that basically give you a degree once you pay them a certain amount of money. The University of Phoenix is a leading example. It is not just in Phoenix; it is everywhere.

Reading 11: Social Class, The Commodification of Education, and Space Through a Rural Lens

By Michael Corbett

> Perhaps the commodity is the product of a new kind of labour, and claims to satisfy a newly arisen need, or is even trying to bring forth a new need on its own account. (Marx, 1977, p. 201)

Since my undergraduate days I have been attracted to Marx's analysis of social class, to the abstract nature of his argument and to the concrete nuances that he used to create what remains a compelling method for understanding the way that capitalism works. Like many educational theorists I have struggled to understand what this vision and this method might mean to my discipline beyond the rather stark structural readings of sociologists like Bowles and Gintis, Bourdieu and Passeron, and Althusser and Willis, as well as Marxist curriculum theorists like Apple, Giroux, and McLaren. Through it all, there are two omissions that I would like to speak to in this essay. The first is a pervasive assumption that the rural represents a precapitalist formation out of which industrializing societies emerge. This idea is most famously articulated by Marx himself who saw the demise of what he called "rural idiocy" as one of the chief achievements of the capitalist mode of production. What he meant by this was a conception of "idiocy" in the Greek sense of the entirely private person. The dissolution of rural idiocy then was essentially driven by the displacement of village and tradition-bound peasants from their relatively isolated existence in the urbanizing industrial economy of 19th-century Europe. What follows from this view is a conflation of the urban and the educational, a gloss that Ching and Creed (1997) identified in their study of rural identity. The theme statement from the 2011 Berlin meetings of the European Educational Research Association is illustrative:

> Cities are greenhouses for educational change and educational reform all over the world and also in Europe. Cities have always been regarded as leading elements in Europe; they are modern, progressive and networked. They

are producers and traders; they are a medium for political and cultural development. Historically, cities have encouraged hopes as well as doubts concerning educational matters.

In this essay I attempt to emulate Marx's own analysis by moving from the abstract to the concrete and back again. I begin with an analysis of some debates around social class in contemporary sociology and particularly the question of whether or not social class is any longer important. I argue that it continues to be, but that social class has always been a spatial phenomenon and not one that floats in the abstract. From there I analyze three specific classrooms that represent different locales in which social class is played out in schools. One of these is a rural school. I then look at the problem of commodification, which I argue serves to create a money-like calculus for comparing the relative value of different schools. This is an analysis, though, that will typically put rural places at a disadvantage so long as education is viewed through a metro-centric, standardized lens. Finally, I return to the concrete in an analysis of rurality, focusing primarily on bell hooks's return to her rural home place in Kentucky, a process that has left her wondering about place, identity, rurality, race, and spatial marginalization (hooks, 2009).

Marx's Ghost and the Simultaneous Hardening and Softening of Social Class

What difference does social class make in education? This question has been a resilient one, and relentlessly problematic. In the *Communist Manifesto*, Marx (1848/1998) wrote about a specter he saw haunting Europe. This image of a ghostly presence conjures an ever-present doubt in the midst of development, growth, economic ups and downs, and fantasies of consumption. For Marx the ghost was communism itself, or the provocative idea that the whole monstrous edifice of capitalism might come crashing down under its own weight and internal contradictions. While at one level this revolutionary imagery is now widely dismissed, the idea that our activities both collectively and individually are contributing irrevocably to our ultimate peril and even demise remains alive and well (Zizek, 2011). It is alive in environmental and ecological discourse that posits all species at risk. The loss of biodiversity, the increased pace of climate change, and the emergence of extreme weather events have now become normal and accepted features of life on Earth.

In addition to the large urban and rural underclasses—which have effectively given up on their own prospects and the idea that they might effectively contribute to their societies—the spectral image of the zombie finds a home amongst a disenfranchised middle-class youth. They have played the game well and yet find themselves, university degrees in hand, unable to find appropriate and stable employment. One of the grand ironies of our age is that commodification and choice are all around us while at the same time for many people it seems as though all of the real choices have been made for them—well in advance of their own agency. Everyone has a certain range of choice, there is no doubt. But at the same time, the structures of wealth and poverty through which resources are distributed seem remarkably resilient and impenetrable, confounding the trite slogans of not only the advertising industry and its consumer dreams, but also those of the institutional face of the dream machine (like the school and the ballot box) that provide us all with at least the theoretical possibility of positive change, unpredictable outcomes, and personal as well as social progress. All of this longing and frustration is haunted by the dreaded thought that the game might just be rigged, and the structures essentially intractable.

But of course the game (or history) is never over. Most contemporary sociologists now see social actors navigating the challenging and shifting ground that lies between two conditions: the influence of structure (a structure that everyone feels even if they cannot always articulate its presence and power) and the drive for autonomy and individuation. In late modernity, that drive has become the most important imaginative work most of us do (Appadurai, 1996). And in the space where we do this work, social class is neither a life sentence nor is it a fiction. Research in the sociology of education has taken two separate and contradictory tacks with respect to the development of class analysis. First of all, the Marxist vision presents a framework in which the positions represented by social class *harden* over time as capitalist relations of production generate increasing inequality. For those who follow Marx, ever-increasing inequality becomes more and more difficult to hide as time goes on. Together, the result of the combined agency of an alienated and impoverished working class supported by a revolutionary cadre of intellectuals (in this case educator-intellectuals or teacher-intellectuals; Giroux, 1987) will be an enhanced and even revolutionary class-consciousness. Thus will emerge an emancipatory potential contained in a convergence of an "alienated and discontented" activist community-intelligentsia and a "deprived and dispossessed" underclass (Harvey, 2009, pp. 241–242).

The other grand narrative of social class is the liberal story that is essentially the tale of a *softening* of social-class positions in an increasingly fluid social structure. In fact, the idea of a social structure itself is sometimes dismissed as a fiction, as in the work of Ulrich Beck (1992, 2006) and Bruno Latour (1993, 2005) or, more famously, in Margaret Thatcher's pronouncement that society itself is a fiction. Indeed, Anthony Giddens (2008), perhaps the most influential sociological proponent of this view, has commented that it is impossible to look at the world today and not conclude that things have gotten better for the majority of the world's people. Here is the polarization that has dogged class analysis for generations. Is the world indeed getting better for most of us, or is the opposite the case? The data are marshaled on both sides and cases are made in one direction or the other. Goldthorpe (2010) has suggested that the main problem with this bifurcation of class analysis is that neither narrative is correct. Indeed, it is undeniable that social class has never, as Marx predicted, hardened and narrowed to form a revolutionary proletariat in any developed capitalist society. At the same time the liberal narrative is equally flawed because the life chances of individuals in these same developed capitalist societies are demonstrably rife with social inequality that runs along social class, racial, regional, gender, and other structural and spatial lines (Harvey, 2009).

The problem, then, if one accepts Goldthorpe's analysis—and I generally do—is to think about social class in terms of the complex tension between embedded and resilient structures; individuals skillfully composing lives in the burgeoning real and virtual social spaces of contemporary capitalism; and dreams for a better world that sit at the heart of many educational projects (decent ones, real ones). Three things need to be said here. First of all, I take social class to be a spatialized phenomenon. In vulgar forms of both liberal and Marxist analyses, all places will be similarly transformed by the forces of time represented by the playing out of a revolutionary historical materialist teleology, with revolution of one sort or another marking the beginning of our "real" history. In the neoliberal camp there is an equally universal homogenizing "end of history" argument (Fukuyama, 1992) with its allegedly democratic vision of an essentially placeless globalization—placeless because all places come under the sway of hegemonic Western ideas. Critical geographers following from Lefebvre (1991) and Tuan (1977) have helped clarify the way that space is *not* an inevitable given, not a mere container or backdrop against which history occurs. Places themselves are transformed by multiple spatial practices that range from the construction of personal identities (e. g., Bettis and Adams's *Geographies of Girlhood* [2005] or Aitken's *Geographies of Young People* [2001]) and the organization of a room in a house (Bachelard, 1994; Lefebvre, 1991) to the removal of entire mountain tops for buried minerals, to the global machinations of advanced capitalism (Harvey, 2009). Space is produced and places are shaped by agency through time. In fact, one way to understand what capitalism is and does is to think of the way that new conceptual spaces are created, recreated, and built one upon the other. Examples of this range from the feverish demolition and rebuilding in Shanghai to the proliferation of networked virtual spaces.

Second, I take social class to be a question of consciousness. Theorists as diverse as Bourdieu, Lefebvre, E. P. Thompson, and Zygmunt Bauman have each helped us understand social class as a cultural, geographic, and identity location that brings social actors into conversation with one another in spaces they create to realize their ends. Even when the particular location for action is as regulated and generic as a franchised fast-food restaurant, ordinary social actors *imaginatively* make the actual space what it *actually* is. So stressed parents indulge their children with greasy or sweet foods against their better judgment because they are too busy to cook, while seniors gather for camaraderie and to avoid the loneliness of an empty apartment. At the same time, youth construct these places as hangouts that might in turn invite drug dealers to use them as illicit business locations—all of these practices illustrating how space is partly imagined, just as Lefevbre argued. Note that space is also relational. All places exist in relationships with other places and while each place represents a "pause" in dynamic, fluid space (Tuan, 1977), they are each neither still nor silent.

Another way to express this idea is to say that class practices are inevitably spatial practices. Third, and finally, the core narrative of Western educational policy and practice for the past 30 years has been a massive shift of energy and emphasis toward making systems *more* commodified, accountable, and comparable across different spatial scales: more "productive" and more firmly managed (Ball, 2012; Luke, 2011; Spring, 2008). There is no longer any strong sense that educational institutions should somehow sit outside the market providing noncommodified service. States and corporate influences, working on educators, have attempted to rationalize educational institutions in order to make them serve the increasingly globalized economic and social machinery of capital in an efficient way. I think what class analysis in education can do is to demonstrate the complexity if not the impossibility of the task of rationalizing education by showing how there is no single "machine," but rather a diverse set of locations that function very differently under the single rubric of "school." There is no single school; there are many schools, each of which effectively reflects the differences in capital held by adults in societies driven by class distinctions (contingent on power, culture, geography, and identity).

Different Geographies: Three Classrooms

I begin by looking at three distinct educational sites in Atlantic Canada. These sites are narrative amalgamations of actual classrooms I have visited in the past 10 years as a researcher and supervisor of student teachers. Each is considered in its community to be a good school. What school research has demonstrated is that the contextual factors connected with children's schooling appear to make much of the difference in academic achievement (Berliner, 2006; Riordan, 2003). Indeed, the classroom itself is a social context for children's lives and learning and it sits within the larger context of neighborhood, community, province (state), region, and nation. To understand better the effects of social class in education, it makes sense to think carefully, as Nespor (2004) argues, in an attempt to understand the interplay between the classroom and the wider environment. To make the point in a concrete way, I will look at three classrooms in three schools in three parts of Atlantic Canada.

Civility and Order

The first school is urban, serving approximately 200 elementary school–age children. The original part of the building dates from the 1920s or 1930s, but there have been several additions tacked on to the original building over the years. The school "fits in" to the neighborhood architecturally with its newer stone and brick construction, mirroring commercial and some residential construction that appears to have developed over an extended historical period. The original school building, however, does not fit into its landscape as well, representing instead the dignified architectural statement of the "palace schools" of the late 19th and early 20th century (Bennett, 2011). The schoolyard is quite small, and it is fenced in on all sides. Traffic buzzes around the perimeter of the site.

The neighborhood might be described as middle class. The houses are generally two-story structures built very close to one another along residential streets that branch off main city thoroughfares. Concrete sidewalks rim the streets, and shops dot corner lots and dominate the main streets. When we enter the school, we see an unobtrusive sign directing visitors to the main office. It is difficult to find, though, because the office occupies a converted classroom, with a door indistinguishable from any of the others inside the building. The hallways are neat and silent. The ceilings are high, there are large windows, and the air is fresh. The space feels bright, large, open, and relaxed. Children move through the building and smile at us. Classrooms are also active yet quiet workspaces in which children moving about appear to be working on various sorts of projects. The building itself is not new, but it is well maintained and obviously cared for.

Inside the classroom that we enter, we notice that the children work collaboratively on mathematics problems in "stations." Each station is a seating area containing a set of manipulative materials designed to help reinforce concepts. A problem is set for students on a brightly colored card, and at each station children work together to solve the task given them. The students ask one another questions, offer help and suggestions, occasionally tell a joke or make a funny comment, but the general atmosphere is one of productive engagement. The teacher is hard to find at first, but we find him hunched over a desk working with a couple of students at one of the stations.

When the math period has run its course, the children unobtrusively gather up the materials at the stations, return them to a portable trolley, and then reclaim their seats. One child takes the portable trolley and replaces materials in the corner of the room where mathematics materials are stored in labeled bins and on shelves. We notice that each curriculum subject area seems to have its own section in the classroom. The room contains a well-stocked library in a corner devoted to reading. There is a couch and a cushioned living room chair in the library corner. Another area of the room contains science materials. Yet another corner of the room houses the children's violins. All of the walls are decorated with children's work, as well as with instructional posters describing and displaying learning principles and ethical slogans to inspire the children. A great deal of student work—particularly writing and artwork—is posted.

Once the children have returned to their seats, the teacher assumes a more traditional role, conducting a discussion that relates to the issues children were dealing with at their stations—in this case statistical probability and sampling. Afterward, the class is dismissed for lunch and the children leave, chatting in pairs or small groups.

This classroom conveys a sense of civility and order: the children are neat in their appearance and orderly and mannerly in their verbal interventions and physical movements. They discourse seriously with one another in small groups and pairs, and with their teacher in formal, whole-group discussion. They also move quietly and in a careful way about the classroom. Each child has an area of his or her own for the storage of materials and for independent work; these workspaces are respected and cared for. On the playground the children are exuberant: the older children organize ball games and other forms of coordinated play, whereas the younger children occupy a separate playground. Their play is typically more free-form. When parents collect their children, many arrive in late-model cars. Nearly as many fathers as mothers appear at school. These parents converse easily with the teachers, and in fact they strongly *resemble* the teachers in their dress and physical manner; the men are often dressed in business suits.

Controlled Chaos

Our second school is situated in a suburban community. It is a relatively large elementary school by provincial standards, serving approximately 200 elementary children and their families. This school was constructed in the 1980s, and its exterior is brick. The surrounding community consists of older small wood-frame dwellings and subdivisions of newer bungalow-style residences (i.e., modest single-family houses). Some houses are freshly painted, but many are not. Few trees line the streets in the surrounding neighborhood, and the houses are closely packed together on very small lots. By both provincial and by national standards, the school serves a community that is economically disadvantaged.

Situated on a hill and surrounded by large play areas, the school is imposing: well constructed, relatively new, and from a distance seemingly well maintained. An architectural anomaly in its surroundings, it sits in a neighborhood of modest houses. Streets lack sidewalks, and there is little evidence of commercial activity near the school. The entrance contains several glassed-in offices from which secretaries and administrators can maintain surveillance of the main entry and exit. In the school office several children sit on a long bench awaiting discipline. Other students mill about in the foyer and are seen in the hallways around classroom doors even though classes are in session. As we pass by classrooms, some children emerge to greet us or just to look at us. Apparently adult visitors are not a common sight. A long narrow window constructed of heavy meshed glass borders each classroom door. Some doors are open, but many are closed. Some of these windows are covered with paper material, obscuring the view of the classroom from the hall.

The classroom we enter is tidy, but it is spartan in learning materials and furniture. Students sit at individual desks, and the teacher presents material from the front of the room. Following teacher presentations in this room, students work independently at their desks or occasionally in pairs and small groups. The classroom has few decorations except inspirational posters sponsored by corporations or by the state. One poster, for instance, features the unlikely image of an ice hockey player standing in full protective gear reading a book. The room contains several shelves of textbook series, and there is a magazine-style rack for paperback books. One corner of the room contains the teacher's desk, bookshelf, and personal effects.

The children in this school appear to function in two principal modes: high-energy *active* and static *passive*. The latter mode predominates: during teacher presentations and through much classroom seatwork, students are for the most part passive. Student body language varies from intense engagement to total disregard. Many students squirm in their seats and look around. Very infrequently do students intervene or participate in teacher presentations and classroom discussions, and when they do, their responses are short. Students do not appear to engage in conversation with teachers, but rather to offer the verbal equivalent of fill-in-the-blank responses.

In fact, this is the format for their classroom work: in their seatwork, students read passages and then answer questions in very brief sentences. They keep scribblers, binders, paper, and work supplies, along with snacks and other things, inside their metal frame desks.

A feeling of *controlled chaos* pervades this space. Students appear restrained, and indeed the measure of the skill of a teacher in this school is often couched in terms of his or her ability to "control" the class. The hallways do not display student work (commercial posters are hung instead) and no student artwork is present, whether in the classroom or in common areas. There is a trophy case mostly for athletic awards in the entryway of the school. Students appear shy with strangers—and even with their teachers. Indeed, most of them make little effort to engage adults and they respond marginally to attempted engagement by adults. When students move about the room, they seem, by contrast, unrestrained, as though they have been released from captivity. The children's movements are quick and jerky overall. The girls tend to form small groups and converse in an animated fashion, often bursting into peals of laughter and occasionally calling out loudly to individuals or to other groups. These patterns prevail among girls outside the classroom—on the playground, and on the school bus or the walk to and from home. Boys converse in monosyllables, and they strike poses common to action heroes and professional athletes, particularly wrestlers. They mime aggressive movements, including hand-to-hand combat with one another.

One sees little evidence of parental presence in the school. Many children walk home from school at lunchtime, unaccompanied by adults. When a parent appears at school, it is almost always a female. In my own time in the school I witnessed not a single conversation between parents and staff. Parents typically meet their children in cars parked on the street adjacent to the school property, waiting for the boys and girls to emerge from the building.

One Big Family

Our third school is in a rural community. It is a relatively small wood-frame structure built in the late 1950s as part of a rural school amalgamation (i.e., consolidation) program. The building sits on a hill at one end of a small village, where it draws just 100 children from a geographic catchment radius of some 35 square kilometers (i.e., 13. 5 square miles). The school was originally built to accommodate a much larger population, so the feeling inside the building is one of considerable space. The parking lot here is often filled with the cars of parent volunteers who run a school lunch program or assist in classrooms. The building is used in the evenings and after school for a variety of community programs. It thus seems likely that local people regard the school as community property.

Visually, the school is somewhat consistent architecturally with the other buildings in the vicinity, which are for the most part well-maintained 19th and early 20th century homes mixed in with newer bungalow-style dwellings. The local economy is based on a primary resource industry, and this fact is evident in the equipment and outbuildings near many houses. Pickup trucks are as common here as automobiles. The entry and foyer of the school feature photographs of the school's children engaged in a variety of activities in and around the school. The presence of adults in the photographs gives the impression that adults are often present for school functions and activities involving children. In the foyer we are greeted by students who are shy but who seem comfortable engaging adults. As in the second school, children appear animated and even manic as they move about the building. Some young boys run about, occasionally crashing into one another as they move out of the building onto the playground. The school seems to work hard to convey the impression that it is a central community institution and that indeed the school itself is the "heart of the community." This is more than a myth because for generations many important community gatherings have indeed taken place in the school. In fact, the language of community is prominently and explicitly invoked on school letterhead and on printed material throughout the building. The term "community" is, in an important sense, defined by the geography of the school's catchment area, created when the provincial school system was "modernized" in the late 1950s (Bennett, 2011). That effort amalgamated a dozen small schools that operated in the local villages hereabouts.

Today, when the school has been threatened with closure—as on several occasions over the past two decades—members of the community have rallied to keep it open. Their rationale is the importance of the school to the community. Inside, adults mingle with children. There are playground supervisors and lunch ladies, all of whom know every student (and parent) by name. Everyone in the school seems to be on a first-name basis. Most of the adults in the picture are women, and when men do appear at the school, they often seem uncomfortable. School is, for the most part, a woman's place in this community.

The curriculum combines traditional book-learning, which is carried on partly in whole-group teaching sessions not unlike the ones at the other schools. There is also evidence of more active project-based learning and community engagement in the form of a school greenhouse, an art production area, and workshop-like areas throughout the school. The atmosphere is happy, convivial, and active; many of the students claim to like working with their hands. Listening to the nonstandard English spoken by the students, it is perhaps not so difficult to understand why, as a group, they struggle in language subjects—and which subjects are not language subjects? Teachers often spend large amounts of time with particular children working to "bring them up to grade level," but most of the teachers understand that the testing will result in a below-average assessment for the majority of students. This circumstance raises for me a number of questions, including what "grade level" is in the first place. Each of these three schools seems to perform a similar age-stage pedagogy very differently. Nonetheless, the constructed space of the school and its "grades" are fundamental to the organization of children in all of them, and in schooling generally. Other misgivings surface as well, such as, questions about the characteristic approaches to language and schooled literacy, approaches that effectively push too many rural children and youth to the margins (Corbett, 2010).

Commodification and Comparison of Apples and Oranges

So how can these schools be compared? The first move is to create a mechanism for this comparison, which is the fundamental problem of commodification that Marx (1977) laid out in the opening chapter of *Capital*. The genius of capitalism lies in its ability to facilitate exchange through the creation of a device that renders every specific object interchangeable. The corporeal "touchability" of the object is magically transformed into an abstract value, or as Marx put it, "all that is solid melts into air" (1998, p. 38). In effect, the commodity form makes possible and functional the comparison of apples and oranges. In the marketplace, money serves this purpose and becomes the universal yardstick with which different commodities can be compared in terms of the value they hold relative to each other. What is fundamental is the way that cognition shifts onto the discursive terrain created by the commodity. In other words, we learn to think and value in terms of the *medium of commodification* (i.e., money). A sensible consumer knows the approximate cost of everything in view. A good consumer is strategic and knows *a deal*.

In educational terms this facility means an inevitabe longing for the comparison of scholastic apples and oranges through the means of *a symbolic equivalent of money*. Throughout the developed world these mechanisms have been relentlessly and meticulously constructed and reconstructed, generating what amounts to a multiscalar stock market of educational capital (credentials, test scores, rankings, grading). Thus, to answer in a simple way the complicated question about which of the three schools is the "best," one can consult the educational marketplace. I am sure I do not have to tell you which school posts the highest scores. But in the case of the rural and suburban schools, this answer will not do. Its appropriateness even for the first seems therefore dubious. This process of commodification allows neoliberal subjects (i.e., you and me) to compare and contrast, to strategize, and to choose.

The magic of commodification creates an illusion of objectivity and allows for the nuances of place to be set aside, and usually ignored entirely. At the same time, and ironically, places are raised in importance via the grading and ranking of the relative educational "performance" of schools. Different schools (each differently located) are relentlessly thrown into comparison against one another both by consumer-parents who as subjects of neoliberal discourse demand *to know the score* and by the neoliberal state that claims devotion to transparency (rather than to the commodification of schooling)."Commodification" is outside the neoliberal vocabulary and can hardly be mentioned within it, and (we) neoliberal subjects can therefore hardly understand it, true and accurate a characterization though it may be. One of the most common uses of standardized test results for schools is in the real estate market when middle-class parents seek out "safe" educational spaces for their children, using test scores of a school as a proxy for the social class composition of its student body.

Contemporary middle-class parenting practices now include the use of data to inform the optimal consumption of educational commodities in increasingly marketized delivery systems. This whole process rests on the idea that all things can (and should) be measured, including educational performance and individual pathology or deviance (Foucault, 1977). As Basil Bernstein (1996) noted four decades ago, the classification of people has thus become the central focus of contemporary education systems.

Marx's project was to demonstrate two things: (1) how quantification and commodification (which requires quantification) have come to dominate life under capitalism and (2) how scientific analysis of the operation of this system of quantification and commodification can be challenged by a revolutionary movement that will lead to a better world ruled by human values, equitable distribution, and genuine free choice rather than by the commodity. It's a durable project. The power of commodification, however, lies in its ability to dismiss other ways of thinking. Under capitalism it becomes difficult to imagine anything that cannot or should not be commodified. Labor time in particular is measured and valued as workers are forced into the singularity of narrow occupational roles and quantifiable production routines carried out in specialized production facilities. The idea that the worth and productivity of a person should be measured is entirely ordinary to our thinking. The fragmentation of experience into narrow, self-contained, and abstracted specialties is a complex process that begins with schooling. It is here that children and youth learn to be who they are "meant to be" and to develop what is called today "an identity," effectively the construction of a coherent yet dynamic sense of consumption and production practices (which are increasingly "cognitive" [Peters, 2011]) suitable to one's social class location.

In rural places, this process tends toward what Mingay (1989, p. 103) calls "an urbanization of the mind," which is a preparation for mobile, placeless sophistication. All these processes are subject to focused measurement that mimics the broader commodification necessary to the "marketplace" and to (our) actions within it. It is intriguing that despite Marx's well-known dismissal of rural idiocy as a primary casualty of capitalism, the only explicit vision of a post-capitalist world he offered looks distinctly rural. In this famous passage from the *German Ideology*, Marx writes of the worker under capitalism that:

> He is a hunter, a fisherman, a herdsman, or a critical critic, and must remain so if he does not want to lose his means of livelihood; while in communist society, where nobody has one exclusive sphere of activity but each can become accomplished in any branch he wishes, society regulates the general production and thus makes it possible for me to do one thing today and another tomorrow, to hunt in the morning, fish in the afternoon, rear cattle in the evening, criticize after dinner, just as I have a mind, without ever becoming hunter, fisherman, herdsman or critic. (1970, p. 53)

The uniqueness of individual schools that I have tried to illustrate earlier is relevant to the enterprise of modernist education because it represents the range of problems to be solved. As David Harvey, Edward Soja, and others have been pointing out for years, social class is not an abstraction; it is instantiated in different ways in different places, as in the example of the fast-food restaurant, given previously. *Social class is spatial.* Contrary to this reality, as citizens and educators we confront the neoliberal theory and practice of judging schools on the basis of a standard metric. And we are further convinced (socialized to a belief) that the legitimate role of the state is to make these rankings transparent. In the case of the low-SES suburban school I described, the problems of spatialized poverty, the historical ghettoization of a marginal labor force, and the attendant educational underperformance that this particular configuration of conditions represents elicits a predictable response (especially under the prevailing neoliberal outlook). Educators in that school (as in many others like it) deploy a combination of low expectations, remedial drill and practice, and hard-edged directive discipline. If these practices can be shown to *raise test scores*, then the school is considered to be "successful." In terms of social class, the successful school is doing its bit by preparing students for exodus from their disadvantaged urban community and their families' lowly position in the social class structure. When this outcome fails to transpire, the schools are blamed for not subverting the machinery of social inequality and transforming individual fortunes.

In the case of the rural school, things are not entirely different. Remedial drill and practice aimed at underperforming children is often administered with a strong community focus. Because it is a "community school," there is a greater expectation, however, that curriculum will connect with place. A central tension in the vision of educational success in this community thus exists between the conflicting desire to sustain the community and to prepare youth to leave it (Corbett, 2007). This tension inflects the problem of social class and schooling here, and in many rural places. Social mobility has a focused spatial meaning if escape is the clear mandate: a host of films about urban teachers and schools work essentially on this assumption. The children featured in *Waiting for Superman* (Guggenheim, 2010) were presumably trying or vying to get on track for leaving their home places. The only possible exception to this might be Geoffrey Canada's *Harlem Children's Zone* (2013), where school improvement seems to be part of a coordinated strategy for neighborhood improvement, a project that also involves considerable careful attention to the spatialized nature of social class and poverty in Harlem.

Making Do As They See Fit: Drilling Down Into Rurality, Place, and Social Class With Bell Hooks

I have been arguing here that educational problems so often come back to spatial questions. The concreteness that results from stepping off the merrygo-round of commodified macro-analyses of educational space can indeed be jarring. In a recent book, bell hooks (2009) describes and analyzes her return to Kentucky through a meditation on rurality. In fact, hooks takes us into a place that is not unlike the third school I mentioned previously, a village school that hangs on in a small and shrinking rural community. Because she grew up in rural Kentucky, hooks remembers a place where embodied experience in nature trumped the categories of social oppression. Class, race, and gender did not matter there in the same way that they did in the city to which she moved as a child. What mattered was the division between the country and the city. In the country of hooks's childhood everyone was subject to the power and affordances of the natural world. Nobody dominated nature in the world of her childhood, and the people who lived in the Kentucky hill country of her youth were in a position that compelled them to find a space of their own, a space of self-reliance and self-determination. It seems as though they were too busy making a living and at the same time forging their own particular relationships with nature to worry too much about dominating one another.

This is a vision of the rural place in which everyone was essentially the same, a story I have heard countless times in my own ethnographic work in rural Atlantic Canada. It is a story I have tended to dismiss because I thought it obscured the multiple layers of difference in the rural community. But hooks does not dismiss it. Apart from the fact that this is a surprising characterization of the racial politics of that time and place, hooks's account locates the generator of core social divisions of class, gender, and race *in the city*. There, the rules were not made by independent people to govern themselves but by those whom hooks calls "unknown others" (2009, p. 8). Moving from country to city, hooks came within the ambit of these rules, experiencing for the first time a racially segregated community.

In the rural community where one framed one's most fundamental connections with nature, and where land was experienced directly as a provider of sustenance, individuals were relatively autonomous, often passionately and knowledgably so. They "made do" and acted "as they saw fit." I continue to live in a rural community where social class distinctions can be complicated by similarities of life practices that wealth would elsewhere obscure. Here, across the "objective" lines of income difference, we grow food, prepare it, store it for the winter, cut our own firewood, shoot deer and rabbits for meat, fix our own vehicles, put up outbuildings, and undertake many similar engagements little appreciated elsewhere. These values are celebrated formally and collectively in rural fairs (Eppley, 2013), churches, and other community spaces; and informally in multiple practices and discourses of what Howley and Howley (2010, pp. 47–48) call "self-provisioning." Rural practitioners take up each of these discourses—ways of using land, tools, time, and space—to do identity work and to build and develop regimes of self-care that allow for independence. Each person chooses what skills to develop, and many still share their skills amongst one another. Although my neighbors, and indeed I myself, do not ordinarily describe these activities in such terms, I choose here to interpret them this way. My choice means I take these practices as identity and lifestyle decisions, as skill development, and ultimately as pride in self-sufficiency and a job well done, and not Bourdieu's (1984, pp. 372–398) disparaging "making a virtue of necessity." hooks puts it this way, too, locating rural life practices in a way that is similar to James Scott's (1999) idea of "metis"—life practices that are resistant to the juggernaut of urbanized, commodified modernity. Indeed, hooks comes very close to arguing that social class is actually an urban phenomenon:

> Oppositional habits of being learned during childhood forged a tie to my native place that could not be severed. Growing up, renegade black and white folks who perceived the backwoods, the natural environment, to be a space away from man-made constructions, from dominator culture, were able to create unique habits of thinking and being that were in resistance to the status quo. (2009, p. 19)

This is not entirely different from Marx's utopian quote from the *German Ideology*, a view also consistent with those put forward by Scott (1999), Lefebvre (2002), and deCerteau (1984), all of whom focus on spatial practices of resistance (tantamount to Scott's more generic "metis"). Indeed we can add to this list Aristotle's poiesis or act of pragmatic creation more recently manifested in "maker culture or in the DIY movement. To my mind, this deep rural sensibility suggests potential for rural educational practices that reflect and valorize those resistant rural life practices that have not yet been schooled away or decultured out of existence. Place-sensitive educators (e. g., Gruenewald, 2003; Theobald, 1997) have long understood the importance of a resistant educational ethic of stewardship and care.

Social Class and Social Space

What I have attempted to argue here is that social class analysis needs to be complicated by spatial analysis and by considerations of rurality. The dynamics of change and the transformation of places are chronic features of social production, we are currently struggling to bring them to bear on our analysis of the often static categories like social class, race, gender, and indeed education itself. But all of these, of course, are also subject to change and transformation. The point is that place (space, geography) is a critical, and largely ignored, dimension of that change. My rural home place is changing rapidly and is in fact becoming increasingly diverse and thoroughly infused by consumer capitalism. Indeed, big-box stores are probably more of a rural than an urban phenomenon. This sad development puts the lie to the notion that large urban spaces replete with independent locally owned boutiques and restaurants are more globalized than the countryside! This said, it is important to remember that all places are in flux and contain what Massey (2005, 141) calls "thrown-together" character. Like hooks, Aimee and Craig Howley, myself, and a handful of academics, Massey actually *lives* in a rural village. But there is no bucolic, preservationist, or communal illusion in the way she depicts contemporary rural places, which must be understood as nexus points of mobilities, regulation, flows of information unleashed from wherever they are produced, and the global circulation of goods and services. Massey used the location of her village to illustrate the way that it is now necessary to think about space in multiple scales and in complex terms. She writes:

> There can be no assumption of pre-given coherence, or of community or collective identity. Rather the thrown togetherness of place demands negotiation. In sharp contrast to the view of place as settled and pre-given, with a coherence only to be disturbed by external forces, places as presented here in a sense necessitate intervention; they pose a challenge. (p. 141)

If the past generation of social research has taught us anything, it is that everything is in motion, including the structural tools we have used to think about how we are together. To take up the creative challenge of negotiating a way forward is a problematic of spatial politics, or what Edward Soja (2010) calls "spatial justice." It is on the ground in changing communities that schools operate. And on the ground where people choose to capitulate or challenge, to demand access to enclosed and exclusive spaces and to mobility. Contemporary understandings of space in education (Green & Letts, 2007; Leander, Phillips, & Taylor, 2010) raise new questions about the way that geographies from the scale of the classroom to that of the globe are plastic and mutable, but at the same time different and distinct. In inner cities and deep rural communities, large-scale commodified assessments rather predictably sow the seeds of paranoia and self-loathing that in turn tends to certify and reproduce a multigenerational underclass. Attempts to circumscribe and close down innovative possibilities in educational spaces are the face of domination that, it seems to me, call progressive and radical educators to resistance. As Massey puts it, "For the future to be open, space must be open too" (2005, p. 12). The closing-down of space is accomplished today through a widespread and thorough commodification of educational practice and assessment that cries out for critique.

Who knows how space will open up as we lurch from crisis to crisis? The class structure and geography of advanced capitalist societies rests on the uncertain foundation of stable markets; cheap energy; easy credit; and mass-produced goods, services, and entertainment—all of which are founded on massive exploitation of resources from rural places. Often these rural places are drained of people (or at least people who care about the place) to make this exploitation easier to accomplish. These elements taken together have created environmental conditions that are immensely precarious, causing many of North America's most profound artists and social critics to imagine dystopian future worlds. Examples include the fictional rural dystopias of James Kunstler's (2008) return to the 18th century in *World Made by Hand*, Margaret Atwood's (2009) end of days after a viral plague, and Cormack McCarthy's (2006) horrendous post-peak oil road scenario.

These tales can be read as a warning. Could it be (turning Bourdieu on his head, so to speak) that not-quite-dead rural virtues of stewardship, deep place-sensitive knowledge, and making do as one sees fit on known and loved land and sea will become the new necessities? Rather than making a virtue of necessity, it makes more sense to speak of making a necessity of the new virtues represented by sustainable bioregional ecological self-defense. Let us not forget that utopia too tends to be rural with foundational Christian Garden of Eden imagery, Marx's intellectual primary producer, or Aldous Huxley's (1962) *Island* (1962) where schoolchildren study philosophy, play, and learn to live together harmoniously and sustainably.

References

Aitken, S. C. (2001). *Geographies of young people: The morally contested spaces of Identity*. London: Routledge.

Appadurai, A. (1996). *Modernity at large: Cultural dimensions of globalization*. Minneapolis: University of Minnesota Press.

Atwood, M. (2009). *Year of the flood*. Toronto: McClelland and Stewart.

Bachelard, G. (1994). *The poetics of space*. Boston: Beacon Press.

Ball, S. J. (2012). *Global Education Inc. : New policy networks and the neo-liberal imaginary*. New York: Taylor & Francis.

Beck, U. (1992). *Risk society: Toward a new modernity*. London: Sage.

Beck, U. (2006). *Cosmopolitan vision*. Cambridge, UK: Polity Press.

Bennett, P. (2011). *Vanishing schools, threatened communities*. Black Point, NS, Canada: Fernwood.

Berliner, D. (2006). Our impoverished view of educational reform. *Teachers College Record, 108*(6), 949–995.

Bernstein, B. (1996). *Pedagogy, symbolic control, and identity: Theory, research, critique*. London: Taylor and Francis.

Bettis, P., & Adams, N. (2005). *Geographies of girlhood: Identities in between*. Mahwah, NJ: Erlbaum.

Bourdieu, P. (1984). *Distinction: A social critique of the judgment of taste*. Cambridge, MA: Harvard University Press.

Canada, G. (2013). The Harlem Children's Zone web page. Retrieved from www.hcz.org/hcz-home.php.

Ching, B., & Creed, G. (1997). *Recognizing rusticity: Identity and the power of place*. New York: Routledge.

Corbett, M. (2007). *Learning to leave: The irony of schooling in a coastal community*. Black Point, NS, Canada: Fernwood.

Corbett, M. (2010). Wharf talk, home talk and school talk: The politics of language in a coastal community. In A. Jackson & K. Schafft (Eds.), *Rural education in the 21st century* (pp. 115–131). College Park: Pennsylvania State University Press.

deCerteau, M. (1984). *The practice of everyday life*. Berkeley: University of California Press.

Eppley, K. (2013). My roots dip deep: Literacy practices as mirrors of traditional, modern and postmodern ruralities. In M. Corbett & B. Green (Eds.), *Thinking rural literacies: International and comparative perspectives* (pp. 75–92). New York: Palgrave Macmillan.

Foucault, M. (1977). *Discipline and punish*. New York: Pantheon.

Fukuyama, F. (1992). *The end of history and the last man*. New York: Penguin.

Giddens, A. (2008). *Globalization and communication*. Lecture to the Annenburg School of Journalism. Retrieved from www.youtube.com/watch?v=n-9rDFN2zPU&feature=.

Giroux, H. (1987). *Teachers as intellectuals: Toward a critical pedagogy of learning*. New York: Praeger.

Goldthorpe, J. (2010). Class analysis and the reorientation of class theory: the case of persisting differentials in educational attainment, *British Journal of Sociology*, *61*, 311–335.

Green, B., & Letts, W. 2007. Space, equity and rural education: A "trialectical" account. In K. Gulson & C. Symes (Eds.), *Spatial theories of education: Policy and geography matters* (pp. 57–76). London: Routledge.

Gruenewald, D. A. (2003). The best of both worlds: A critical pedagogy of place. *Educational Researcher*, *32*(4), 3–12.

Guggenheim, D. (2010). *Waiting for Superman*. New York: Paramount Vantage and Participant Media.

Harvey, D. (2009). *The enigma of capital and the crises of capitalism*. New York: Oxford University Press.

hooks, b. (2009). *Belonging: A culture of place*. New York: Routledge.

Howley, C., & Howley, A. (2010). Poverty and school achievement in rural communities: A social class interpretation. In K. Schaaft & A. Youngblood (Eds.), *Rural education in the twenty-first century: Identity, place and community in a globalizing world* (pp. 34–50). College Park: Pennsylvania State University Press.

Huxley, A. (2009). *Island*. New York: HarperPerennial. (Original work published 1962)

Kunstler, J. (2008). *World made by hand*. New York: Grove.

Latour, B. (1993). *We have never been modern*. Cambridge, MA: Harvard University Press.

Latour, B. (2005). *Reassembling the social: An introduction to actor-network theory*. Oxford, UK: Oxford University Press.

Leander, K., Phillips, N., & Taylor, K. (2010). The changing social spaces of learning: Mapping new mobilities, *Review of Research in Education, 34*, 329–394.

Lefebvre, H. (1991). *The production of space*. London: Wiley Blackwell.

Lefebvre, H. (2002). *Critique of everyday life: Foundations for a sociology of the everyday*. London: Verso.

Luke, A. (2011). Generalizing across borders: Policy and the limits of educational science. *Educational Researcher*, *40*(8), 367–377.

Marx, K. (1970). *The German ideology*. New York: International Publishers.

Marx, K. (1977). *Capital, Volume 1*. New York: Vintage.

Marx, K. (1998). *Communist manifesto: A modern edition*. London: Verso. (Original work published 1848.)

Massey, D. (2005). *For space*. London: Sage.

McCarthy, C. (2006). *The road*. New York: Knopf.

Mingay, G. E. (1989). *The rural idyll*. New York: Routledge.

Nespor, J. (2004). Educational scale-making. *Pedagogy, Culture, and Society*, *12*(3), 309–326.

Peters, M. (2011). *Cognitive capitalism: Education and digital labour.* New York: Peter Lang.

Riordan, C. (2003). *Equality and achievenent.* New York: Prentice Hall.

Scott, J. (1999). *Seeing like a state: How certain schemes to improve the human condition have failed.* New Haven, CT: Yale University Press.

Soja, D. (2010). *Seeking spatial justice.* Minneapolis: University of Minnesota Press.

Spring, J. (2008). *Globalization of education: An introduction.* New York: Routledge.

Theobald, P. (1997). *Teaching the commons: Place, pride and the renewal of community.* Boulder, CO: Westview Press.

Tuan, Y. (1977). *Space and place: The perspective of experience.* Minneapolis: University of Minnesota Press.

Zizek, S. (2011). *Living in the end times.* London: Verso.

Questions to Think About

1. How do systems of education differ in agricultural, industrial, and postindustrial economies?
2. Why is human capital theory not useful in explaining the value of education on worker productivity?
3. What are the consequences of having a highly credentialed education system?
4. How does Sanderson use nation-building and credential inflation theories to describe the ways in which educational systems in postindustrial economies benefit the upper classes?
5. Why does Corbin dislike the idea of examining schools as commodities?
6. What are the effects of location to a school environment?
7. What is the difference between Marxism and neoliberalism? What theoretical paradigms do each fall under (conflict, structural-functionalist, symbolic interaction)? How can you tell from Corbett's essay?

Resources

 A tale of two schools: video of education inequalities in Long Island, NY: http://www.eraseracismny.org/resource-center/video-gallery/175-tale-of-two-schools-race-and-education-on-long-island

 National Center for Educational Statistics:
http://nces.ed.gov/

 US. Department of Education:
http://www.ed.gov/

 WorldBank:
http://data.worldbank.org/

SECTION VII
URBAN ISSUES

Introduction

The two readings in this section focus on issues often prevalent in urban areas. Urban areas are places where large numbers of people live, work, and socialize, usually in very close proximity. Thus, issues that may be ignored in less densely populated rural—and many suburban—areas tend to bubble to the surface in cities. Because of the nature of urban areas, people are able to communicate with a wide variety of individuals, police can observe large numbers of people in a short period, and problems with spatial segregation and housing often develop due to a competition for space and resources. Issues of stratification and social class create an atmosphere in which tensions between groups lie close to the surface.

Because of the organization of urban areas, they are usually places where social movements begin. A social movement occurs when a group of individuals see a condition in need of change and seek to create that change. In the article "No There There: Social Movements and Urban Political Community," Chris Rhomberg contends previous models of social movements are insufficient in describing the full extent of the emergence of social movements. Traditional political sociology focuses on the social structures causing a need for social change. Issues of inequality and a competition for scarce resources, such as housing and jobs, create a cauldron in which social movements begin to form. According to Rhomberg, this cauldron is not enough. The traditional theories assume social movements occur in areas where all the players have equal standing but fail to take into account the effects of institutions.

Rhomberg argues that in order for social movements to be completely understood, several theories taken together develop a better picture. New institutionalism and regime theories offer an understanding of the political structures that must be present along with the social dynamics for social movements to occur. New institutionalism theory explores the ways politicians and political systems do not represent the will of the masses, but rather the will of their own interests, and the political landscape reflects those interests and lays out the "rules of the game." Regime theory, a byproduct of new institutionalism, explores the ways political regimes—or groups of politicians, business elite, and elite social alliances—form to create policies benefiting the advantaged groups. Because political regimes consist of the most powerful people in the community, they have the strength to oppress interests that oppose them. Social movements then rise to challenge the power of the regime.

Both of the previous theories explore the conditions making social movements likely, but Rhomberg argues they do not explain why the contesting groups emerge and mobilize. Social movements theory examines the social context allowing for resource mobilization and activism. Urban areas open opportunities to mobilize resources because of the numerous opportunities for civic discourse. The prime areas for this discourse are in the neighborhoods of individuals living in the urban community and in the workplace. Social movement organizations then intervene to bring these diverse groups together for a single cause, drawing on the group's shared culture and collective identity. These three theories, taken together, form a more comprehensive framework for understanding the conditions making social movements possible along with ways in which urban areas provide unique opportunities for mobilization.

Another common urban problem is homelessness. People who become homeless can be found anywhere, but are most visible in urban areas. Although being homeless is, in itself, not a crime, the policies and laws enacted in urban areas often criminalize the behavior of homeless individuals. For example, laws making sleeping in public spaces illegal make sleeping virtually illegal for unhoused individuals. In "Portland's Response to Homeless Issues and the 'Broken Windows' Theory," Tracy J. Prince examines how cities use broken windows policies to "control their homeless populations." She then provides a case study of Portland, Oregon, to discover whether similar strategies are used. Broken windows theory is used in many urban areas to "clean up" crime in the cities. The premise is that focusing on petty crimes such as vandalism or loitering will keep other, more harmful crimes from occurring. In the case of the homeless, applying a broken windows approach means police would aggressively question, ticket, and/or imprison any person who violates a loitering, sleeping, panhandling, or other small violation that a city enacts. The result would, theoretically, be a reduction of the homeless, or at the least concentrating homeless individuals in a small area. Also, many cities apply the magnet theory of homelessness, which states people who are homeless will be attracted to cities with good services. Under this premise, many cities have reduced the services they provide so they do not act as "magnets." This theory disregards the fact it is difficult for those without means to research their options, much less travel from city to city seeking homeless services.

Although Portland has a reputation of being a progressive city, it also has low wages, large unemployment rates, and a large number of homeless. After exploring the policies of

New York, Seattle, and San Francisco, which have implemented broken windows-type policies and policing, Prince finds the strategies Portland uses to deal with homeless issues more often fall in line with its reputation as a progressive city. Although there are several statutes limiting the activity of its downtown homeless, the city has yet to fully implement broken windows policing. The city acknowledges the lack of affordable housing and the need for services, and has, along with some of the "broken windows" policies, enacted some progressive measures—such as a large, well-organized tent city—that focus more on seeking help for the homeless and less on policing them.

Reading 12: No There There

Social Movements and Urban Political Community

By Chris Rhomberg

On the night of May 5, 1922, a crowd of some fifteen hundred men wearing white robes and masks gathered silently in a valley in the hills above Oakland, California. Rows of parked cars lined the nearby road, and two searchlights beamed across the sky as a fiery cross burned behind an altar draped with the American flag. At a given signal, five hundred more unmasked men marched four abreast toward the altar to take their oaths and be initiated into the order of the Knights of the Ku Klux Klan. Newspaper reporters were brought in to record the scene, and hooded Klansmen from as far away as San Francisco, Sacramento, Fresno, San Jose, and Los Angeles came to join their Oakland brethren for the ceremony.[1]

In the early 1920s, a powerful Ku Klux Klan movement burst forth in many American cities, targeting immigrant Jews and Catholics as well as people of color and attracting an estimated four to six million members, in what some consider to be the largest right-wing movement in our nation's history.[2] By 1924, the Oakland Klan alone enrolled at least two thousand members, including such prominent and ordinary citizens as Protestant clergy, small businessmen, professionals and managers, salesmen, skilled workers, public employees, and even the son of a U.S. Congressman. A year later, the *Oakland Tribune* reported that eighty-five hundred Klansmen and women and their supporters from across the country filled the Oakland Auditorium to witness the swearing-in of five hundred members joining the national order.[3]

Blending prejudice with advocacy on issues like Prohibition and opposition to urban machine politics, the Klan enjoyed significant support in Oakland, a city whose population in 1920 was more than 90 percent white. Local Klan leaders won election as county sheriff in 1926 and city commissioner of streets in 1927, and quickly established their own patronage networks in city hall. Their power was finally broken in a celebrated graft trial prosecuted by Alameda County District Attorney (and later U.S. Supreme Court Chief Justice) Earl Warren.

The scandal achieved such notoriety that it led directly to a major reform of the Oakland city charter in 1930 that abolished the city commissions and created a city-manager form of government.

Fast-forward to 1946. By this time, Oakland had already experienced the economic and political upheavals of the Great Depression and New Deal eras, including the 1934 General Strike across the bay in nearby San Francisco. World War II accelerated the process of change, stimulating production in local shipyards and factories and attracting a massive influx of new workers to labor in the defense industries. By 1945, Oakland's population had increased by as much as a third and its black population had more than tripled, reaching almost 10 percent of the total number of city residents.[4]

Nationally, the end of the war was followed in 1946 by a wave of strikes, the largest in American history, involving more than four million workers.[5] In Oakland, however, class polarization emerged not from the factories or the waterfront but from a strike of downtown retail clerks, most of whom were women. In late 1946, a majority of workers at Kahn's, a department store, and Hastings, a men's store, struck to demand recognition of their union. Local drivers from the International Brotherhood of Teamsters honored their picket line and refused to deliver goods to the stores during a busy holiday season. The retail business elites then pressured the city government to break the picket, and a massive display of police force sparked a citywide General Strike by the city's American Federation of Labor (AFL) unions in protest. For two and a half days, an estimated one hundred thousand striking workers from 142 unions shut down factories, shipyards, construction sites, most retail shops, and virtually all transportation in the city. Crowds estimated at between five thousand and twenty thousand people rallied in downtown Oakland in largely peaceful demonstrations outside the struck stores.

Labor insurgency carried over through the following spring, when four union-endorsed candidates won upset elections to the city council, despite a vigorous Red-baiting campaign led by the *Oakland Tribune*. The popular challenge in city government lasted until 1950, when politics in Oakland again split into two camps. Backed by the AFL Central Labor Council, the local Congress of Industrial Organizations (CIO), and the National Association for the Advancement of Colored People (NAACP), the city council voted to authorize the construction of three thousand units of federally subsidized public housing, as part of a comprehensive plan to remove urban "blight" in the central city. Opponents attacked the plan as "socialistic" and, led by the Apartment House Owners Association and the Oakland Real Estate Board, launched a recall campaign against the progressive councillors. The result was the defeat of one of the councillors, the withdrawal of the housing proposal, and the end of the liberal coalition on the city council.[6]

Turn again to twenty years later. The city's African American population had grown steadily during the postwar decades, but racial segregation in housing kept it concentrated initially in the West Oakland ghetto, where unemployment and poverty were at least two to three times the city average.[7] By the 1960s, however, continued population growth, along with displacements resulting from highway construction and urban renewal projects, pushed black residents toward other areas of the city. Tensions in racially transitional neighborhoods led to increased intervention by the city's social service and law enforcement agencies to control juvenile delinquency and manage problems of "social disorganization." These early efforts in Oakland later expanded under (and served as a model for) national urban social programs sponsored by the Ford Foundation and the federal government's War on Poverty.[8]

As the civil rights movement of the '60s spread from the southern states to cities in the North and West, such programs frequently became the catalysts for black community organization and political mobilization.[9] In Oakland, struggles emerged for control of the city's Community Action Agency and Model Cities programs, centering on demands for jobs, housing, and social services, as well as long-standing grievances over police conduct in the black community. The latter, especially, helped give rise to the Black Panther Party for Self-Defense, founded in Oakland in 1966.[10]

Racial polarization persisted for years in Oakland, as a conservative white political elite held on to power in city government and black community organizations engaged in a "long march" through the corridors of an array of urban public bureaucracies. Unlike many other American cities, no major riot occurred in Oakland during the period, but the city did not escape violence, including several fatal shootouts between Black Panther members and police. Yet despite the imprisonment or exile of many leading members between 1967 and 1973, Black Panther Party chair Bobby Seale's 1973 campaign for mayor won a stunning 37 percent of the vote, in the largest turnout for a regular municipal election in Oakland's history.[11]

What's Goin' on? Protest and Discontinuity in American Society

One city, three periods of popular insurgency. Each movement touched on above is radically different from the others; each one arises from a different social location or base, adopts a different form, and articulates a different collective identity, centered on ethnicity, class, and race, respectively. Yet all three occurred in the same place and within a relatively short span of about fifty years—in effect, one person's adult lifetime. How could that be? We are accustomed to thinking of cities as almost organic entities, each with its own unique biography and personality, the history of their physical development embodied in their streets, skylines, and neighborhoods, their collective memory held together by the accumulated ties of community.

But what kind of community could repeatedly undergo such diverse moments of mass polarization? It is almost as if we were talking about three different cities. The sheer juxtaposition of these movements in one place challenges our understanding and raises at least two questions. First, what explains their rapid disjuncture? Even if we allow for substantial social change in Oakland between periods, that only begs the second question: What were the lasting effects, if any, of each movement on subsequent periods and on the local community?

These questions are not just a puzzle for sociological theory, nor is Oakland an isolated case. Each one of these episodes occurred as part of nationwide social and political mobilizations that swept across twentieth-century urban America. In the 1920s, a resurgent white nativist (or "Second") Klan prospered not only in the Old South but also in Indianapolis, Denver, Los Angeles, and other cities and towns across the northern and western United States. Contrary to popular perceptions, urban Klan members came from a wide range of socioeconomic strata; many had solid social standing, and the movement was strongest where native white Protestants were a majority or rising group, not a backward or declining one. Alongside racial and ethnic intolerance, Klan leaders frequently espoused mainstream middle-class values, calling for good government, better law enforcement, and improvements in public schools and city services, and they gained considerable support through participation in electoral politics.[12]

A few years later, urban workers were at the forefront of protests against the economic crisis of the 1930s. In 1934, strikes of factory hands in Toledo, truck drivers in Minneapolis, and stevedores in San Francisco sparked mass uprisings and bore witness to the revival of labor militancy throughout the country. In the mill towns of New England and in the auto and steel hubs of the industrial Midwest, CIO union drives galvanized virtually entire communities, while in the metropolitan port cities of the West and East, long-shore, maritime, and transportation workers challenged local elites for power. With the end of World War II, the nation's streets filled with discharged soldiers, migrant war workers, and striking union members, and in 1946, citywide general strikes broke out not just in Oakland but also in Stamford, Connecticut; Lancaster and Pittsburgh, Pennsylvania; Houston, Texas; and Rochester, New York.[13]

Finally, African American experiences of migration and urbanization in the postwar period formed the social bases for the rise of the modern civil rights movement. Urban black communities provided the crucible, as sociologist Aldon Morris observes, for the "institutional building and the proliferation of dense social networks across localities and across neighborhoods in cities through which the movement was mobilized and sustained."[14] Conditions in cities also transformed the movement as it spread from the South to the racial ghettoes of the North, charting a trajectory of protest from civil rights to black power. Across the era as a whole, these changes are remembered by their urban landmarks: Montgomery and Greensboro; Birmingham and Selma; Watts, Newark, and Detroit.

"As an urban nation," political scientist John Mollenkopf writes, "urban development issues have been a primary, if not exclusive, factor in our national political development."[15] Similarly, in this book I argue that each one of these movements both reflected and called into question the experience of urban political community at distinct moments in the past century. Each represented a crucial struggle over the boundaries of the polity and the meaning of popular civic participation, and all were pivotal historical junctures in the patterning of race, class, and urban politics in the United States. Each is significant in its own right, but my aim here is to bring all three together in one place, in order to examine their relationships with one another and the dynamics of mobilization and community in urban space. And by focusing on the puzzle of their *discontinuity*, I believe an analysis of these movements can help shed light on the conditions of political community in our country today.

Social Movements and Political Community: An Analytic Framework

If the theme of this study is discontinuity, then what do these diverse movements have in common? What theoretical guidelines or tools can we use to trace their causes and consequences, and to fit them into a comparative frame? How may we identify the key actors, the conditions affecting them, and the outcomes of their interaction? In this book, I employ an explanatory framework built on three basic analytic dimensions: socioeconomic structure, institutional politics, and urban civil society.[16] To specify these I introduce here concepts drawn from three corresponding, well-known paradigms in sociology and political science: (1) traditional political sociology, grounded in the social bases of groups; (2) the "new institutionalism," with its central focus on the state; and (3) social movement theory, highlighting processes of group formation and mobilization in civil society. Each of these theoretical approaches helps explain part of the story, but each is by itself incomplete. Only by looking at it from all three perspectives together can we fully grasp the historical relationship between social movements and political community.

Socioeconomic Structure: Traditional Political Sociology

Let us begin with the old school. Traditionally, the field of political sociology took as its starting point the social origins of politics, and specifically the emergence of groups and interests from positions in an underlying social structure. This was true of classical Marxism, with its antagonistic classes arising from the societal division of labor; but it was no less true for the American pluralist social science of the 1950s and '60s, in which groups of individuals from various social strata developed different political values and interests, expressed in voting preferences and other behavior.[17] For both, macrostructural conditions in the economy and society produced the bases for the formation of groups, whose interests were translated more or less directly into the polity and into political outcomes.[18]

This approach has been subject to much criticism, of course, most often for its "reduction" of politics and culture to mere reflections of socioeconomic structure. Notwithstanding these criticisms, for our purposes the traditional paradigm continues to offer an essential point of departure. The analysis of social structure calls attention to categorical inequalities among groups, in terms of their access to and control over resources.[19] Structures embody enduring, unequal, and contradictory relationships, and therefore generate recurring problems of integration and social order, the solutions to which raise questions of political power.[20] Thus, a structure of wage labor creates problems for employers of recruiting, paying, and controlling a labor force, and problems for workers of securing jobs, income, and the regulation of work. Structures of urban settlement create shared circumstances of collective consumption for residents of an area, as well as competition with other users of the spatial environment. In each case, the structural position of actors may systematically afford or deprive them of resources or advantages in pursuing different goals.

Processes of structural change likewise affect the configuration of social relations found in the city. Geographers have examined the ways in which mobile capital investment and successive rounds of development produce uneven "layers" of urban economic and spatial structure.[21] Others have studied the entry of generations of urban migrants and their descendants into various occupational or labor market niches.[22] The distribution of residential housing also defines groups through the segregation of urban neighborhoods by class and race or ethnicity.[23] These processes are all visibly illustrated in Oakland, where the peculiarities of the city's industrial and occupational structure, the means of access to its labor and housing markets, and its patterns of migration and urban growth produced the bases for spatial differentiation and social inequality among groups.

A structural approach, therefore, identifies important societal cleavages and the unequal conditions affecting different groups. By itself, however, structural analysis does not explain each group's concrete political *interests,* their alignment with or against other groups, the strategic opportunities for action, or the particular shape of state institutions or policy. Nor does it explain processes of group formation and mobilization, or the outcomes of actual events of collective action. In short, socioeconomic structures are necessary but insufficient determinants of group formation and political conflict. Throughout the twentieth century, the city of Oakland underwent substantial structural change, much of it driven by external forces, as during the rapid transformation of the region during World War II. Nevertheless, local actors still had to negotiate the form and impact of these changes within the community. How they did so must be explained with reference to the other two analytic dimensions.

The State: The "New Institutionalism"

More recent generations of political theorists have developed an alternative perspective, sometimes referred to as the *new institutionalism*.[24] This paradigm shifts the burden of explanation from the structural bases of groups to the organizational field of politics, centered on the institutions of the state. In this view, state actors and political institutions do not simply reflect social forces but possess powers and interests of their own, and actively shape the political terrain for all groups. Unlike traditional political sociology, this theory holds that groups do not enter the political arena with predetermined capacities or goals. Rather, the political terrain itself determines the prevailing "rules of the game," deciding who counts as an actor, what is or can become an "issue," and how power is to be exercised.[25]

At the level of the city, this approach may be specified using the concept of urban political "regimes," as developed by political scientist Clarence Stone and others.[26] In this model, local political actors build alliances with private economic and social groups in order to promote urban development and govern more effectively. Power is viewed as coordinating capacity within governing coalitions, rather than as direct command or control; constituent group interests are negotiated within the dominant coalition, which determines those policy alternatives that are deemed practically achievable and how groups may benefit from them. The alliances in the regime are held together by formal and informal ties extending into civil society, which facilitate the cooperation of actors around a unifying policy agenda and overall political project.[27]

The regime model links the formal institutions of the state with the composition of its constituent groups, their mode of cooperation, and the resources they can coordinate.[28] Established regimes are self-reinforcing, with considerable power to suppress opposing interests, not so much through direct force as through the preemptive weight of the regime's accumulated relations of coordination. Subordinate or excluded groups face the daunting task of contesting not only more powerful actors but also the principles of organization in the regime. As Stone writes, "Challenging a regime is not simply a question of mobilizing opposition. It means restructuring the ways in which people and groups are related to one another and providing new avenues of cooperation between them."[29]

The periods of protest in Oakland, I will argue, each occurred under distinct urban political regimes. The Klan mobilized against a regime characterized by *machine patronage*, organized by ethnic politicians like Alameda County boss Michael Kelly. In the '30s and '40s, labor insurgency rose up against the power of what I call *business managerialism*, personified in the figure of J. R. Knowland, the conservative Republican publisher of the *Oakland Tribune*. In the '60s, the civil rights and black power movements encountered a racial order regulated by *bureaucratic insulation*, administered through the city government, quasi-independent local authorities, and federal programs. In each case, the organization of the regime embodied a specific set of political alliances and defined the dominant terrain of politics for the period.

Institutionalist state and urban regime theories tell us much about the boundaries of inclusion and exclusion in the polity, the interests and alignments among political actors, and how groups become established or hegemonic in different political or governmental arenas. But they still do not explain the *origins* of insurgent movements, how oppositional identity develops within excluded groups, or how the latter sometimes do in fact challenge regimes. Neither structural change nor political institutions alone can explain mobilization, as it develops through a historical process of self-organization among groups, and as it is revealed in the episodic pattern of collective action observed in Oakland. To understand this process we must look to the third analytical dimension, the arena of civil society, using social movement theory as a guide.

Civil Society: Social Movement Theory

Current sociological theories of social movements generally incorporate elements of the structural and political-institutional perspectives described above, as causal factors shaping the context for mobilization. Thus macrosocial changes like urbanization, industrialization, and migration affect groups' mobilization potential through changes in population size and demographic patterns, relative societal location, spatial concentration, and means of communication.[30] Similarly, the political terrain affects the strategic opportunities for action and the articulation of concrete issues and interests. Where social movement theory makes a distinctive contribution, however, is in its focus on processes of mobilization in civil society.

By *civil society* I mean the "middle ground" of social relations between the socioeconomic structure and the state. This refers to the broad field of private, formal voluntary association— including the variety of social, cultural, and community organizations, churches, labor unions, neighborhood associations, advocacy groups, and others—as well as the more informal world of family and friends, personal networks of mutual dependency and support, and the spontaneous conviviality of the "daily round."[31] Relations in civil society support the emergence of various public spaces in which people learn about, discuss, and form opinions on social and political concerns independently of the state and of the formal institutions of the public sphere (e.g., mass media, legislatures, courts).[32]

These social spaces correspond to what social movement theorists call "micromobilization contexts," and they function as arenas or sites for the collective formation of social identity and political opinion.[33] Participants in these spaces engage in an open-ended "cultural and ideological contest or negotiation" that includes the content of public affairs, their identities as speakers, and the location of boundaries between the public and private worlds. As a whole, civil society is a "multi-organizational field" that encompasses diverse streams of public discourse, whose interactions create the possibility for innovative or oppositional cultures.[34]

In the urban environment, two crucial arenas where association and group formation occur are the workplace and the neighborhood.[35] In the railroads and shipyards, machine shops and warehouses, canneries and department stores, and street corners and agency offices, groups of Oakland workers interacted with one another and developed traditions and habits of organization and collective identity. At the same time, uneven patterns of housing and urban development both united and divided groups, from the old ethnic working-class neighborhood in West Oakland, to the white middle-class housing tracts in the foothills of East Oakland, to the growing division by race throughout the city after World War II. These spatial settings formed the scene for the routines of everyday life and the experience of urban community.

Social movements are constituted in and through this medium of civil society, through the collective working out of constructions of identity, solidarity, and public awareness. But civil society does not automatically produce political insurgency. Subordinate groups may be internally stratified, fractured by structural contradictions, or divided by legacies of prior organization and political conflict.[36] Public spheres are often fragmented or dominated by elite interests, while civil society itself harbors exclusionary and hierarchical relations of private power.[37] The ambivalence of civil society underlines the importance of specialized social movement organizations as strategic agents, who intervene in civil society to make groups into collective *actors*.

Movement organizations do this by employing select repertoires of associational forms, resources, and tactics, including the cultural symbols deployed to inspire and maintain group solidarity.[38] Resources are concentrated through an often difficult process of organization building, alliance formation, and outreach among the indigenous networks and relationships of persons within subordinate populations.[39] At the same time, movement organizers try to unify the group through discursive strategies of "framing"—articulating a sense of collective identity and shared grievance—that draws on the group's own culture and the discursive possibilities in the public sphere.[40] Movement organizations act as intermediaries between the mobilization of identity in society and the negotiation of interests in the polity. To paraphrase sociologist C. Wright Mills, they turn private troubles into public issues, transforming common experiences of group inequality into cohesive oppositional identities and specific goals, alliances, and political demands.

My analysis of Oakland focuses especially on the role played by social movement organizations against the backdrop of group formation in civil society. So, for example, the Klan used the familiar model of the secret fraternal society to promote a nativist ideology that combined Protestant moralism, urban reformism, and racial and ethnic chauvinism into a persuasive collective identity and mobilizing force. Labor unions gave an organizational form and voice to workers who had endured the Depression, migration, and war, transforming their hopes and fears into mass militancy and political action. The civil rights and black power movements drew on forms of ghetto neighborhood organization and racial solidarity to unite African American residents and challenge the city to overcome racial segregation and inequality.

This brings us to the question of urban political community. As we have seen, structural forces concentrate diverse populations in urban space, creating interdependencies of work, consumption, and residence in a local economic area, as well as shared interactions with local government and political institutions. Beyond these linkages, such populations form a political community through their formal and informal recognition of mutual rights and responsibilities to participate in collective self-governance.[41] The *content* of their community, however—its meaning and boundaries—remains historically variable and often politically contested. Who belongs to the community and how they recognize their rights and responsibilities to one another are critical questions not only for analysis but for the participants themselves. For us, the answers to these questions will be most clearly revealed in events of collective action.

Collective Action and the Struggle for Political Community

The analytic dimensions of socioeconomic structure, institutional politics, and civil society provide the theoretical scaffolding for my narrative account of events in Oakland. Within this framework, a comparison of the three movements reveals not an invariant outcome but a recurring problem. Urban political elites govern through the construction of regimes, organizing selective ties among actors in the state and society through the mechanisms of machine patronage, business management, or bureaucratic insulation. These regimes define the boundaries of community and the dominant terrain of political power, in the cases described here along the lines of ethnicity, class, and race. Structural changes can and do destabilize regimes, however, creating opportunities for excluded groups. Challenging actors mobilize on the field of civil society, building up group solidarity, articulating their collective identity, and reaching out to a larger public. In the course of insurgency, challengers bring to bear strong new claims of political community on actors in the urban setting, in order to win recognition and achieve their demands.

In so doing, movement actors must create or expand the public spaces needed to make their challenges heard. Yet these public spaces are highly fragile, political institutions are normally exclusive, and privileged groups turn away from public dialogue toward the protection of private interests and domains. Under normal conditions, regime hegemony rests not on any strong consensus but on the demobilization or dispersal of opposition—hence the explosiveness of polarization when it occurs. And urban civil society in the United States is itself a deeply fragmented terrain, divided historically by race, class, and other social fissures. The fragmentation of urban civil society undermines the capacity of the local civic arena to bind actors together in a mutually responsive political community.

Social movement organizers maneuvering on this terrain face difficult tasks: maintaining group unity, keeping coalitions together, and contending with more powerful actors. Moments of collective action are inevitably uncertain and involve real risks of repression, disintegration, or defeat. In the absence of a strong civic community, movement organizers turn instead to institutional strategies, attempting to secure their gains by incorporating group demands into the political fabric of the regime. The turn to institutionalization leads on the one hand to the decline of mobilization, and on the other to the redrawing of the boundaries of institutional power. Subsequent challenges, then, emerge from groups with different identities affected by different dimensions of exclusion, who face the legacy, and the limits, of previous rounds of reform. Thus discontinuity.

Again and again—through protests and strikes, and in key local elections—challenging actors in Oakland sought to enlarge the sphere of public discourse, and to gain access and entry to the polity. Yet, as often, the strength of the political community was insufficient to sustain the actors' engagement with one another. There was not enough *there* there; civil society remained divided, coalitions broke apart, and participation declined as movement actors settled into institutional reform. The outcomes produced the demobilization of collective actors and the reconstitution of urban regimes, not a continuing dialogue among groups in a dynamic political community.

Discontinuity, however, also means that boundaries and identities are not fixed. The institutional settlements affected the formation of actors but failed to eliminate the structures of inequality. As new structural changes occurred, or as relations among groups broke down, so the conditions of political community were again transformed. Social movements remained crucial vehicles in this process, reconfiguring identities and mobilizing collective actors in new forms.

The Problem of Discontinuity: Historical Perspectives

In a nutshell, this model describes the relationship I observe in Oakland between social movements and urban political community. How does my analysis compare to other accounts of these dynamics? To be sure, more traditional interpretations take a different view. Among the latter are what might be called the assimilationist, cyclical disorder, and social capital models of political community. Each of these draws from and lends itself to broad historical readings of American politics and society, and each offers a different explanation for social movement discontinuity. Yet none adequately distinguishes the three dimensions of socioeconomic structure, institutional politics, and civil society.

The Traditional Paradigm: Assimilationism

Perhaps the most familiar version is the traditional assimilationist paradigm, in which periods of mobilization merely reflect the temporary pressures associated with the accommodation or entry of new groups into the American polity. In this model, cities are the great melting pots of American democracy, where members of incoming groups find opportunities for education and social mobility; develop multiple, cross-cutting social ties; and learn to participate in a unifying, public-regarding "civic culture."[42] Movements are but symptoms of the individual and social adjustments that occur in this process, which results in the progressive incorporation of groups into an open, liberal, and pluralist institutional arena.

In this view, the Klan serves as a negative case: Traditional accounts portray it as a reactionary extremist movement, the "last desperate protest of a nineteenth-century Protestantism in the course of eclipse."[43] Attracting mainly isolated, downwardly mobile or lower-middle-class persons on the margins of urban society, the Klan's bigotry and intolerance offered symbolic relief for its supporters' status anxieties, but the organization ultimately collapsed, along with its disappearing social base. By contrast, the labor struggles of the '30s and '40s captured the democratic aspirations of the rising urban immigrant working classes and delivered them into the high tide of political incorporation under the New Deal. Under the auspices of the 1935 National Labor Relations Act, unions became partners in the formation of an industrial welfare state, gaining a permanent status as an interest group aligned with the Democratic Party.[44]

What the labor movement did for ethnic working classes, by analogy, the civil rights movement did for blacks. As African Americans migrated from the rural South to the urban centers, they followed in the footsteps of the European immigrants, first organizing in their own communities and eventually pressing for the recognition of their rights. The civil rights movement won by appealing to established democratic values, earning northern liberal support against the archaic racial caste system of the Old South. With the passage of federal civil and voting rights laws in the 1960s, African Americans finally secured entry as equal members of the polity, fulfilling the promise of American democracy.[45]

The assimilationist tradition rightly puts social movements in the context of macrostructural processes and periods of institutional change. But the ideology of progressive liberal incorporation often fails to understand how structural forces affect the social bases of groups, both before and after the process of "entry." A growing body of historical research now shows that urban Klansmen were *not* disproportionally lower-class or marginal individuals, but instead roughly paralleled the general population in their communities.[46] The organization of labor unions often both reflected and reinforced exclusionary labor markets and racial-ethnic divisions within the urban working class. And behind the achievements of the civil rights movement were persistent patterns of socioeconomic stratification, between blacks and whites and within the black population, some of which have since become even more pronounced.[47]

Just as important, the concept of an integrative civic culture presupposes that interests are represented more or less equally or transparently within a liberal political sphere. But civic and political institutions can be highly selective about which interests gain access and how they are represented. In the '20s, the Klan's racial and ethnic prejudice often proved no barrier to its political legitimacy, but rather mirrored prevailing public opinion among white Protestant middle classes, merging rhetorically with other elements of so-called progressive municipal reform. Conversely, labor historians have observed the institutional constraints imposed by the legal regulation of collective bargaining, notwithstanding the real gains that workers achieved. Capital mobility and limitations on workers' rights to organize meant that firms could abandon older unionized industrial cities and states for nonunion areas in the suburbs and in the South and West, where rapid postwar growth sustained the regional bases for the alliance of conservative Republicans and southern Democrats in the U.S. Congress. Throughout the postwar era, the unions were unable to alter these substantive constraints, despite their allegiance to the majority Democratic Party.[48]

Other scholars have emphasized the racial boundaries that characterized New Deal politics and policies from their beginnings.[49] Later, as black migration increased to the urban North and West, federal and local housing and urban renewal programs systematically segregated or discriminated against African Americans.[50] These and other government actions served to perpetuate informal but entrenched societal relations of racial exclusion in housing, employment, and education. Nondiscrimination laws alone proved insufficient to undo these relations, leading to the introduction of affirmative action and other types of state intervention to achieve integration and racial equality. These policies have had mixed success, however, and are themselves now increasingly under attack.[51]

In short, the simple ebb and flow of mobilization cannot be taken as a sign of stable liberal assimilation. The fate of the New Deal and civil rights coalitions underlines the impermanence of their political settlements; contrary to the image of steady, progressive inclusion, relations among groups have seen periods of democratic expansion and conservative retrenchment. In the city, actors are made, unmade, and remade, altering not only the balance of power among interests but also the culture of the civic community.

The Limits of Assimilation: Cyclical Disorder Theory

A second, more skeptical, view of discontinuity might be labeled *cyclical disorder* theory. In this model, democratic institutions are if anything *too* open and subject to popular pressures.

For political scientist Samuel Huntington, American political culture is defined by a historically constant system of beliefs or "creed," identified with values of liberty, equality, individualism, and democracy. Periodically, Americans are seized by an intense moral fervor for these ideals, yet such moments of "creedal passion" raise excessive and contradictory demands that no government can practically satisfy. The result is an inevitable cycle of disappointment, cynicism, and political retreat, which then prepares the ground for renewed outbursts of creedal intensity.[52] Political scientist James Morone argues that reformers in American politics win support by invoking a myth of "the people" as a united community, participating directly in the control of their own affairs. Once the desired reforms are actually implemented, however, the image of community dissolves into a maze of fragmented government bureaucracies and competing, self-interested groups.[53] In these theories, democratic participation leads not to assimilation but to conflict and political gridlock, while collective action ends mainly in unintended consequences. Radical protest undermines established authority without realizing the reformers' ideals, and other critics have blamed social movements, particularly those of the '60s, for contributing to the breakdown of civic solidarity and urban moral order.[54]

Cyclical disorder theorists correctly point to the limits of assimilation, and of the political system's capacity to mediate contradictory demands. But they do not adequately explain how or why political institutions have the distinct capacities that they do. In Oakland, as we shall see, the machine politics of the '20s, the business managerialism of the '30s and '40s, and the large-scale bureaucratic administration of the '60s were all different ways of organizing the polity, and each generated different kinds of responses. By contrast, the idea of a constant, invariant cycle does not capture the historical stakes involved in each period, and obscures significant differences in the development of political institutions and their relation to groups in society.[55]

Similarly, broad, abstract notions of "creed" or "people" do not account well for the complex ways in which ethnic, class, and racial identities operated at each juncture. After all, the Klan was hardly egalitarian, unions did not preach individualism, and the civil rights movement showed no liberal fear of government. Likewise, pessimism about protest does not allow for how mobilization might actually express collective agency or effectively bring about change, notwithstanding its varied consequences. In each period, movement actors articulated specific identities, grievances, and alternative visions of the urban future. We will do better to trace more closely who the actors were in each case, their paths of formation, and their roles in the struggle to define their political community.

The Collapse of Community? Social Capital and Civic Engagement
Over the past decade, scholarly and public debates in the United States have again turned to problems of community and politics, although this time for very different reasons. Unlike the earlier periods of mobilization, in the 1990s researchers were more likely to note a disturbing

decline in popular civic and political participation.[56] In contrast to both the assimilationist faith in liberal integration and the cyclical theorists' distrust of democracy, Americans seemed to be losing their sense of political community altogether.

One of the more prominent figures in this "civic disengagement" debate has been political scientist Robert Putnam. In a series of publications, Putnam has argued that Americans have experienced a historic loss of individuals' "social capital," by which he means those "features of social life—networks, norms, and trust—that enable participants to act together more effectively to pursue shared objectives." For Putnam, social capital is the key to a healthy civil society, the essential precondition for bringing citizen action together with public policy and "making democracy work." The collapse of a broad social connectedness has deprived citizens of vital links with their communities, thereby diminishing their attachment to public concerns.[57]

What has caused this decline of community? The demands of modern organizations of work, the sprawling pattern of urban growth, and the effects of television and mass media on leisure time have all played a part in eroding the ties among individuals. But for Putnam the most important factor is a generational gap in the socialization of persons into the norms and networks of social trust. In order to revive democratic participation, Putnam advocates revitalizing local grassroots forms of voluntary association, as a way to increase social capital and as a forum for popular civic education.[58]

The debate over civic engagement has raised serious questions about the current state of American political community, yet the analysis of social capital shares some of the weaknesses of the earlier theoretical approaches. The benign vision of local civil society discounts the historical weight of both structural group conflict and institutional power.[59] Putnam's model implicitly recalls the older sociological theory of social disorganization, in which individuals' atomization leads to anomic dysfunctions and the failure to integrate into a consensual civic culture. Correspondingly, his programmatic stress falls on the education and socialization of individuals, not on the structural forces that unequally distribute resources and actively produce disorganization, or on the institutional barriers that discourage participation and disempower certain groups. Indeed, under some circumstances, comparatively higher levels of civic engagement might well take the form of polarization and mass protest, as we will see in Oakland.

The metaphor of social capital makes community a marketlike commodity, but the logic of markets does not spontaneously create democratic institutions.[60] Putnam is right to bring our attention to the lived experience of everyday life in neighborhoods, workplaces, and other "face-to-face" associational settings typical of urban civil society.[61] But the social capital approach blurs the transition from private voluntarism to political action, from civil society to public politics. The focus on individuals' norms and behavior neglects the role of *collective* actors in sustaining participation and in forging the bonds of political community. People engage in the life of their communities not only through private affiliations but also as members of mobilized groups, through strikes, demonstrations, elections, and other forms of collective action in the public sphere. These are often concentrated in highly contentious and pivotal events, whose outcomes shape our understanding of the *content* of political community.

The assimilationist, cyclical disorder, and social capital theories all fail to account adequately for the problem of social movement discontinuity. All underestimate the effect of structural forces on the social bases of groups, and on the resources available to them. All presume an open, neutral, and liberal civic and political arena, without adequately theorizing the institutional capacities, organization, or biases of the state. Finally, none provides an appropriate framework for understanding social movements, or political community, as a relationship among collective actors.

Oakland: A Case Study

This book offers a case study of these three social movements in Oakland, from the point of view of urban political development in twentieth-century America. As a case study, it draws on that tradition of social research, associated with Max Weber, which is grounded in the causal explanation of social action in specific historical contexts.[62] In this tradition, as Charles Ragin writes, sociological analysis aims at generating "limited historical generalizations that are objectively possible and cognizant of enabling conditions and limiting means—of context." The approach is case-oriented because it looks to the configuration of causes and conditions in a given historical setting, interpreted as a whole. The in-depth study of particular cases can allow us to uncover those social mechanisms—or what Charles Tilly calls "recurrent causal sequences of general scope"—that are analogous across cases or relevant in other settings.[63]

My focus is on the struggles of groups and actors to forge a political solidarity and community in an urban context. As a window onto these processes, the city of Oakland has certain advantages. Founded in the middle of the nineteenth century, it grew rapidly to its mature size during the period of this research, in the early and mid twentieth century. A medium-size city, with a population of 384,575 in 1950, it is large enough to feature problems of concentration, industrialization, and population change typical of American urban centers, yet small enough to permit observation of its social and political relations more or less as a whole. Moreover, the prominence of all three movements in the city's history makes it an especially useful case, displaying the more pronounced aspects of polarization and discontinuity that are my specific concerns.

At the same time, no claim is made here that Oakland is representative, statistically or otherwise, of all American cities. By identifying its unique circumstances, however, we can establish comparative standards for analyzing similar and different conditions in other cities and regions in the United States. Nor do I assume that all relevant contextual factors are enclosed within the city itself: Larger economic forces, state and national politics, broader cultural traditions, and even global events like World War II—all exerted enormous influence. But whatever these external forces were, local actors still had to negotiate their impact on group relations and politics within Oakland, and they often did so in highly conscious and deliberate ways. That is the process that I will examine here.

Because of my interest in mobilization, I divide the overall time frame in Oakland into three periods, each associated with a specific movement and its dominant political terrain: roughly 1900 to 1930, 1930 to 1950, and 1950 to 1977. Although these periods do not perfectly separate each movement in time, arranging Oakland history in this manner serves my analytical purposes in two ways: First, it allows for an individualizing comparison between periods, calling attention to their distinctive characteristics and differences; and second, it provides a longitudinal comparative design for inquiry into the sequential relationship between periods of movement activity.[64]

My central problem is to explain change—discontinuity—across periods in the same place, and correlatively to ask what effects earlier periods had on later ones. Hence, I depart from the traditional variable-based causal models that are standard in much of contemporary social science. Such models require strong assumptions of equivalence and independence between cases in order to test the validity of uniform hypotheses generalized for all cases. This would require assuming, at the outset, that each period had no effect on the others—in other words, that at three successive times, Oakland really was simply three different cities, all subject to the same causal forces. Regardless of whether such a claim were plausible, it would immediately assume away an investigation into what I am really interested in—namely, the discontinuity and sequence, or change, between periods.[65]

Moreover, in variable-based methods, cases do not operate as *contexts*, or configurations of parts in interrelated wholes, that are subject to reflexive action or internal transformation. Instead, cases are assumed to be drawn from a population of fixed entities with analytically separate attributes. The researcher hypothesizes that some of these attributes affect other attributes, and the hypothesized causal factors act largely independently from one another to produce constant effects across all cases.[66] Again, this abstracts from the very features with which I am most concerned: the relations between groups and actors in the temporal unfolding of events.

Therefore, I adopt a narrative analytic method, in order to capture what sociologist Larry Griffin describes as "the mutually constitutive interplay of agency and social structure, a dynamic continuously occurring in time and through time."[67] From this perspective, causal social forces are embedded in the sequences of interactions between actors and their historical context, understood as a set of enabling conditions, influences, and constraints. This approach allows for the possibility that actors and events may alter their environments, that outcomes in earlier periods may affect conditions for later ones, and that the institutional settings for and meanings of action can change, for example, as the central axis of political conflict shifts from one set of identities to another (see the methodological appendix).

The Plan of this Book

In the story that follows, I begin my study of each period by surveying the socioeconomic structural conditions generating the social bases of unequal groups. I then describe the organization of the dominant political regime, its member groups and their mode of coordination, and the ways these factors define the boundaries of inclusion and exclusion in the urban polity. I observe the paths of group formation on the field of urban civil society, focusing especially on the rise of new or newly mobilized collective identities and forms of organization.

At crucial junctures, the paths of these groups intersect in urban public space. I follow the interactions of movement actors and established elites in sequences of mobilization and conflict, tracing the steps that lead to polarization and political crisis. In such moments, the opposition between the goals of the movement and the mechanisms of reproduction in the regime highlight the choices at stake and their implications for the future pattern of urban development. The outcomes of these events, in turn, shape the political terrain for subsequent periods of regime-making and social movement challenge.

For clarity of exposition, each period is divided into two chapters. The first describes the context of mobilization under the existing regime, and the second concentrates on events leading to increasing polarization and its outcomes. Chapter 2 begins by drawing a baseline of economic, political, and social development in Oakland from the beginning of the twentieth century to 1920, showing how these forces generated the principal contending groups and the dominant political terrain. On the one hand, an old corporate elite and an ethnic (Catholic) working class were united through a system of urban machine patronage, while on the other, a rising downtown merchant class and white Protestant middle class experienced exclusion from this regime and increasingly mobilized for reform. Structural changes up through World War I destabilized these actors and their alliances, leading to a brief upsurge of working-class militancy, which was largely defeated after the war.

This review sets the stage for the events of the '20s, described in chapter 3. Rapid commercial and residential growth greatly increased the size and strength of both downtown business and the white middle class, the latter providing the social base for the emergence of the Ku

Klux Klan. Taking the form of a secret fraternal society (a common form of grassroots social and political organization at the time), the Klan mobilized opposition to the machine using a discourse of ethnic nativism. Once in power, however, the Klan leaders themselves succumbed to the institutions of machine politics, becoming simply one more corrupt faction. Middle-class whites then transferred their allegiance from the Klan to the downtown business leaders, who pushed through a series of reforms that effectively eliminated machine politics from city government.

These reforms produced a major break and reorientation in the relations between the local government and societal actors. Oakland shifted from a political terrain dominated by ethnicity to one more strongly defined by class power. Chapter 4 begins with the consolidation of a new regime, which I describe here as business managerialism. Led by *Oakland Tribune* publisher Joseph Knowland, the downtown elite intervened more or less directly in the control of Oakland's economic development, while the reformed city council maintained a middle-class "caretaker" government oriented toward low taxes and homeowner services. At the same time, the crisis of the Great Depression stimulated a return of working-class militancy, marked by the rise of unions affiliated with the CIO. During the '30s, however, organizational rivalry between the CIO and the older, larger AFL unions kept the working-class challenge in check, helping to preserve the power of the urban regime.

In the '40s, wartime industrialization brought a massive new influx of working-class population, socially isolating the business regime and creating the conditions for class polarization. In chapter 5, I analyze the events leading up to and during the General Strike, and the political mobilization that followed. In the General Strike, Oakland workers demonstrated an extraordinary class solidarity, allowing the unions to defend themselves successfully in a showdown with the downtown elite. The pursuit of democratic reform in city government, however, called for more complex alliances on a difficult terrain, and the unions' inability to bridge divisions of class and race, even within their own ranks, limited their ability to achieve broader institutional change.

Chapter 6 picks up the third case. By the early '50s, the downtown elites had weathered the postwar working-class challenge, and they began to pursue their own agenda of urban and regional redevelopment. This included major changes in housing, economic, and transportation infrastructures, administered by an array of new bureaucratic public authorities. Redevelopment led to the displacement of the growing yet politically excluded black population and to the dissatisfaction of white homeowners who opposed the movement of black residents into their neighborhoods. Political elites responded by adding separate layers of administrative social programs, largely funded by the federal government and premised on the principle of bureaucratic insulation. While offering opportunities, these programs also channeled black mobilization toward a parallel form of bureaucratic enfranchisement and reinforced the compartmentalization of black demands.[68]

The failures of this form of incorporation helped drive the racial polarization of the late '60s, discussed in chapter 7. In particular, controversies surrounding the issues of unemployment and relations between police and the community formed the local context for the emergence of the black power movement. This took shape in several forms: in the rise of the Black Panther Party among black youth, in the radicalization of protest in the city's federal Community Action and Model Cities programs, and in the turn to demands for community control. Official resistance on the part of the city government to these pressures maintained the atmosphere of racial polarization in Oakland, setting the stage for the electoral campaigns of Bobby Seale for mayor and Elaine Brown for city councillor in 1973.

The final chapter recaps the dynamics that lead to social movement discontinuity, focusing on the problem of urban political community, and explores some of the theoretical implications of the results. I compare the historical experiences in Oakland with those in other American cities and examine some of the changes that have occurred in Oakland in the 1980s and '90s. Finally, I reflect on the significance of the analysis for current debates on civic and political engagement and the future of democratic participation in the United States. Throughout the book, my deepest concern will be to understand not only the way things are, but how they can change.

Notes

1. *Oakland Post-Enquirer*, May 6, 1922; *San Francisco Examiner*, May 7, 1922.

2. Seymour M. Lipset and Earl Raab, *The Politics of Unreason: Right-Wing Extremism in America, 1790–1970* (New York: Harper & Row, 1970), p. 21.

3. *Knights of the Ku Klux Klan, Inc., v. Leon C. Francis et al.*, case file no. 81245, Civil Division, California Superior Court, Alameda County, 1925; *Knights of the Ku Klux Klan, Inc., v. East Bay Club of Alameda County*, case file no. 82470, Civil Division, California Superior Court, Alameda County, 1925; *San Francisco Chronicle*, August 12, 1924; *Oakland Tribune*, August 24, 1925.

4. Commonwealth Club of California, *The Population of California* (San Francisco: Parker, 1946), pp. 105–120, 169; U.S. Bureau of the Census, *Special Reports*, Series CA-3, no. 3: *Characteristics of the Population, Labor Force, Families and Housing, San Francisco Bay Congested Area: April, 1944* (Washington, D.C.: GPO, 1944), pp. 7, 14; idem, *Special Census of Oakland, California: October 9, 1945* (Washington, D.C.: GPO, 1946).

5. Joel Seidman, *American Labor from Defense to Reconversion* (Chicago: University of Chicago Press, 1953).

6. Marilynn Johnson, "Mobilizing the Homefront: Labor and Politics in Oakland, 1941–1951," in *Working People of California*, ed. Daniel Cornford (Berkeley: University of California Press, 1995), pp. 344–368; *Oakland Tribune*, July 21, 1949; *San Francisco Chronicle*, February 27 and 18 and March 2 and 5, 1950.

7. U.S. Bureau of the Census, *1970 Census of the Population, Supplementary Report: Negro Population in Selected Places and Selected Counties* (Washington, D.C.: GPO, 1971), p. 5. Oakland City Planning Department, *West Oakland:A 701 Subarea Report* (Oakland: City Planning Department, 701 Division, May 1969).

8. Ralph Kramer, *Participation of the Poor: Comparative Community Case Studies in the War on Poverty* (Englewood Cliffs, N.J.: Prentice-Hall, 1969).

9. J. David Greenstone and Paul Peterson, *Race and Authority in Urban Politics: Community Participation and the War on Poverty* (New York: Russell Sage Foundation, 1973).

10. Bobby Seale, *Seize the Time* (New York: Vintage, 1968); Gilbert Moore, *Rage* (New York: Carroll and Graf, 1993 [orig. 1971]), p. 193.

11. Rod Bush, *The New Black Vote: Politics and Power in Four American Cities* (San Francisco: Synthesis, 1984), pp. 323–324.

12. For review essays, see Leonard Moore, "Historical Interpretations of the 1920's Klan: The Traditional View and the Populist Revision," *Journal of Social History* 24 (Winter 1990): 341–357; and Stanley Coben, "Ordinary White Protestants: The KKK of the 1920s," *Journal of Social History* 28 (Fall 1994): 157–165.

13. George Lipsitz, *Class and Culture in Cold War America: "A Rainbow at Midnight"* (New York: Praeger, 1981).

14. Aldon Morris, "A Retrospective on the Civil Rights Movement: Political and Intellectual Landmarks," *Annual Review of Sociology* 25 (1999): 517–539.

15. John Mollenkopf, *The Contested City* (Princeton, N.J.: Princeton University Press, 1983), p. 11.

16. Other political theorists have called for a similarly explicit tripartite approach. See Margaret Somers, "Citizenship and the Place of the Public Sphere: Law, Community, and Political Culture in the Transition to Democracy," *American Sociological Review* 58 (October 1993): 587–620; Jean Cohen, "Interpreting the Notion of Civil Society," in *Toward a Global Civil Society,* ed. Michael Walzer (Providence, R.I.: Berghahn Books, 1995), pp. 35–40; Mustafa Emirbayer and Mimi Sheller, "Studying Publics in History," *Comparative and Historical Sociology* 11, no. 1 (Fall 1998): 5–6; Iris Marion Young, "State, Civil Society and Social Justice," in *Democracy's Value,* ed. Ian Shapiro and Casiano Hacker-Cordon (Cambridge: Cambridge University Press, 1999), pp. 141–162.

17. Robert Dahl, *Who Governs?* (New Haven, Conn.: Yale University Press, 1961); S. M. Lipset, *Political Man* (New York: Doubleday, 1960); David Truman, *The Governmental Process* (New York: Knopf, 1953). See also David Held, *Political Theory and the Modern State* (Cambridge: Polity Press, 1989), pp. 57–58.

18. Although cultural and institutional forces were acknowledged, for traditional political sociologists the most important structural force was undoubtedly the economy. See Reinhard Bendix and Seymour Martin Lipset, "Political Sociology," *Current Sociology* 6 (1957): 79–99.

19. Charles Tilly, *Durable Inequality* (Berkeley: University of California Press, 1998).

20. Roger Friedland and Robert Alford, "Bringing Society back In: Symbols, Practices, and Institutional Contradictions," in *The New Institutionalism in Organizational Analysis,* ed. Walter W. Powell and Paul DiMaggio (Chicago: University of Chicago Press, 1991), pp. 232–263.

21. Doreen Massey, *Spatial Divisions of Labor: Social Structures and the Geography of Production* (London: Macmillan, 1984); Alan Warde, "Spatial Change, Politics and the Division of Labor," in *Social Relations and Spatial Structures,* ed. D. Gregory and J. Urry (London: Macmillan, 1985), pp. 190–212.

22. Roger Waldinger, *Still the Promised City: African Americans and New Immigrants in Post-Industrial New York* (Cambridge, Mass.: Harvard University Press, 1996).

23. Douglas Massey and Nancy Denton, *American Apartheid* (Cambridge, Mass.: Harvard University Press, 1993).

24. Paul DiMaggio and Walter W. Powell, "Introduction," in *The New Institutionalism in Organizational Analysis,* ed. Walter W. Powell and Paul DiMaggio (Chicago: University of Chicago Press, 1991); James G. March and Johan P. Olsen, *Rediscovering Institutions: The Organizational Basis of Politics* (New York: Free Press, 1989); Theda Skocpol, "Bringing the State back In: Strategies of Analysis on Current Research," in *Bringing the State back In,* ed. Peter Evans, Dietrich Rueschemeyer, and Theda Skocpol (Cambridge: Cambridge University Press, 1985), pp. 3–37.

25. Theda Skocpol, "A Society without a 'State'? Political Organization, Social Conflict, and Welfare Provision in the United States," *Journal of Public Policy* 7, no. 4 (1987): 349–371. Among the ways the state used to shape the political terrain are its repressive powers of social control; its "infrastructural" activity, including the selective promotion and extraction of resources from the economy and population under its authority; its administrative ability to formulate and carry out policy; and its regulation of the channels through which groups claim access to the state. See J. Craig Jenkins, "Social Movements, Political Representation, and the State: An Agenda and Comparative Framework," in *The Politics of Social Protest,* ed. J. Craig Jenkins and Bert Klandermans (Minneapolis: University of Minnesota Press, 1995), pp. 14–38.

26. Stephen Elkin, "Twentieth Century Urban Regimes," *Journal of Urban Affairs* 7, no. 2 (1985): 11–28; Clarence Stone, *Regime Politics: Governing Atlanta, 1946–1988* (Lawrence: University Press of Kansas, 1989).

27. See also the model of institutional power in Hanspeter Kriesi, "The Political Opportunity Structure of New Social Movements: Its Impact on Their Mobilization," in *The Politics of Social Protest,* ed. J. Craig Jenkins and Bert Klandermans (Minneapolis: University of Minnesota Press, 1995), pp. 167–198.

28. Clarence Stone, "Urban Regimes and the Capacity to Govern: A Political Economy Approach," *Journal of Urban Affairs* 15, no. 1 (1993): 1–28.

29. Idem, *Regime Politics,* p. 229. Gerry Stoker adds, "A regime once established is a powerful force in urban politics. Opponents 'have to go along to get along' or face the daunting task of building an effective counter-regime"; Stoker, "Regime Theory and Urban Politics," in *Theories of Urban Politics,* ed. David Judge, Gerry Stoker, and Harold Wolman (Thousand Oaks, Calif.: Sage, 1995), p. 65.

30. Doug McAdam, *Political Process and the Development of Black Insurgency* (Chicago: University of Chicago Press, 1982); Roberta Ash Garner and Mayer Zald, "The Political Economy of Social Movement Sectors," in *Social Movements in an Organizational Society,* ed. Mayer Zald and John D. McCarthy (New Brunswick, N.J.: Transaction, 1987). pp. 293–317.

31. Manuel Castells, *The City and the Grassroots: A Cross-Cultural Theory of Urban Social Movements* (Berkeley: University of California Press, 1983), p. 294; John Logan and Harvey Molotch, *Urban Fortunes* (Berkeley: University of California Press, 1987), p. 20.

32. Nancy Fraser, "Rethinking the Public Sphere: A Contribution to the Critique of Actually Existing Democracy," in *Habermas and the Public Sphere,* ed. Craig Calhoun (Cambridge, Mass.: MIT Press,1992), pp. 109–142; Jean Cohen, "Does Voluntary Association Make Democracy Work?" in *Diversity and Its Discontents,* ed. Neil Smelser and Jeffrey Alexander (Princeton, N.J.: Princeton University Press, 1999), pp. 263–291. Contemporary theorizing about the "public sphere" is inspired, of course, by Jürgen Habermas, *Structural Transformation of the Public Sphere* (Cambridge, Mass.: MIT Press, 1989).

33. Doug McAdam, "Micromobilization Contexts and Recruitment to Activism," *International Social Movement Research* 1 (1988): 125–154; John McCarthy, "Constraints and Opportunities in Adopting, Adapting and Inventing," in *Comparative Perspectives on Social Movements,* ed. Doug McAdam, John McCarthy, and Mayer Zald (Cambridge: Cambridge University Press, 1996), pp. 141–151; Hanspeter Kriesi and Dominique Wisler, "The Impact of Social Movements on Political Institutions: A Comparison of the Introduction of Direct Legislation in Switzerland and the United States," in *How Social Movements Matter,* ed. Marco Guigni, Doug McAdam and Charles Tilly (Minneapolis: University of Minnesota Press, 1999), p. 60; Richard Wood, "Religious Culture and Political Action," *Sociological Theory* 17, no. 3 (November 1999): 307–332.

34. Fraser, "Rethinking the Public Sphere," p. 125, and Geoff Eley, "Nations, Publics, and Political Cultures: Placing Habermas in the Nineteenth Century," in *Habermas and the Public Sphere,* ed. Craig Calhoun (Cambridge, Mass.: MIT Press,1992), pp. 289–339; Doug McAdam and Ronelle Paulsen, "Specifying the Relationship between Social Ties and Activism," *American Journal of Sociology* 99 (1993): 640–667; Aldon Morris, "Political Consciousness and Collective Action," in *Frontiers in Social Movement Theory,* ed. Aldon Morris and Carol Mueller (New Haven, Conn.: Yale University Press, 1992), pp. 351–373.

35. Ira Katznelson, *City Trenches: Urban Politics and the Patterning of Class in the United States* (Chicago: University of Chicago Press, 1981).

36. See, for example, Ira Katznelson and Aristide Zolberg, eds., *Working Class Formation* (Princeton, N.J.: Princeton University Press, 1986); Kim Voss, "Labor Organization and Class Alliance: Industries, Communities and the Knights of Labor," *Theory and Society* 17 (1988): 329–364; Eric Arnesen, *Waterfront Workers of New Orleans: Race, Class and Politics, 1863–1923* (Oxford: Oxford University Press, 1990).

37. Young, "State, Civil Society, and Social Justice"; Alejandro Portes and Patricia Landolt, "The Downside of Social Capital," *The American Prospect* 7, no. 26 (May–June 1996): 18–21, 94.

38. Mayer Zald and John D. McCarthy, "Social Movement Industries: Conflict and Cooperation among SMOs," in *Social Movements in an Organizational Society,* ed. Mayer Zald and John D. McCarthy (New Brunswick, N.J.: Transaction, 1987), pp. 161–180; Ruud Koopmans, "The Dynamics of Protest Waves: West Germany, 1965 to 1989," *American Sociological Review* 58 (October 1993):637–658;Charles Tilly, "Repertoires of Contention in America and Britain, 1750–1830," in *The Dynamics of Social Movements,* ed. Mayer Zald and

John McCarthy (Cambridge, Mass.: Winthrop, 1979), pp. 126–155, and idem, "How to Detect, Describe, and Explain Repertoires of Contention," Working Paper 150 (New York: Center for Studies of Social Change, New School for Social Research, 1992); Elisabeth Clemens, "Organizational Repertoires and Institutional Change: Women's Groups and the Transformation of U.S. Politics, 1890–1920," *American Journal of Sociology* 98, no. 4 (January 1993): 755–798.

39. Aldon Morris, *The Origins of the Civil Rights Movement* (New York: Free Press, 1984); McAdam, *Political Process*, pp. 124–145.

40. David Snow et al., "Frame Alignment Processes, Micromobilization, and Movement Participation," *American Sociological Review* 51 (1986): 464–481; David Snow and Robert Benford, "Master Frames and Cycles of Protest," and Verta Taylor and Nancy Whittier, "Collective Identity in Social Movement Communities: Lesbian Feminist Mobilization," both in *Frontiers in Social Movement Theory*, ed. Aldon Morris and Carol Mueller (New Haven, Conn.: Yale University Press, 1992), pp. 133–155 and 104–129, respectively.

41. Michael Walzer, *Spheres of Justice* (New York: Basic Books, 1983), p. 60; Elizabeth Frazer, *The Problems of Communitarian Politics* (Oxford: Oxford University Press, 1999), pp. 203–210.

42. Dahl, *Who Governs?* pp. 34–36; Gabriel Almond and Sidney Verba, *The Civic Culture* (Princeton, N.J.: Princeton University Press, 1963).

43. Lipset and Raab, *The Politics of Unreason*, p. 114. See also John Higham, *Strangers in the Land* (New York: Atheneum, 1971 [orig. 1955]), pp. 276–294; Richard Hofstadter, *The Age of Reform: From Bryan to FDR* (New York: Knopf, 1977 [orig. 1955]), p. 291; George Mowry and Blaine Brownell, *The Urban Nation: 1920–1980*, rev. ed. (New York: Hill and Wang, 1981); David Burner, *The Politics of Provincialism* (New York: Knopf, 1968), pp. 42–28, 74–102; Arnold Rice, *The Ku Klux Klan in American Politics* (New York: Haskell House, 1972).

44. Arthur Schlesinger Jr., *The Age of Roosevelt: The Politics of Upheaval* (Boston: Houghton-Mifflin, 1960); Samuel Lubell, *The Future of American Politics,* 3d ed. (New York: Harper & Row, 1965); Robert Dahl, *Pluralist Democracy in the United States: Conflict and Consent* (Chicago: Rand McNally, 1967), pp. 430–450; Lipset, *Political Man*, pp. 92–93.

45. Nathan Glazer and Daniel Moynihan, *Beyond the Melting Pot: The Negroes, Puerto Ricans, Jews, Italians, and Irish of New York,* 2d ed. (Cambridge, Mass.: MIT Press, 1970); Stephen Thernstrom and Abigail Thernstrom, *America in Black and White* (New York: Simon and Schuster, 1997).

46. Leonard Moore, *Citizen Klansmen* (Chapel Hill: University of North Carolina Press, 1991); Christopher Cocoltchos, "The Invisible Empire and the Search for the Orderly Community," and Shawn Lay, "Imperial Outpost on the Border: El Paso's Frontier Klan No. 100," in *The Invisible Empire in the West,* ed. Shawn Lay (Urbana: University of Illinois Press, 1992), pp. 97–120 and 67–95, respectively; William Jenkins, *Steel Valley Klan: The Ku Klux Klan in Ohio's Mahoning Valley* (Kent, Ohio: Kent State University Press, 1990); Nancy MacLean, *Behind the Mask of Chivalry* (Oxford: Oxford University Press, 1994); Kathleen Blee, *Women of the Klan: Racism and Gender in the 1920s* (Berkeley: University of California Press, 1991); Robert Goldberg, *Hooded Empire: The Ku Klux Klan in Colorado* (Urbana: University of Illinois Press, 1981); Kenneth Wald, "The Visible

Empire:The Ku Klux Klan as an Electoral Movement," *Journal of Interdisciplinary History* 11, no. 2 (Autumn 1980): 217–234.

47. Sheldon Danziger and Peter Danziger, *America Unequal* (Cambridge, Mass.: Harvard University Press, 1995); Richard Freeman, *The New Inequality* (Boston: Beacon Press, 1999); Massey and Denton, *American Apartheid;* William J. Wilson, *The Declining Significance of Race,* 2d ed. (Chicago: University of Chicago Press, 1980).

48. Nelson Lichtenstein and Howell John Harris, eds., *Industrial Democracy in America: The Ambiguous Promise* (Cambridge: Cambridge University Press, 1993); Christopher Tomlins, *The State and the Unions: Labor Relations, Law, and the Organized Labor Movement in America, 1880–1960* (Cambridge: Cambridge University Press, 1985); Michael Goldfield, *The Decline of Organized Labor in the United States* (Chicago: University of Chicago Press, 1987), pp. 26–38.

49. Landmark acts like the NLRA, the 1935 Social Security Act, and the 1937 Fair Labor Standards Act all excluded agricultural labor and domestic service, where three-quarters of all African American workers were still concentrated during the '30s. Jill Quadagno, *The Color of Welfare* (Oxford: Oxford University Press, 1994); G. William Domhoff, *The Power Elite and the State* (New York: Aldine de Gruyter, 1990).

50. Arnold Hirsch, *Making the Second Ghetto* (Cambridge: Cambridge University Press, 1983); Thomas Sugrue, *The Origins of the Urban Crisis: Race and Inequality in Detroit* (Princeton, N.J.: Princeton University Press, 1996).

51. Cedric Herring and Sharon Collins, "Retreat from Equal Opportunity? The Case for Affirmative Action," in *The Bubbling Cauldron: Race, Ethnicity, and the Urban Crisis,* ed. Michael Peter Smith and Joe R. Feagin (Minneapolis: University of Minnesota Press, 1995), pp. 163–181.

52. Samuel P. Huntington, *American Politics: The Promise of Disharmony* (Cambridge, Mass.: Harvard University Press, 1981), p. 147.

53. James Morone, *The Democratic Wish: Popular Participation and the Limits of American Government* (New Haven, Conn.: Yale University Press, 1990).

54. Arthur Schlesinger Jr., *The Disuniting of America* (New York: W. W. Norton, 1992); Frederick Siegel, *The Future Once Happened Here: New York, D.C., L.A., and the Fate of America's Big Cities* (New York: Free Press, 1997).

55. Doug McAdam, Sidney Tarrow, and Charles Tilly, *Dynamics of Contention* (Cambridge: Cambridge University Press, 2001), pp. 65–67.

56. Stephen Craig, "The Angry Voter: Politics and Popular Discontent in the 1990s," in *Broken Contract? Changing Relationships between Americans and Their Government,* ed. Stephen Craig (Boulder, Colo.: Westview Press, 1996), pp. 46–66; Stephen Nichols, David Kimball, and Paul A. Beck, "Voter Turnout in the 1996 Election: Resuming a Downward Spiral?" in *Reelection 1996: How Americans Voted,* ed. Herbert Weisberg and Janet Box-Steffensmeier (Chappaqua, N.Y.: Chatham House, 1999), pp. 23–44.

57. Robert Putnam, "The Strange Disappearance of Civic America," *The American Prospect* 7, no. 24 (Winter 1996): 34–48. See also idem, "Bowling Alone: America's Declining Social Capital," *Journal of Democracy* 6, no. 1 (January 1995): 66.

58. Idem, *Bowling Alone: The Collapse and Revival of American Community* (New York: Simon and Schuster, 2000).

59. Cohen, "Does Voluntary Association Make Democracy Work?"; Theda Skocpol and Morris Fiorina, "Making Sense of the Civic Engagement Debate," in *Civic Engagement in American Democracy*, ed. Theda Skocpol and Morris Fiorina (Washington, D.C.: Brookings Institution, 1999), pp. 13–14.

60. Stephen Samuel Smith and Jessica Kulynich, "It May Be Social, but Why Is It Capital? The Social Construction of Social Capital and the Politics of Language," *Politics and Society* 30, no. 1 (March 2002): 149–186; Dietrich Rueschemeyer, Evelyn Huber Stephens, and John Stephens, *Capitalist Development and Democracy* (Oxford: Polity Press, 1992).

61. Christopher Beem, *The Necessity of Politics* (Chicago: University of Chicago Press, 1999), pp. 170–172.

62. Max Weber, "'Objectivity' in Social Science and Social Policy," in his *The Methodology of the Social Sciences*, trans. and ed. E. A. Shils and H. A. Finch (New York: Free Press, 1949), pp. 49–112.

63. Charles Ragin, *The Comparative Method* (Berkeley: University of California Press, 1987), pp. 3, 31; Tilly, *Durable Inequality*, p. 7; see also John Walton, *Western Times and Water Wars* (Berkeley: University of California Press, 1992), p. 2; and Arthur Stinchcombe, *Theoretical Methods in Social History* (New York: Academic Press, 1978), pp. 21–22.

64. Walton, *Western Times and Water Wars*, p. 7; Jeffrey Haydu, "Making Use of the Past: Time Periods as Cases to Compare and as Sequences of Problem Solving," *American Journal of Sociology* 102, no. 2 (September 1998): 339–371.

65. Ragin, *The Comparative Method*, p. 49; Michael Burawoy, "Two Methods in Search of Science: Skocpol versus Trotsky," *Theory and Society* 18 (1989): 759–805; Haydu, "Making Use of the Past," p. 348.

66. Andrew Abbott, "From Causes to Events: Notes on Narrative Positivism," *Sociological Methods and Research* 20, no. 4 (May 1992): 428–455; idem, "What Do Cases Do? Some Notes on Activity in Sociological Analysis," in *What Is a Case?* ed. Charles Ragin and Howard S. Becker (Cambridge: Cambridge University Press, 1992), pp. 53–82; Ragin, *The Comparative Method*, pp. 59ff.

67. Larry Griffin, "Narrative, Event-Structure Analysis, and Causal Interpretation in Historical Sociology," *American Journal of Sociology* 98 (March 1993): 1094–1133. See also Abbott, "What Do Cases Do?" pp. 62–63; Jill Quadagno and Stan Knapp, "Have Historical Sociologists Forsaken Theory?" *Sociological Methods and Research* 20, no. 4 (May 1992): 481–507.

68. Susan Fainstein and Norman Fainstein, "Economic Change, National Policy, and the System of Cities," in *Restructuring the City*, ed. Susan Fainstein, 2d ed. (New York: Longmans, 1985), pp. 1–26.

Reading 13: Portland's Response to Homeless Issues and the "Broken Windows" Theory

By Tracy J. Prince

All across America cities are adopting the "broken windows" theory in their dealings with homeless people. City councils, mayors, and business improvement districts eagerly embrace the promises of a whitewashed downtown, sometimes without realizing the profound shift in tax dollars this approach requires or analyzing whether or not this is an efficacious or even humane community investment. While the rhetoric sounds wonderful—who doesn't want better "quality of life?"—the results of this policy bring many cities to the dark ages of social justice and simply sweep poverty, hunger, and homelessness away from public sight. The not so hidden cost of broken windows–inspired policies shifts tax dollars from addressing the causes and effects of homelessness toward the criminal justice system, since many of the daily activities of the homeless are criminalized. How does Portland fit into this changing national climate? What are the current and historical responses to homelessness in Portland? How do Portland's policies compare to those of its west coast neighbors—particularly Seattle and San Francisco whose cities have somewhat similar demographics, weather, and political leanings? At a time when cities are rushing blindly to embrace a policy that—whether they realize it or not—is social Darwinism, declaring, "if you can't fend for yourself, if you don't have a place to urinate or sleep, you must be removed," is Portland, which prides itself on its tolerance, any different?

The Broken Windows Theory

In 1969 Stanford psychologist Philip Zimbardo conducted an experiment testing what would happen to two cars left abandoned in two different neighborhoods—both 1959 Oldsmobiles. "The license plates of both cars were removed and the hoods opened to provide the necessary releaser signals" (Zimbardo 1969). In one affluent and one nonaffluent neighborhood, the results were the same, although the vandalism took a little longer in the affluent neighborhood. In the Bronx, the car was completely vandalized in three days, with 23 separate incidents of vandalism. In Palo Alto, California (the wealthy neighborhood where Stanford University is located), the car was not touched for one week, but once Prof. Zimbardo and his graduate students helped things along by bashing the car a bit, people in the neighborhood quickly helped finish off the destruction.

In a 1982 *Atlantic Monthly* article titled "Broken Windows: The Police and Neighborhood Safety" political scientist James Q. Wilson and criminologist George L. Kelling (and Kelling and Catherine Coles's 1996 book on the same subject *(Fixing Broken Windows)*) expanded upon Zimbardo's study drawing the conclusion that broken windows on abandoned cars and in the cityscape seemed to signal that "no one cares." They drew a further correlation that social ills left publicly broken lead to more social ills. Some say this is an illogical assumption since they used one experiment with abandoned cars as the basis of an argument essentially claiming, among other things, that evidence of broken people in public spaces creates crime. Saying that the best way to fight "quality-of-life" crimes is to fight the disorder that precedes it, they called for more community policing and proactive efforts to prevent crime before it happens. While community policing and crime prevention sound quite reasonable, they also suggested that police pay more attention to the type of crimes often overlooked—public drunkenness, panhandling, public urination, graffiti, uncollected trash, and unrepaired buildings—in order to create a blight-free public space, which would then, conceivably, lower crime rates. "Therefore, the objective for preventing street crimes is to prevent the first window from getting broken, or prevent the first graffiti marks, or prevent the first drunkard from a public display. This has led to Neighborhood Watch programs and increased police foot patrols. These measures have not had a significant impact on crime, but they have succeeded in making neighborhood residents feel safer" (Williams 1998).

Wilson and Kelling's theory received an enormous boost when New York City mayor Rudolph Giuliani adopted the broken windows theory with a community-policing strategy focused on what he called "quality of life" and maintaining order—and crime rates dropped. Like George W. Bush's "compassionate conservatism" rhetoric, Mayor Giuliani spoke of his compassion when discussing his homeless policies. Giuliani's campaign was led in large part by powerful Business Improvement Districts such as the Times Square Business Improvement District, the Fifth Avenue Association, the Alliance for Downtown New York, the Madison Avenue B.I.D., the Grand Central Partnership, and the 34th Street Partnership. The rhetoric of this campaign referred to a "war on crime" aiming, in part, to "reduce sidewalk congestion" with "zero tolerance" on such issues as unlicensed vendors, loiterers, panhandling, and outdoor camping. "Community courts" and "quality of life" debates were often thinly disguised xenophobia against unhoused people, with an obvious focus on removing them completely from sight. Times Square was cleaned beyond recognition, graffiti was regularly washed from subway cars, subway turnstile-jumpers were arrested, trash was picked up, homeless people were arrested and moved along, and many of the effects of homelessness were removed from public sight. Giuliani's police commissioner, Howard Safir, encouraged the arrest of homeless people should they refuse shelter or police assistance. In *Sidewalk*, (1999) an excellent ethnography of the impact of Giuliani's policies on homeless people, Mitchell Duneier reveals the dirty underbelly of such policies. Although usually considered in the domain of human services, homeless people and issues in New York City are now frequently dealt with by the criminal justice system, as yet another "broken window." Furthermore, it has been argued by many that these campaigns simply moved the homeless to other boroughs and to New Jersey.

Nevertheless, focusing on these minor crimes seemed to work since crime rates dropped and in 2002 Manhattan experienced the lowest murder rate in 100 years (Salon.com 2002). Since New York City had such apparent success with these strategies, cities the world over began emulating their tactics. Many cities make it clear that they have fully accepted the view of homeless people as broken windows who need to be removed from public sight. However, other cities use the buzzwords "broken windows" with no apparent understanding of the term or the true social costs of implementing NYC-inspired policies. Santa Monica restricted homeless feeding programs in 2002 to discourage homeless people from coming to or staying in Santa Monica. Los Angeles police chief William Bratton brought his New York City training with him and implemented quality of life broken windows policies. He has said that he would like to corral all the homeless people into skid row so that they can be more easily controlled. The Hollywood Entertainment District business improvement group fully supports his ideas (Winton and Sauerwein 2003). Even historically tolerant San Francisco has embraced a hard-line approach to homeless policies and made enormous changes cleaning up the human broken windows in their city. Billboard campaigns to support drastically reducing homeless benefits with 2002's Proposition N (sponsored by the Hotel Council of San Francisco and other business groups) declared: "I want to be able to walk down the street without being asked for money," and "I don't want to have to hold my breath every time I pass an alley." Yet rates of violent crime have been dropping since the 1980s in American cities, well before Giuliani's tactics became popular. The Center on Juvenile and Criminal Justice (2002) debunked the commonly accepted idea that the implementation of the broken windows theory resulted in reduced crime rates. They found that since 1995 San Francisco, for example, reported a 33% reduction in violent crime rates even though during most of this time their policy was not to pursue aggressive arrests, prosecutions, and prison terms for homeless people. In comparison, during this time, New York City's experienced a 26% decrease in violent crime rates.

Criminalizing the Homeless: Expensive, Ineffective, and Inhumane

Homeless advocates argue that criminalizing homelessness is exorbitantly costly, doesn't reduce homelessness, doesn't lower crime, and forces people into nightmarishly never-ending cycles of homelessness. For example, the taxpayer's expense for a night spent in jail is far higher than for a night in a shelter, which in turn is more costly than tax dollars spent on low-income housing. A prison bed averages $20,000 per year; typical rent subsidies average $4,500 to $6,000 per year; and the average annual cost for emergency shelter is $15,000 for singles and $25,000 to $30,000 for families (Culhane et al. 2002). The National Coalition for the Homeless argues that "the cost of arresting, processing and jailing homeless people is higher than the cost of creating housing . . . [and] criminalization of homelessness leads to increased barriers to accessing shelter and housing due to a criminal record and unpaid fines" (National Coalition for the Homeless 2002). In a "Policy Guide on Homelessness," the American Planning Association (2003) observes that the true costs of homelessness are masked in the budgets of law enforcement, corrections, health care, welfare, education, and other systems. In Portland, homeless advocate Rob Justice (2003), executive director of JOIN, makes the case that criminal records and fines for quality of life tickets would create a huge barrier to ending the cycle of homelessness. JOIN is an outreach group specializing in housing assistance for people who either do not utilize or are turned away from shelters and camp or sleep outdoors.

Oregon's History of Poverty and Homelessness

In considering Portland's homeless community, it is important to have a snapshot of poverty in Oregon and contingent issues that lead to homelessness. The effects of Oregon's struggling economy are clear in the strain on social services and the increase in homeless people turned away from shelters. In 2002–2003 the state ranked number one in the nation in unemployment (Oregon Employment Department). Furthermore, even fully employed people find themselves struggling to make ends meet in today's economy. Oregon Housing and Community Services estimated in 2001 that a living wage needed for basic expenses ranged from $10.07 per hour for a single adult to $16.36 for an adult with two children. Yet 40% of the jobs advertised in Oregon pay less than the bottom end of this living wage scale. Consequently, the Oregon Food Bank reports that in 2002 Oregon was ranked as the hungriest state in the nation and continues to hover near the top of the list. The Oregon Center for Public Policy shows that poverty rates among Oregon's working families with children have doubled since the late 1970s, and the gap between the rich and the poor in Oregon grew four times faster than the country as a whole (Leachman 2001).

Figure 13.1. People seeking shelter nightly in Multnomah County.

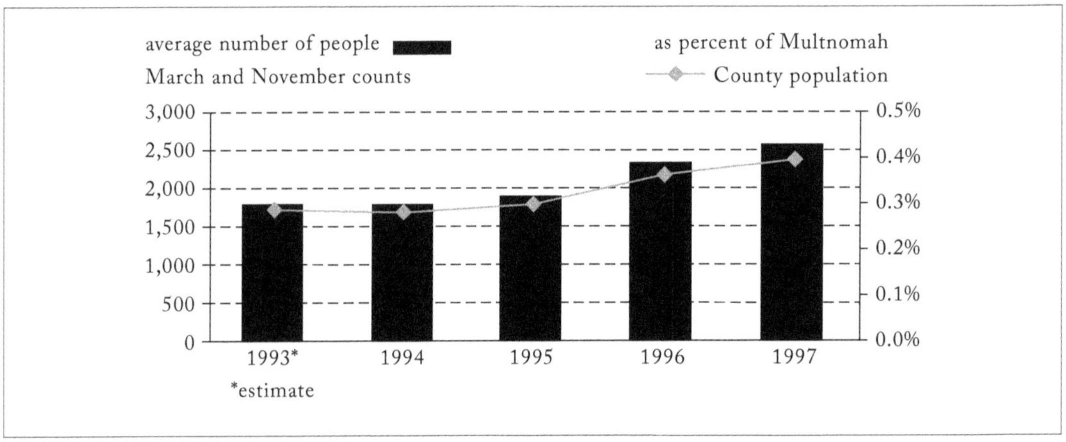

Source: Multnomah County Department of Community and Family Services, (November 1997).

Although Oregon has been quite progressive in providing medical care for the uninsured (over 1 million uninsured Oregonians have received medical, dental, mental health, and chemical dependency services coverage under the Oregon Health Plan), this coverage has been seriously eroded in the enormous budget cuts of the past few years. The effects of these cutbacks are felt profoundly among the homeless and near homeless, especially those served by mental health and chemical dependency assistance. Of course, the difficult economic climate can be seen in dramatic increases in people seeking help from homeless service providers. Since 1993, the estimated number of single women turned away because of lack of space has increased 203% since shelter space has not kept pace with demand. Multnomah County reports a 38% increase in homeless families since 1993 and a 90% increase in those turned away from shelters (Graham 2003). Figure 13.1 reflects Multnomah County's research tracking a marked increase in people seeking shelter from the early to late 1990s.

In counting the numbers of homeless people, the city and county rely on two systems. One count is derived from Multnomah County's "one night shelter count," which counts only people seeking shelter assistance from public and private facilities in the county. The March 2003 count recorded 1,340 households and 2,220 individuals seeking emergency shelter, housing vouchers, rental assistance, or transitional housing assistance. One hundred and eighty households and 337 individuals were turned away because the shelters had reached capacity (Multnomah County Office of School and Community Partnerships 2003). The second count is conducted annually by JOIN, which only counts people sleeping outdoors or camping in Portland. In spring 2003 JOIN counted 1,571 homeless people.

Sisters of the Road Cafe, a homeless advocacy and outreach nonprofit, believes this number to be low. "Over 100 more homeless persons, 1,672 to be exact, were counted by JOIN in 2002;

Figure 13.2. Age and race of people seeking shelter.

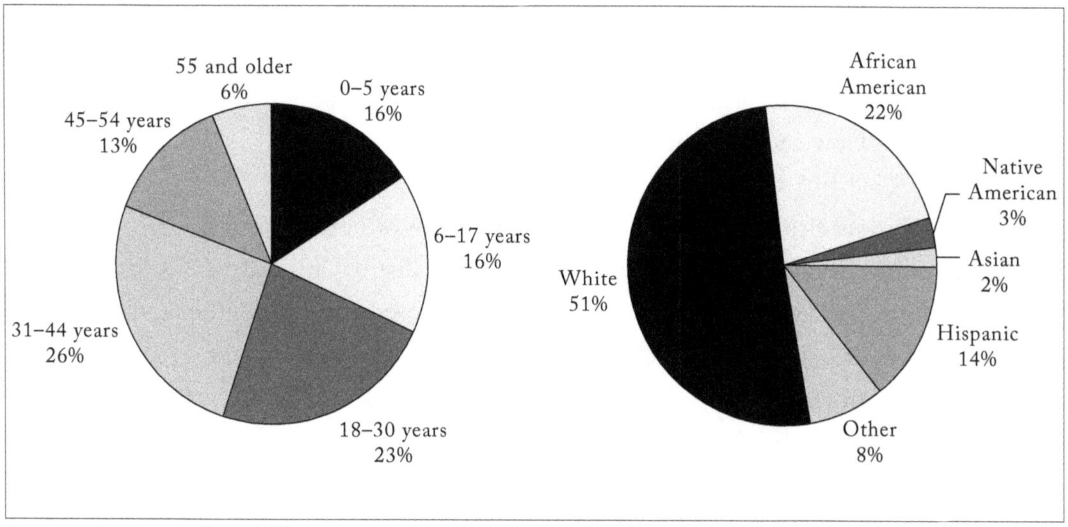

Source: Multnomah County Department of Community and Family Services, (November 1997).

and from the increased demand upon social services there is little reason to assume that fewer homeless people are here now. Also, because JOIN was low on funding this year, it was unable to allocate a sufficient number of outreach people to conduct a thorough count" (2003a). They also point out the difficulty of counting homeless adults and families who are sleeping in cheap motels, rooming houses, or on a friend's couch or who opt to remain hidden deep within parks, in vehicles, or in abandoned buildings.

Likewise Multnomah County argues that 100% accuracy is impossible when counting the homeless because of undercounting (not all homeless people can be found) and double-counting (those who make multiple attempts to find shelter on the same night are counted with each contact made). Regarding the racial demographics of homeless people, the Portland–Multnomah Progress Board (1999), referring to the above chart, found that although more whites seek shelter than any other racial group, they also make up about 86% of Multnomah County's population (see Fig. 13.2). They point out that this means that the percentages of African Americans, Native Americans, and Hispanics seeking shelter are disproportionately overrepresented.

Portland's History of Homeless Politics

Carl Abbott writes in *Greater Portland: Urban Life and Landscape in the Pacific Northwest* (2001) about the strong history in Portland of creating policies through consensus practices. Yet he points out the flip side of Portland-style consensus politics that rewards less confrontational activists—bringing "into the conversation 'well-behaved' advocacy groups that have gained attention. Once at the table, such groups can trade acquiescence with long term land redevelopment goals for substantial public commitments to low-income housing and social services." Abbott gives an example of how this consensus process has unfolded with debates about homelessness and low-income housing:

> In the 1980s, agencies serving the homeless population of Portland's skid road agreed to a cap on shelter beds in the Burnside/Old Town district in return for a go-slow approach to redevelopment and an active program for relocating shelters and social services. A charismatic advocate for the homeless who declined to sign on found that contributions quickly dried up while newspapers headlined his own flaws of character and abusive behavior. In contrast, the Northwest Pilot Project monitors the loss of low cost downtown housing and repeatedly chides the city for neglecting the poor in its plans for a bright new downtown, but it also works within the framework of Portland progressivism to build coalitions among government, foundations, businesses, and social service agencies. In 1995, the Portland Organizing Project (POP) forced consideration of low income housing as a component of the River District north of downtown. Once the development leadership recognized the power of POP's populist appeal, however, they moved rapidly to enfold low income housing and its more consensus-minded advocates into the planning process (leaving POP on the outside and favoring the somewhat poor over the very poor). (151–152)

Mayor Bud Clark

In important homeless-related policies of recent history, Mayor Bud Clark introduced community policing in the late 1980s, and his 1987 12-point homeless plan drew national attention, although it eventually achieved only half of its goals (Schrag 1984). It used city money to build much-needed shelters. Previously, shelters were run almost exclusively by faith-based programs. After a few years, though, it became clear that those shelters ended up cycling through, not moving out, the homeless. Thus, a new approach was needed.

Commissioner Gretchen Kafoury

In her terms as both county and city commissioner, Gretchen Kafoury had enormous impact on Portland's homeless and low-income and affordable housing policies. In 1993 she appointed a task force on Strategies for Fair Housing (to respond to the Fair Housing Amendment Act of 1988), which was charged with making recommendations to the city council concerning homelessness and housing. A primary emphasis for the task force was to situate low-income housing throughout the city instead of ghettoizing it. In December 1993, the city council adopted their recommendations including changes to the zoning code, certification standards for homeless shelters, and a location policy regarding geographic concentrations of poverty. These three recommendations were designed to address community concerns while also making it, in some cases, easier to locate special needs housing. This was a crucial achievement by Kafoury's task force since locating special needs housing is always a difficult negotiation with the neighbors. As the APA points out, despite evidence in 20 years of numerous studies that such projects contribute to rather than detract from neighborhoods, NIMBY arguments often prevent supportive housing from being accepted in neighborhoods. A 1999 Urban Land Institute report, for example, indicates that supportive housing does not decrease property values or increase criminal activity (quoted in APA 2003).

The city chose to achieve the goals suggested by the task force by controlling funding for low-income housing in "impact areas." The funding sources include Housing and Urban Development's (HUD's) HOME funds (the largest federal block grant to state and local governments to create housing for low-income households), HUD's Community Development Block Grant (CDBG) funds providing funding for housing and community development projects, HUD's Housing Opportunities for Persons With AIDS (HOPWA) funds, and other low-interest loan programs. "Impact areas" are defined as areas with high concentrations of poverty, where more than 50% of the households in a census tract block group earn less than 50% of median income or 20% or more of the housing units are pubic and assisted (PDC 2003). But Commissioner Kafoury is perhaps best known for her "shelter reconfiguration plan," which the city has operated under for the past decade. This plan created separate shelters for men, women, families, youth, mentally ill, and domestic violence victims and included a component to provide permanent housing (although this housing, the Ritzdorf Court Apartments, wasn't completed until 2002). These shelters are now at full occupancy year-round with long waiting lists in the winter.

Commissioner Erik Sten

Kafoury protégé, City Commissioner Erik Sten, oversees housing issues and is making his mark with collaborative community discussions toward a 10-year plan to end homelessness, following the lead of others nationwide including the National Alliance to End Homelessness. A major component of this plan focuses on a "housing first" strategy. The idea is to first assist people with stable housing, then address other issues such as mental health or addictions. This is the polar opposite of most current shelter programs in which sobriety and stability must be achieved first before people are allowed to transition into more permanent housing.

Although now being discussed more nationally, the housing first model has existed since 1992 with JOIN's highly successful program. Of the 770 people placed into housing with JOIN's rental assistance program in 2001, 92% remained in housing a year later. This surprising success rate was achieved even though 70% of the participants had physical, mental, substance abuse, or criminal justice problems that their caseworkers thought might impair their ability to consistently pay for housing.

Though JOIN began its life in 1992 in a very confrontational mode with the city and the police, it has since developed collaborative ties with the city. The police in particular became an active part in helping find solutions for homeless people. Police Chief Charles Moose was supportive of police officers working closely with JOIN case managers when dealing with a homeless person. As a result of this collaboration the police found they needed fewer officers to respond to incidents (Anderson 2003). This collaboration has diminished somewhat since Chief Moose left in 1999.

Sten's "housing first" focus puts the city's concern with creating more low-income and affordable housing options on the front burner. However, the question is: Where will the funding come from? Homeless people and activists like those at Sisters of the Road Cafe are concerned that funding will be pulled from shelters and meal providers and are working with Commissioner Sten to make sure these concerns are addressed. Sisters of the Road, for example, was invited by Sten to participate in developing the City's official plan, so they are holding grassroots meetings to collect ideas from Portland's homeless community.

Homeless Programs and Policies

Collaborations on Homeless Youth Services

Multnomah County currently provides services for 1,000 homeless youth per year in Portland. In 1998 the Citizen's Crime Commission and the Association for Portland Progress questioned Portland's system of services for homeless youth, claiming that it was fragmented, lacked accountability, and was grossly underfunded. Under the influence of the HUD Continuum of Care model (which has required cities to act together to create collaborative and innovative responses to homelessness, analyze community needs, prevent gaps and possible overlaps of services provided, and make decisions about funding priorities at a local rather than national level) and the influence of Portland's historically collaborative climate, a Downtown Homeless Youth Continuum was formed. (The Continuum of Care components are prevention, outreach and assessment, emergency shelter, transitional housing, permanent supportive housing, permanent affordable housing, and supportive services.) Community stakeholders, human service providers, business leaders, government agencies, homeless youth, and researchers provided input on ways to restructure the system and transition homeless youth off the streets. As a result of their efforts, between 1999 and 2001 the City of Portland and Multnomah County funding devoted to homeless youth services increased from $820,000 to $2,584,000. This additional funding allowed such improvements as more case management, more shelter and transitional housing space, a 24-hour access center, and other services (Multnomah County Auditor's Office 2001).

Low-Income and Affordable Housing Policies

Since the affordability of housing is a clear factor in the ability to be permanently housed, low-income and affordable housing policies are an important part of addressing homelessness (see Chap. 9, Howe). Refuting the commonly held belief that addictions and the deinstitution-alization of the mentally ill have contributed to the rising rates of homelessness, Wright and Lam (1987) draw a direct link between the reduction in low-income housing opportunities in America and the rise of homelessness. Citing the lack of low-income and affordable housing as a major impediment for a community to end homelessness, the APA argues that planners can play a role in reducing homelessness by "determining local housing needs through their comprehensive plans, removing regulatory and legal barriers to the development of affordable and supportive housing, and fostering community support for permanent housing for the homeless" (2003). The APA's suggested tools to achieve more low-income and affordable hous-ing are: promoting infill incentives, property tax abatement, density allowances, land assembly, and fast track permitting.

The APA also reminds us that the American Institute of Certified Planners (AICP) Code of Ethics requires that a planner "must strive to expand choice and opportunity for all persons, recognizing a special responsibility to plan for the needs of disadvantaged groups." In Portland, this message sometimes seems to ring true, with some focus on preserving low-income and affordable housing and alternatives to the ghettoization of poverty, and with some city council members, the Portland Development Commission (PDC), Multnomah County, and numerous homeless service providers moving to a "housing first" focus. However, this has not always been the case (see Chap. 3, Gibson). The Northwest Pilot project estimates that since 1974 downtown Portland has lost 863 units of low-income housing to gentrification. Clients may wait three years for the subsidized housing that remains (Transition Projects, Inc. 2001). Reportedly, there is a shortage of 10,500 units of housing for low-income households in Multnomah County (Silverman 1999).

Opponents of the gentrification that is blamed for reducing stocks of low-income and affordable housing point to neighborhoods such as Albina, a historically African American neighborhood with interesting older homes in desirable proximity to downtown. In this neighborhood, average housing values doubled between 1990 and 1996 while, at the same time, the white population increased 12% or six times as fast as the African American population (Oregon Environmental Council 2003). These statistics point to displaced African American residents and gentrification rapidly changing a neighborhood. However, the Fannie Mae Foundation (2000) evaluates a different aspect of gentrification, expanding the tax base:

> The risk of displacement is often raised by critics of gentrification who view the return of middle-income suburbanites to cities as a zero-sum game. While the risk of displacement is real, we think it is outweighed by the even greater risk of losing a chance to secure a larger tax base. Taxing new middle-income residents and spending the money on programs for a general urban population is a benefit that at least partially offsets the pain caused by displacement.

In response to arguments against gentrification and displacement, in 2001 Portland's City Council adopted a "no net loss" policy on housing affordable to low- and moderate-income persons and households in the central city, to retain at least the current number of low-income and affordable housing units (at or below 60% area median income.) A specific goal to achieve the City's Comprehensive Housing Policy, Central City No Net Loss Policy, Consolidated Plan was set at 10,000 units by 2011. An additional goal was made to preserve or replace 1,200 units within the central city by 2006. The Housing Authority of Portland has also committed to no net loss of public housing within the city, and in 2001, Metro adopted a Regional Affordable Housing Strategy. Although in the 1990s the PDC was criticized as not having a comprehensive social agenda for its urban renewal programs (Wollner et al. 2001), in 2003 PDC added 3,550 units to the former 10,000-unit goal. This will be achieved with preserved or new rental units and an increase in first-time homebuyers and will be financed through traditional sources (CDBG, HOME, tax increment financing) as well as partnerships with the city and other organizations for resources through lines of credit, the City Lights Revenue Bond program, the Enterprise Foundation Smart Growth Fund, the Oregon Residential Loan, and the HOME 24 program (PDC Quarterly 2003).

Ordinances Affecting the Homeless in Portland

In 1981 Portland passed the first of its Public Order laws (Portland Municipal Code 14A.50.020), an ordinance prohibiting temporary campsites on public property or public rights of way. Penalties include fines up to $100 and 30 days in jail. Although initially set up to discourage damage to public properties, Sisters of the Road Cafe argues that this code and others impacting the homeless are used to harass and criminalize the homeless. "Time and again law enforcement and city officials tell us that these laws will direct people experiencing homelessness through the community court system and to social services that will get them off the streets," says Rachel Langford, a volunteer with Sisters of the Road's program Crossroads. "At the same time they admit that these social services are overburdened, underfunded, and unable to meet the needs of many homeless citizens" (Newth 2003).

Portland Municipal Code 14A.50.010 prohibits drinking and open containers of alcohol on public property. This type of ordinance is a common civic strategy to reduce homeless loiterers. Portland police usually use this as an opportunity to question homeless people and ask them to move on if they are being disruptive.

Portland's de facto sit/lie law, Ordinance 14A.50.030 restricts people from blocking a doorway or the flow of pedestrian traffic or vehicular traffic. The Portland Police Bureau's enforcement guidelines state that panhandling alone does not violate this code. In 2001 an effort was led by the Portland Business Alliance (a business development group increasingly supportive of criminalization of the homeless) to create a tougher sit/lie law. They looked at Seattle's law as a model—it has restrictions against sleeping, blankets, chairs, etc. This effort failed when homeless advocates lobbied Mayor Vera Katz who announced that the existing laws were sufficient. Reportedly, only four arrests were made in 2002 enforcing this law (Jaquiss 2003).

Portland Municipal Code 14A.50.050 prohibits erecting permanent or temporary structures on public property or public rights of way. The police guidelines on enforcing this code require a 24-hour notice, require that police contact an outreach worker from JOIN, and allow for arrest and confiscation of property (to be held for 30 days) to be used as "evidence" of the crime. Recently added language encourages officers to give JOIN more than 24 hours' notice so that they have time to make contact with the campers (Portland Police Bureau 2003).

Portland Municipal Code 20.12.265 is a Parks and Recreation "trespass." This is usually enforced as a 30-day exclusion from a park. Fines may be assessed up to $600, though this method of enforcement is not the norm.

Like many cities Portland uses "drug free zones" to manage homeless people. Most of downtown is designated a "drug free zone." People may be excluded from a zone based upon arrest for probable cause (Portland Municipal Code 14B.20.030). In recent years Portland police have also discussed creating a "transient free zone" where arrests could be made, but homeless advocates and Commissioner Erik Sten have prevented this from proceeding further.

Recent Flashpoints in Portland's Homeless Issues

Several events keep homeless issues in the public light in Portland. St. Francis Park in the SE Portland Buckman neighborhood has business leaders, police, neighborhood leaders, and the church at odds about homeless people who hang out in the park adjacent to the St. Francis Church. Like all Catholic organizations dedicated to the ideals embodied by St. Francis, it has a historical outreach to the hungry and homeless. In September 2003 the police declared the park a "chronic nuisance" and demanded that the church come up with a solution to help address day camping, loitering, and crimes occurring in or near the park. This situation is reminiscent of a similar neighborhood/human services provider conflict that occurred in 2001 at the Sunnyside Centenary United Methodist Church—another meal provider in Southeast Portland. That dispute drew attention from national advocacy groups when the city council put a limit on how many people would be allowed to worship there (Homeless People's Network 2000, *World Faith News* 2000, *Jewish World Review* 2000). St. Francis is still negotiating with neighborhood leaders to come up with an acceptable plan to reduce the impact on the neighborhood (Hannum 2002).

Dignity Village, a cooperative homeless campsite, was created in 2000 after Portland's 19-year-old camping ban was overturned. An editorial by Jack Tafari in *street roots*, a paper written by members of Portland's homeless community, called for people to organize and form a tent city. The idea captured the imagination of homeless people, churches, donors, homeless service providers, the Oregon Law Center, and Mark Lakeman of the collective City Repair who helped create a master plan for the village (City of Portland Office of Neighborhood Involvement 2003). Some of the motivations cited for its creation were to accommodate many of those turned away from overcrowded shelters, to provide alternatives to shelters that require attendance at religious services, to provide a place for homeless people who own pets, and to band together to prevent police harassment and street crimes. The city has moved the village several times because of NIMBY (not in my back yard) issues and public versus private property issues. A highly organized group, Dignity Village has had the benefit of excellent pro bono legal and community design work. They have also created savvy publicity opportunities such as marching as a "Homeless Front" shopping cart brigade while moving to a new site, thereby drawing the attention of every news channel in town. After strong initial resistance, the city began working with the community to help locate an acceptable site. As of 2004, the camp is located near the Portland airport on part of a leafcomposting facility, leased from the city at $2,000 per month. This fee is to offset the city's loss of income from the lost space and thus lost leafcomposting revenue. The village has council meetings, rules of behavior, showers, educational opportunities, gardens, and hosts numerous visitors such as

Portland Public School children who want to learn about their philosophy. Their stated aim is to be a self-governing, green, sustainable urban village. They continue to look for a permanent location.

Lastly, in 2003 an Oregon and Washington pizza chain decided to be creative about home-less handouts. It paid homeless people with pizza, soda, and a few dollars for holding a sign for about 40 minutes reading "Pizza Schmizza paid me to hold this sign instead of asking for money." Pizza Schmizza founder Andre Jehan said: "I got tired of not being able to make eye contact with these people. I thought, 'What skills could they have?' Holding a sign was an obvious one." Although an advertising watchdog group founded by Ralph Nader thought it was exploitation, Peter Schoeff, a 20-year-old homeless man who took them up on their offer said, "I think it's a fair trade. We're career panhandlers, that's the only way we can get money" (CNN.com 2003, Salon.com 2003, *Seattle Times* 2003).

The Magnet Theory

The magnet theory is the idea that good homeless services in a city act as a magnet to draw homeless people from around the country. The Coalition on Homelessness in San Francisco (1999) points out the many cities that like to use this argument by posting names of places where civic leaders allege that their services draw more homeless people, including Akron, Ohio; New York City; Philadelphia; Portland, Pennsylvania; and Alexandria, Louisiana to name a few. The Sisters of the Road Cafe talks about this problem of perception and points to the reality that most users of homeless services are long-term residents:

There is a misconception in City Hall, the Portland Police Bureau, and the Portland Business Alliance that homeless people and other "vagrants" flock to Portland because the supportive services are so plentiful. Yes, there is a strong matrix of support services in Portland, but there are many other cities with a similar support infrastructure. Where the misconception lies is that people don't come to Portland simply for its "vaunted" services. Many low-budget travelers pass through Portland because it is a scenic city with a vibrant underground culture and arts scene. Those folks typically are on the move to other places, even though they may frequently return to visit. Many people come because they are attracted to the bohemian lifestyle promised by districts such as Belmont, Hawthorne, Northeast 28th, and Northeast Alberta. Yet, for all those who come and stay, just as many leave for better opportunities elsewhere. Few will deny that decent-paying jobs are difficult to come by here. Finally, there is a significant number of homeless people here who don't take advantage of the services system at all. Perhaps the best answer is that the great majority of homeless people in Portland have been here for years. Although they may lack housing, they are full-time long-term residents. (2003b)

Seattle and San Francisco in Comparison

In the Seattle–Bellevue–Everett Primary Metropolitan Statistical Area (PMSA) the population is 2.4 million; 82% are white. The Seattle/King County Coalition for the Homeless (2003) estimates that there are 7,980 people who are homeless in King County, Washington. Each year they conduct a one-night count, including a street count and counts at shelters and transitional housing programs. In 1993 and 1994 Seattle implemented several Civility Laws to help control the homeless people downtown. Under these laws, for example, a repeat offender who urinates in public can be fined up to $1,000 and jailed up to 90 days and a first time offender for aggressive panhandling can receive the same punishment (City and County of San Francisco Board of Supervisors 2002). Seattle's sit/lie ordinance restricts people from sitting or lying on sidewalks in certain business districts between 7 a.m. and 9 p.m., including sitting on a blanket or stool (Seattle SMC 15.48.040). If police notify individuals that they are breaking the law and they refuse to move they may be fined up to $50. If the ticket isn't paid or the offender doesn't appear in court the penalty reverts to up to 90 days in jail and up to $1,000. The sit/lie ordinance has been challenged in court several times but has not been struck down. Leaving no doubt about the influences driving these recent changes in Seattle, the Seattle Police Department Web site actually provides a brief lesson on the broken windows theory (Seattle Police Department 2003).

In the San Francisco PMSA the population is 1.7 million; 62% are white. In 2002 the San Francisco Mayor's Office on Homelessness counted 8,640 homeless people. This total has been highly debated, with activists claiming the homeless count is double this amount. The *San Francisco Chronicle* estimates that between 8,500 and 15,000 homeless people live in San Francisco but acknowledges that no one really knows the total. Proposition N (also known as the "Care not Cash" initiative), which passed with almost 60 percent of the vote in 2002, dramatically changed the city's response to homelessness. It authorized the city to reduce monthly checks to the almost 3,000 able-bodied homeless adults who don't qualify for state or federal aid, from about $395 to $59 (Lelchuk 2003). They are being told that they will receive shelter and food instead. The problem is that the resources are limited, shelters are overcrowded, and service providers are stretched to their limits. Thus it is impossible for the city to fulfill its promise. In another brutal effort to rid themselves of the homeless, the Matrix, also known as the "Quality of Life Enforcement Program," is the name for police operations to remove the homeless from downtown San Francisco via criminalization tactics. Laws prohibit public urination and drinking, camping, aggressive panhandling, and "intending to lodge." The police are moving along or arresting homeless people and often dump their belongings in the garbage. San Francisco's Coalition on Homelessness (1999) studied 80 cities and their efforts to criminalize homelessness under the guise of quality of life crimes or the broken windows theory. One hundred percent of the communities studied lacked enough shelter beds to meet demand, yet 90% are implementing antipanhandling laws.

Portland at the Crossroads

It seems that Portland has not yet fully joined its neighbors, Seattle and San Francisco, to throw enormous criminal justice resources at running the homeless out of town or out of sight. While its downtown business district seems to be attempting to follow in the steps of New York City's Business Improvement Districts, the Portland Business Alliance has not yet succeeded in having the broken windows theory dictate policy or in criminalizing homelessness to the extent reached in many other cities. Portland's homeless advocates point to many egregious problems (lack of low-income housing, insufficient service provider funding, and gentrification leading to displacement are at the top of the list), but Portland has a history of long-range and progressive thinking about homelessness that may yet lead to a model to end homelessness—provided a "transient-free zone" isn't set up first!

Yes, the conditions are ripe for heading toward more criminalization of the homeless, and flashpoints such as the St. Francis/Buckman neighborhood debate demonstrate how conflict-ridden the climate remains. But this is also the same climate in which police are required to work with outreach workers from JOIN to help campers find permanent housing, where funding more than doubled for homeless youth after a community consensus was reached on restructuring homeless youth services, where the city council, the Housing Authority, Metro, and the Portland Development Commission have a no net loss policy for low-income and affordable housing, where after initial conflict the City of Portland and Dignity Village have created productive practices and dialogue, and where for over a decade the city has maintained policies to prevent geographic concentrations of poverty. It will be interesting to check back in a few years to see which way the winds have blown and how much Portland planners have involved themselves in these issues. Portland has established a national reputation for planning an egalitarian and sustainable community. Will it be able to foster a model for addressing homeless issues that rejects the politics of fear created by the broken windows theory? It seems quite reasonable to not want to smell urine on public streets and be endlessly panhandled in the urban center. But can Portland find an answer that addresses society's human tragedies rather than simply sweeping them out of sight? It seems clear that it is not an effective use of tax dollars to funnel people and thus funds through the criminal justice system. Perhaps the 10-year plan to end homelessness can find answers to both the business community's interest in a cleaned-up urban core and the social service community's interest in humane responses to homelessness, especially during these harsh economic times.

References

Abbott, Carl. 2001. *Greater Portland: Urban Life and Landscape in the Pacific Northwest.* Philadelphia: University of Pennsylvania Press.

American Planning Association. 2003. *Policy Guide on Homelessness.* http://www.planning.org/policyguides/homelessness.htm?project (accessed 11 November 2003).

Anderson, Jennifer. 2003. Life turnabout hinges on basic premise: Housing. *Portland Tribune,* 22 April. http://www.msnbc.com/local/vcolptld/M289418.asp (accessed 11 November 2003).

Center on Juvenile and Criminal Justice. 2002. *Shattering "Broken Windows": An Analysis of San Francisco's Alternative Crime Policy.* http://www.cjcj.org/pubs/windows/windows.html (accessed 1 July 2003).

City and County of San Francisco Board of Supervisors. 2002. *San Francisco's "Quality of Life" Laws and Seattle's "Civility" Laws—11 Jan 2002. Legislative Analyst Report* (File No. 011704). http://www.sfgov.org/site/bdsupvrs_page.asp?id=5100 (accessed 23 February 2003).

City of Portland Office of Neighborhood Involvement. June 2003. *Planning at the Roots: Low-Income and Communities of Color in Portland, Oregon.* Portland: Office of Neighborhood Involvement.

CNN.com. 2003. *Pizza Company Hires Homeless to Hold Ads.* 17 June. http://www.cnn.com/2003/US/West/06/17/offbeat.pizza.ap/ (accessed 11 November 2003).

The Coalition on Homelessness in San Francisco. 1999. *Looking at America through "Broken Windows."* http://www.sf-homeless-coalition.org/799brokenwindows.html (accessed 1 July 2003).

Culhane, Dennis P., Stephen M. Metraux, and Trevor R. Hadley. 2002. Public service reductions associated with placement of homeless persons with severe mental illness in supportive housing. *Housing Policy Debate* 13 (1): 107–163.

Duneier, Mitchell. 1999. *Sidewalk.* New York: Farrar, Straus and Giroux.

Fannie Mae Foundation. 2000. Target marketing can help attract city residents. *Housing Facts and Findings* Spring 2 (1). http://www.fanniemaefoundation.org /programs/hff/v2i1-marketing.shtml (accessed 11 November 2003).

Graham, Rachel. 2003. Homeless for the Holidays. *Willamette Week,* 14 Mar. http://www.wweek.com/html/urbanpulse122899.html#family (accessed 1 November 2003).

Hannum, Kristen. 2002. St. Francis plan for park problems rejected. *Catholic Sentinel,* 31 October. http://www.sentinel.org/articles/2002-44/10660.html (accessed 11 Nov 2003).

Homeless People's Network. 2000. *Portland Church at Center of Gathering Storm.* 11 Feb. http://projects.is.asu.edu/ pipermail/hpn/2000-February/000109.html (accessed 1 November 2003).

Jaquiss, Nigel. 2003. Bulldog. *Willamette Week,* 12 Feb. http://www.wweek.com/flatfiles/allstories.lasso?xxin=3620 (accessed 1 July 2003).

Jewish World Review. 2000. *Zoning Out Religious Freedoms.* 24 Feb. http://www.jewishworldreview.com/michelle/ malkin022400.asp (accessed November 2003).

Justice, Rob. 2003. Interview with author. 20 April. Executive director of JOIN.

Kelling, George, and Catherine Coles. 1996. *Fixing Broken Windows: Restoring Orderand Reducing Crime in Our Communities.* NY: The Free Press.

Leachman, Michael. 2001. *Hunger in Oregon.* Silverton: Oregon Center for Public Policy.

Lelchuk, Ilene. 2003. Ammiano zeros in on 1,350 homeless. *San Francisco Chronicle,* 10 April. http://sfgate.com/ cgi-bin/article.cgi?file=/chronicle/archive/2003/04/10/BA90033.DTL (accessed 1 July 2003).

Multnomah County Auditor's Office. 2001. *Homeless Youth Services Continuum: Review of System Outcomes.* Portland: Multnomah County Auditor's Office.

Multnomah County Office of School and Community Partnerships. 2003. *One Night Shelter Count March 26, 2003.* Portland: Multnomah County Office of School and Community Partnerships.

National Coalition for the Homeless. 2002. *People Need Their Civil Rights Protected.* http://www.nationalhomeless. org/facts/civilrights.pdf (accessed 11 November 2003).

Newth, Dan. 25 Feb 2003. *Dispatch from Portland.* Originally printed in *street roots.* http://www.alternet.org/sns/ story.html?StoryID=15243 (accessed 1 July 2003).

The Oregon Environmental Council. 2003. *Healthy Albina.* http://www.orcouncil.org/reports/Albina/chapters/ chapter3.htm (accessed 11 November 2003).

PDC Quarterly. 2003. PDC increases housing goals. *PDC Quarterly* 5 (2): 4. http://www.businessinportland.org/ pdf/pubs_general/gen_quarterly_spring_2003.pdf (accessed 1 November 2003).

Portland Development Commission. 2003. *Housing: Location Policy and Impact Area Map.* http://www.pdc.us/ housing_serv/general/iam.asp (accessed 1 November 2003).

Portland–Multnomah Progress Board. 1999. *Decrease Homelessness.* http://www.p-m-benchmarks.org/health_ fam/31.html (accessed 11 November 2003).

Portland Municipal Code 14A.50.020. *Camping Prohibited on Public Property and Public Rights of Way.* http://www. portlandonline.com/auditor/index.cfm?c=28513&#cid_15427 (accessed 11 November 2003).

Portland Municipal Code 14A.50.030. *Obstructions as Nuisances.* http://www.portlandonline.com/auditor/index. cfm?c=28513&#cid_15427 (accessed 11 November 2003).

Portland Municipal Code 14A.50.050. *Erecting Permanent or Temporary Structures on Public Property or Public Rights of Way.* http://www.portlandonline.com/auditor/index.cfm?&a=15431&c=28513 (accessed 11 November 2003).

Portland Municipal Code 14B.20.030. *Civil Exclusion.* http://www.portlandonline.com/auditor/index. cfm?c=28513&#cid_15427 (accessed 11 November 2003).

Portland Municipal Code 14A.50.010. *Alcohol on Public Property and Public Rights of Way.* http://www. portlandonline.com/auditor/index.cfm?c=28513& #cid 15427 (accessed 11 November 2003).

Portland Municipal Code 20.12.265. *Trespass.* http://www.portlandonline.com/auditor/index.cfm?&a=17286&c= 28627 (accessed 11 November 2003). Portland Police Bureau. 2003. *Manual of Policy and Procedure.* http://www. portlandpolicebureau.com/directives.html (accessed 11 November 2003).

Salon.com. 2002. *Manhattan Murder Rates Hit 100 Year Lows.* 31 December. http://www.salon.com/news/ wire/2002/12/31/manhattan_murder/index.html (accessed 1 July 2003).

Salon.com. 2003. *Company Pays Homeless Workers with Pizza.* 16 June. http://www.salon.com/news/wire/2003/06/16/ pizza_paycheck/index.html (accessed 1 July 2003).

San Francisco Mayor's Office on Homelessness. 2002. *Homeless Count Report: 25 November 2002.* http://www.sfgov. org/site/homeless_page.asp?id=3930 (accessed 1 July 2003).

Schrag, John. 1984. This Bud's for you. *Willamette Week* http://www.wweek.com/html/25-1984.html (accessed 11 November 2003).

The Seattle/King County Coalition for the Homeless. 2003. *The One Night Count.* http://www.homelessinfo.org/ onc.html (accessed 11 November 2003).

Seattle Municipal Code SMC 15.48.040. *Sitting or Lying Down on Public Sidewalks in Downtown and Neighborhood Commercial Zones.* http://clerk.ci.seattle.wa.us/~scripts/nph-brs.exe?s1=&s2=sit+lie&S3=&Sect 4=AND&1=20&Sect1=IMAGE&Sect3=PLURON&Sect5=CODE1&d=CODE&p=1&u=/~public/code1. htm&r=2&Sect6=HITOFF&f=G (accessed 1 July 2003).

Seattle Police Department. 2003. *The "Broken Window" Theory.* http://www.cityofseattle.net/police/prevention/ Tips/broken_window.htm (accessed 1 November 2003).

The Seattle Times. 2003. Homeless Serving as Billboards. 15 June. http://seattletimes.nwsource.com/html/ localnews/134998925_pizza15.html (accessed 1 November 2003).

Silverman, Rachael. 1999. *Description and Assessment of Portland's Response to Homelessness of Adults.* Portland: Portland Bureau of Housing and Community Development.

Sisters of the Road Cafe. 2003a. *Portland's Anti-homeless Ordinances.* http://www.sistersoftheroadcafe.org/ crossroads/Anticamp.htm (accessed 11 November 2003).

Sisters of the Road Cafe. 2003b. *Frequently Asked Questions.* http://www.sistersoftheroadcafe.org/crossroads/FAQ. htm (accessed 11 November 2003).

Transition Projects, Inc. 2001. *Women's Reality: Single Homeless Women in the City of Portland.* Portland: Transition Projects, Inc.

Urban Land Institute Report. 1999. *The Impact of Supportive Housing on Neighborhoods and Neighbors.* Washington, DC: Urban Land Institute.

Williams, Rebecca. 1998. *Philip Zimbardo: A Psychologist's Experience with Deviance.* http://www.criminology.fsu. edu/crimtheory/zimbardo.htm (accessed 1 May 2003).

Wilson, J. Q., and G. L. Kelling. 1982. Broken windows: The police and neighborhood safety. *Atlantic Monthly,* March. http://www3.theatlantic.com/election/connection/crime/windows.htm (accessed 1 May 2003).

Winton, Richard, and Kristina Sauerwein. 2003. LAPD tests new policing strategy. *Los Angeles Times,* 6 February. http://www.latimes.com/templates /mi...evive2feb02&section=%2Fnews%2Flocal (accessed 1 July 2003).

Wollner, Craig, John Provo, and Julie Schablitsky. 2001. *A Brief History of Urban Renewal in Portland, Oregon.* Portland: Institute for Portland Metropolitan Studies.

World Faith News. 2000. Portland City Council throws out attendance limit for church. 3 March. http://www.wfn.org/2000/03/msg00052.html (accessed 1 November 2003).

Wright, J. D., and J. A. Lam. 1987. Homelessness and the low-income housing supply. *Social Policy,* Spring: 48–53.

Zimbardo, P. G. 1969. The human choice: Individuation, reason, and order versus deindividuation, impulse, and chaos. *Nebraska Symposium on Motivation* 17: 237–307.

Questions to Think About

1. Which theory of social movements seems most accurate? Are there other theories that could describe how or why social movements occur?

2. If politicians are elected to represent the masses, why are social movements needed?

3. In what ways is it easier to form a social movement in cities than in rural areas?

4. What is needed for a social movement to form? What instigates social movements?

5. What are the monetary costs of criminalizing the homeless?

6. How does broken windows policing harm the homeless?

7. Why is it so difficult to know how many homeless are in any urban area? Is there a better way to count the homeless?

8. What are the strategies that Portland uses to deal with homelessness? How is this different from the policies in New York or San Francisco?

Resources

 The Four Stages of Social Movements:

https://www.ebscohost.com/uploads/imported/thisTopic-dbTopic-1248.pdf

 Social Movements in America. A Research Guide, New York Public Library:

http://www.nypl.org/blog/2011/10/18/social-movements-in-america-research-guide

Social Movements and Culture:
http://culturalpolitics.net/social_movements/

 National Coalition for the homeless:
http://nationalhomeless.org/

 Community Policing Dispatch, Department of Criminal Justice:
http://www.cops.usdoj.gov/html/dispatch/January_2009/nugget.htm

 Center for Evidence-Based Crime Policy: http://cebcp.org/evidence-based-policing/what-works-in-policing/
research-evidence-review/broken-windows-policing/

CPSIA information can be obtained
at www.ICGtesting.com
Printed in the USA
LVHW102220210119
604748LV00003B/276/P